Jackson Hole Hikes

Also by Rebecca Woods

Beyond the Tetons
coauthored with Susan Marsh

Targhee Trails

Walking the Winds

Jackson Hole Cooks!

Jackson Hole Hikes

A Guide to Grand Teton National Park,
Jedediah Smith, Teton and Gros Ventre Wilderness
and surrounding national forest land

by
Rebecca Woods

White Willow Publishing
P.O. Box 6464 • Jackson, Wyoming 83002
email:whitewillow@bresnan.net

Warning

By their nature, outdoor activities can be dangerous. It is your responsibility to be aware of potential risks, have the proper equipment and take safety precautions. Changing terrain and weather conditions present a wide range of hazards, including but not limited to: snow and ice fields, avalanches, landslides, caves, falling trees or limbs, high or rushing water, contaminated water, wild animals, severe weather, becoming lost or overexerted, dehydration and hypothermia.

Field conditions can and do change. While every effort has been taken to ensure this book's accuracy, it may contain errors. This guide should not replace your own judgment or decision-making skills.

ISBN: 978-0-9755359-5-0

Table of Contents

Teton Pass, The West Bank and Teton Village

Teton Pass

The West Bank

Teton Village

7

Jackson and Greater Snow King Area

Appendix

Introduction

Jackson Hole has a long tradition of spellbinding those who enter its confines, from the earliest Indians and hunters to the tourists and residents of today's resort community. One of its first visitors, fur trapper William Sublette, is credited with naming the valley in 1829. Turn-of-the-century trappers called valleys ringed by mountains "holes." It was accepted practice to name areas they frequented after themselves. Sublette named the valley "Jackson's Hole" in honor of his partner, Davey Jackson.

Roughly 80-miles long and six- to eight-miles wide, the valley is bound by Yellowstone National Park to the north, Togwotee Pass to the northeast, the Gros Ventre Range to the east, Hoback Canyon to the south, Teton Pass and the Snake River Range to the southwest and, of course, the Teton Range to the west.

The Tetons sheer size, shape and beauty are the most notable feature in the valley geologically and scenically. Shoshoni Indians called the range Teewinot, or "many pinnacles." In 1811 William Price Hunt of the Astorians named the peaks Pilot Knobs. Dr. Ferdinand Hayden said the peaks resembled shark's teeth; men on his 1872 expedition to the region named the highest summit Mt. Hayden in his honor. But it was the name three trappers from the Canadian Northwest Company gave them that stuck: Les Trois Tetons, or three breasts.

The range is one of the most precipitous in the world, completely lacking foothills. Along its 40-mile course, it rises 3,000-7,000 feet above the sage-covered flats of the valley floor. The impressive upsweep of granite is an irresistible magnet to climbers and adventurers. The Grand Teton was officially first climbed in 1898, thirty-one years before the park was established. There is, however, some controversy over this, and it may have been climbed as early as 1872 by Nathaniel Langford and James Stevenson. Since that time an untold number of climbers and hikers have explored the park's peaks and its 260-plus miles of trail.

Just as beautiful in their own right are the national forest lands that ring the valley. The 287,000-acre wilderness area in the heart of the Gros Ventres is home to 20 peaks that soar above 10,000 feet, abundant wildlife, glacier-carved cliffs and colorful polychrome rock bands. One hundred and ten miles of trails criss-cross this, some of the prettiest country in the region.

The Teton Wilderness and the Absaroka Range to the north straddle the Continental Divide. Source of both the Yellowstone and Snake Rivers, that wilderness is almost 900 square miles in size.

Caribou-Targhee National Forest presides over the western side of the range. There, long U-shaped, glaciated canyons allow easier access up western slopes and afford dramatic views of the range as well.

Surrounded by one of the jewels of the National Park system and national forest land in every direction, Jackson Hole is in the enviable position of offering more backcountry to explore than virtually any other area in the lower 48 states.

PLANTS AND TREES

In the mountains of western Wyoming, vegetation is strongly controlled by aspect, especially on the lower slopes. Southern aspects are typically dry and open, dominated by grass and shrubs, while forest blankets north-facing slopes. The vegetation pattern is a response to varying availability of moisture. Snow melts quickly from south-facing slopes, and wind scours them. They may be mostly bare through the winter, supporting drought-tolerant shrubs such as sagebrush, bitterbrush and bigtooth maple. These conditions create ideal winter range for mule deer, elk and other wildlife. Snow remains longer on the protected north and east-facing slopes, giving them enough moisture for conifer forests to survive. An alternating pattern of forest and open hillsides punctuates every draw and canyon along the mountain fronts.

Wildflowers and a mix of shrubs thrive at lower elevations. The highest peaks harbor low alpine wildflowers and stunted trees called krummholz (a German word for "crooked wood"). The same species as those found at lower elevations, krummholz trees have adapted to the harsh conditions of mountaintops by taking on another form. Trees that grow tall and straight on the valley floor will grow no taller than 10 feet on higher, exposed terrain, where wind and desiccation limit their height. Krummholz' height is also an indicator of average snow depth, since foliage that grows higher than protective snow will not survive. The stunted trees often form a dense thicket that may be hundreds of years old.

Alpine tundra—which begins just below treeline and climbs to the summits of the highest peaks—is found along the top of the Teton Range and a few scattered pockets elsewhere in the valley.

Cone-Bearing Trees

It is easy to learn the cone-bearing trees in this area, because there are few species and each has distinctive characteristics. An inventory on the Bridger-Teton done in 1985 established the average and oldest age of each common species found during the survey. This information is listed at the end of each description.

Lodgepole Pine

Lodgepole pine is the most common tree in the area, growing from 6,000 feet to timberline. It has two needles in a bundle, its cones are small and round, and its bark is thin. (Lodgepole bark is a favorite food for porcupines; look for them in lodgepole forest.) The straight trees grow to a height of 70-80 feet, often occurring in pure stands. Indians used its straight trunk for teepees and lodges. Some lodgepole cones pollinate late June, creating a yellow cloud during windy conditions. Other cones are serotinous, or late opening. When exposed to temperatures exceeding 112 degrees Fahrenheit, the pitch encasing the seeds melts, and the seeds are released. In this manner, the trees replant themselves: Lodgepole pine is typically the first tree to thrive after a forest fire or other large disturbance.

Average Age: 121 years
Oldest age: 312 years

Whitebark Pine

Whitebark pine is of great importance to wildlife, since it produces large, nutrient-packed seeds. It has five needles in a bundle, with cones about 2 1/2" long. The cones are a dark purple color, tightly clasped and sealed by gummy pitch; they don't open on their own. Jays, Clark's Nutcrackers and squirrels pry the  cones apart, then gather and cache the seeds for future food. Unused caches sprout and some may survive to grow into trees. This tree is threatened throughout the region due to a combination of drought; white pine blister rust, an introduced fungus that girdles smaller branches and young trees; and epidemic mountain pine beetle activity. Mountain pine beetles are endemic but occasionally they become epidemic—that is, more numerous than their habitat can sustain. The cycles of pine beetle abundance are influenced by the condition of the forest (old trees are more susceptible) and climate factors. The Bridger-Teton Forest has a number of monitoring sites for whitebark pine and has identified seed trees that appear healthy and resistant, from which cones are gathered for regeneration.

Whitebark pine is found above 8,000 feet. Light grey and smooth-barked, it is often irregular and contorted, reaching a maximum height of 60 feet. Near timberline, whitebark pines form much smaller krummholz.

Average Age: 174 years
Oldest age: 350 years

Limber Pine

Limber pine is not widespread. It is usually found as a minor component of dry forests dominated by Douglas fir and juniper. Its needles are 2" long and come in bundles of five. The tree looks similar  to whitebark pine, with the exception of its cones. They  are typically five to six inches long, tan or light brown in color, and stand perpendicular from the branches. They are thick, resinous and woody, and the scales open at maturity. The best way to tell a limber pine from a whitebark is to look for cones. Another way is to notice the habitat. Whitebark are usually found up high, whereas limber pines grow between 5,000 and 8,500 feet. The smaller branches and twigs are very flexible, a characteristic reflected in its name.

Average Age: 161 years
Oldest age: 361 years

Engelmann Spruce

Engelmann spruce (sometimes a cross with Colorado spruce in this area) has singly attached short, stiff needles growing from a woody peg. The peg remains on the branch after the needle falls off, giving its branches a rough texture. The needles have sharp tips, and if you roll the needle between your fingertips, you will feel its edges. Conversely, subalpine fir has flat needles. The spruce's four-inch cones hang from the branch; fir cones stand upright. Engelmann spruce is found between 6,000 feet to treeline. It is the dominant conifer lining many area rivers and creeks.

>Average Age: 167
>Oldest age: 440

Subalpine Fir

Subalpine fir is easy to identify by its narrow, dense form, like a spire. The bark is smooth, blistered, and light silver in color. Its cones stand erect, falling apart a scale at a time. Whole fir cones are seldom found unless they have fallen off green in a windstorm. Subalpine fir occupies the same range as Engelmann spruce, from mid-elevation to timberline, and is often found in mixed stands. It grows in cool, moist areas rarely struck by forest fires. In many places, the subalpine fir stands are old and susceptible to invasion by insects, especially after several years of drought stress. You may see dead and dying subalpine fir throughout the region.

>Average Age: 104
>Oldest age: 240

Douglas Fir

Douglas fir has pendant cones (unlike the upright cones of true firs) distinguished by a three-pronged bract projecting beyond the scales. It is found between 6,000 and 8,500 feet, often growing in open stands. On younger trees, the bark is smooth and gray-brown; on older trees, it is thick, darker and deeply furrowed. Douglas fir can attain heights up to 100 feet. Botanists theorize that the tree's deeply fissured bark—which can grow over 5-inches thick—protects its living tissues from cooler ground fires and thus contributes to its longevity.

>Average Age: 161
>Oldest age: 469

Deciduous Trees

Like cone bearing trees, there are relatively few deciduous trees in the mountainous region of western Wyoming and eastern Idaho. The species most commonly mentioned in this guide are profiled below.

Cottonwood

Cottonwoods are the largest deciduous trees in the region. Both black and narrowleaf cottonwoods are found in the area. Black cottonwood is the larger of the two. It can exceed 80 feet in height and attain a diameter of three feet. The bark of black cottonwoods is smooth and greenish-brown on younger trees, furrowed and dark gray on older trees. The margins of the broadly ovate leaves have many small, rounded teeth and the leaves are dark green above and pale underneath. Narrowleaf cottonwoods typically top out at 60 feet in height and have a trunk diameter of two feet. As the name implies, the leaves are only a half-inch to 1-1/2 inches wide, as pictured to the right. Cottonwoods require a lot of water. They are found bordering rivers and streams up to 8,500 feet in elevation. Their minuscule seeds are attached to silky fibers (the "cotton" of cottonwood) that allow them to be carried long distances by the wind.

Balsam poplar, often confused with cottonwood, grows in small stands away from creeks and rivers.

Average Age: 128 years

Oldest age: N/A: only 9 trees sampled

Quaking Aspen

This slender tree has greenish-white bark marked by black patches and lines. The round to oval, finely toothed leaves are attached to long, flattened stalks that tremble in even slight breezes, giving the tree is name. Aspens are typically 30-60 feet in height and grow on dry to moist lower elevation sites. They typically reproduce by suckering, growing vertical shoots above ground from their large, shallow root system. Suckering produces stands of trees called "clones" that are connected underground and genetically the same.

This interesting tree has photosynthetic bark. A powdery white material that covers the bark protects the tree from ultraviolet radiation. Aspen wood is used to make shingles, chopsticks and, because it resists splintering, sauna benches.

Beaver utilize aspen extensively for food and building material. Elk and deer browse on its twigs and leaves. When food is scare, they eat the bark, which produces the common black scars.

Average Age: 71 years

Oldest age: 228 years

WILDLIFE

The mountains and adjacent valleys support a variety of game animals, birds and smaller wildlife. Black bears are most often seen in the vicinity of Cascade Canyon, near the mouth of Death Canyon and en route to Amphitheater and Surprise Lakes; grizzly bears are resident in Teton Wilderness and the northern end of the valley. You can avoid conflicts by keeping a clean camp, putting away food or coolers when you are not there, and making noise along the trail. Unless habituated to human food, bears generally will try to avoid you.

Generally, the best opportunity to see wildlife is at dawn and early evening when many species browse or move to different feeding areas. Elk are typically viewed in meadows fringed by forest, bighorn sheep and mountain goats in steep cliff areas that help protect them from their predators. Moose inhabit river corridors, where there is an abundance of aquatic plants and willows. Acquainting yourself with preferred habitat improves your chance of seeing particular animals.

For all species, the safest way to watch wildlife is with binoculars. Do not try to "sneak up" on wildlife: this is stressful to the animal and its fight response may result in serious injury to yourself. Be particularly careful in blind canyons and dense willow bottoms, where moose could be resting out of sight, and around wildlife with young. You are likely too close if you see an animal doing one of the following:

▶   it stops what it was doing and looks in your direction
▶   it moves either away from or toward you
▶   it appears nervous or uneasy, pawing the ground, swinging its head, or raising the hair on its neck

Wildlife you may see in backcountry covered by this book include:

Bighorn Sheep

Bighorns are aptly named. Mature rams sport curled horns that can grow as large as 18 inches in circumference and over 40 inches in length. Heavy ridges on the horn indicate annual growth that can be used to determine the age of the animal. Ewes also grow horns. They are short, flat and never curl. Bighorns stand 30-45 inches tall and weigh between 120-340 pounds. They are gray to brownish in color and have a white rump patch. They eat plants and grasses and usually inhabit precipitous slopes and cliff areas that provide protection from predators. In Jackson Hole, they are most often spied on high mountain passes, on steep slopes in the National Elk Refuge near a natural salt lick, far down the Gros Ventre access road and in Hoback Canyon. Ewes typically birth a single lamb in seclusion in late May/early June following a six-month gestation. The pair rejoins the herd within days.

14

Bison

There are presently 600-800 bison in Grand Teton National Park. These large grazers are found on the sage grasslands and low hillsides in the park and in the foothills of the Gros Ventre Range on the east side of the valley. Bison stand 4-6 feet tall and can weigh as much as 2,400 pounds. Their massive head and front legs are covered by shaggy dark brown fur that lightens and becomes shorter behind the shoulders. Both males and females have upward-curving, short black horns. Females typically give birth to one reddish-colored calf in May, following a gestation of 9-10 months. The calves lose their reddish coat by autumn and are weaned by the time they are seven months old. With few natural predators the bison population has grown significantly in recent years, presenting management challenges in both Grand Teton and Yellowstone National Parks.

Coyote

Coyotes are adaptable and live in a wide variety of habitats; you may see them in all but the highest elevations. As the snow recedes, they are particularly active in Antelope Flats and along the meadow-lined Granite Creek access road. Coyotes form packs where food is relatively abundant, roaming a typical 10-mile hunting route, but will range up to 100 miles when food is scarce. Rodents, rabbits, carrion, plants, frogs and insects all satisfy a coyote's voracious palate. This member of the dog family resembles a small to medium-sized German shepherd. Its nose is slightly more pointed and its tail fuller, the latter held between its back legs while running. Coyotes are grey to reddish-grey in color with a whitish throat and underbelly. A short gestation period of two months yields a litter of five to seven pups.

Pronghorn

Over half of the world's pronghorn antelope reside in the Greater Yellowstone Ecosystem. Thousands of animals browse on the vast, rolling sagebrush hills and plains that characterize western Wyoming. Small herds of 12 or more are likely to be spied along the Inner Park Road, Antelope Flats Road and in Hoback Canyon. The tan-and-white animals stand roughly three feet high and weigh between 70-140 pounds. Their underside and rump are white, as are a pair of bands across their throat. Both sexes grow short, gently curved horns with a single prong that projects forward. Noticeably large eyes help them spot potential predators. They give birth to one to three kids in late spring/early summer.

Moose

Moose are the largest member of the deer family. They stand 5-7 feet tall—their height attributed mostly to very long legs—and weigh as much as 1,000 pounds. Males sport massive antlers that are dropped every year, typically between December and February. Moose feed primarily on aquatic vegetation in the summer, and are often seen in willow bottoms, sloughs and beaver ponds, and along watercourses and forested uplands. They also feed on a variety of plants, including antelope bitterbrush, Douglas fir, subalpine fir, whitebark pine, cottonwood, sedges, rushes and spruce.

Solitary most of the year, moose rut in September and October; a single calf is born in May or June following an eight-month gestation. Occasionally a cow will give birth to two calves. Newborns are a light, reddish brown. Though wobbly at birth, by three days they are strong enough to follow their mother.

Moose are often seen near Oxbow Bend, in willowed terrain between Jackson Lake Lodge and Colter Bay and throughout the Snake River corridor.

Elk

Elk are members of the deer family. Their straw-colored rump patch, reddish-brown summer coat, dark brown neck cape, and short tail help identify them. Mature males sport antlers that reach maximum size in early autumn, typically spanning 5 1/2 feet and weighing as much as 25 pounds. These are shed each spring and quickly recycled by rodents who consume the calcium rich bone. Since grasses comprise the bulk of their diet, elk are usually seen in areas of shrub and grass communities, high mountain meadows, and coniferous forest. Typical feeding areas are fringed by forest, providing quick escape for the herd and cover at night.

Recreationists traveling in September and early October may hear bull elk bugling. The high-pitched mating call punctuates crisp autumn days and nights as the rutting season nears its peak. Rubbing their antlers against trees to remove the last vestiges of summer velvet and sparring with rival bulls are all part of the complex mating dance. The results of the rut arrive in late May and June, when females drop their single, 30-pound calves. Calves are mobile within hours of birth and by six months may weigh as much as 250 pounds.

Elk are seen throughout the territory covered by this publication.

Mule Deer

The long, black-tipped ears of the mule deer help identify them, and have given them their common name. Mule deer occupy a variety of habitats at all elevations. Because the primary component of their diet is shrubbery and herbage, they are commonly spotted near dawn and dusk in brushy terrain that contains open meadows, scattered aspen groves and rocky ridges. In winter, they migrate to lower protected valleys and open slopes. They have small seasonal home ranges, and may move extensively during migration and rut.

Mule deer are characterized by a bounding gait in which all four feet leave the ground and come down together. Males are typically 3-4 feet tall and weigh over 200 pounds; smaller females range from 100-150 pounds. The mating season begins in late fall, and is usually completed by the end of December, when bucks may band loosely together. Does and young form their own winter herds. One or two fawns are dropped in June and July. The weak, spotted young are "hidden," with the mother returning to them only to nurse. They gain enough strength to follow their mother in a couple of weeks and are weaned from her by autumn.

Mule deer are often seen on the hillsides above Jackson, south of town, near almost all rivers and creeks valleywide, and on the slopes in lower Hoback Canyon.

Grizzly Bear

A large hump near the bear's shoulders, concave face and white-tipped guard hairs that give the bear a "grizzled" appearance distinguish this bruin. Mature grizzlies range in weight from 240 to over 1,100 pounds. Color varies from almost white, to brownish yellow or nearly black. Because the bulk of a grizzly's diet is composed of roots, bulbs, berries and plant matter, the bears are often seen digging in open meadows and in alpine tundra. Be prepared, however, to encounter them in forested mountain terrain as well.

Grizzlies opportunistically eat fish, small mammals and carrion, which they can smell up to 10 miles away. The bears are quite active in April and May when they emerge from hibernation and seek out winter kill.

Although grizzlies can be encountered throughout the region, hikers should be particularly alert near Emma Matilda and Two Ocean Lakes, Breccia and Brooks Lake Mountain, South Fork Falls, and other hikes near the vicinity of Teton Wilderness.

Black Bear

Black bear are not always black: a variety of colors may be seen among these bears—cinnamon, black, brown, and light tan. Some have white patches in their coats. The profile of a black bear's nose is straight, and the ears are pointed. They stand about 3 1/2 feet high at the shoulder, and average 4 1/2 feet to 6 feet long. Weight can approach close to 600 pounds, with most weighing 250-300 pounds. Males are about 20 percent larger than females. They are not true hibernators, but go into a deep sleep in the winter. They typically emerge from their den in April with up to five, but usually two or three, cubs. The cubs are born and nursed while the sow sleeps, and have thus attained a weight of 4 1/2 to 6 1/2 pounds when they leave the den between five to six weeks old.

Black bears are omnivorous, and actively seek large winter kill and small mammals when they leave the den. The primary component of their diet, however, is plant matter, berries and insects, making them most likely to be encountered in forested areas. Black bears mark trees by raking their curved claws down the bark, and can readily climb trees. Like humans, they use trails for easy access to their favorite feeding spots, and are thus often glimpsed ahead on a path before fleeing through the woods. If surprised, however, they have been known to attack. Travelers in bear country should be acquainted with bear behavioral signs and encounter precautions, outlined in the appendix of this book.

Front
4-1/2 inches long
4 inches wide

Back
6-7/8 inches long
3-1/2 inches wide

Black bear scat: diameter between 1-3/8 inches and 1-1/2 inches

BACKCOUNTRY SAFETY

It is beyond the scope of this book to detail safety aspects of backcountry travel; entire volumes have been written on the subject. Basic skills, first aid and emergency response and rescue procedures are universal concerns best addressed elsewhere. There are, however, several considerations that merit attention.

Trip planning

Trip planning is the key to a safe trip. Let someone know your itinerary. Don't forget to take along backcountry essentials recommended to help you address unexpected problems. They include:

- ▶ Extra clothing (warm, dry, wind-resistant)
- ▶ Extra food
- ▶ Sunglasses
- ▶ Pocketknife
- ▶ Fire starter, like a candle, wax tablets, etc., and matches in a water-tight container
- ▶ Good first aid kit
- ▶ Flashlight with extra batteries.
- ▶ Map of the area you are traveling, preferably a USGS topographic map.
- ▶ Compass or GPS with extra batteries

Maps

National Forest maps can be purchased from the Forest Visitor Center in Jackson, and any of the Ranger District offices. Most outdoor stores in the area also carry maps. These small-scale maps are particularly useful when traveling to trailheads. For backcountry travel, a 7.5-minute topographic map is recommended. Not all the trails and new roads will show up on the map, but the topographic detail will help you find your way if lost. Digital maps uploaded to GPS units are useful...until your battery dies. A paper backup is advised. Delorme, National Geographic and other reputable companies sell digital, seamless topographic map collections covering specific national parks or states that allow you to print out the section you will be visiting. Other sites allow you to download individual topos to your computer free of charge. Visit the useful web sites listing in the appendix of this book for sources. The line maps in this book are intended for general reference only. They lack the detail needed for backcountry travel, and should not be used as such.

Stream crossings

Many of the trails in this book cross creeks where a ford is required. For most of the summer and fall, the creeks are shallow and fording is a safe and refreshing wade through ankle-deep water. The rocks can be slippery, so it is wise to carry a trekking pole and a pair of river runner's sandals or old tennis shoes, since wearing shoes provides better footing than trying to cross barefoot. During high spring flows between late May and early July, some crossings may not be possible.

Water treatment

Even clear cold water can contain tiny cysts of internal parasites like Giardia and Cryptosporidium, which spread from animal or human fecal waste. Drinking untreated water can cause intestinal discomfort and sickness. Unless you know the water source is safe the day you dip into it, boil, filter, or chemically treat your water.

Weather and Lightning

In the mountains, it can snow almost any day of the year and over the course of time probably has. Moreover, mountain storms can come in quickly. It is advisable to check the forecast before you depart on a lengthy outing, and in all cases to be prepared to withstand sudden, severe weather changes. A wool hat, gloves, pile jacket, waterproof layer and emergency "space" blanket should live in your daypack. Period.

Afternoon thunderstorms are common and with them, lightning. Every year approximately 200 people in the United States are killed by lightning strikes, more than the combined total of victims of floods, tornadoes and hurricanes. This underscores the importance of taking refuge in a storm. Avoid meadows, ridges, lone trees, lakeshores, mountaintops and rock overhangs, where an electric charge can bounce to you. If available, seek refuge in groves of trees of uniform size or low-lying areas. Keep away from metal objects such as tent poles, pack frames and walking sticks that can act as lightning rods in an electrical storm.

While 20 percent of the people struck by lightning do not survive, if CPR is administered immediately to a victim of a lightning strike—even if he or she appear dead—chances are the victim may be revived.

Trail right-of-way

Hikers, bikers and horse packers use the trails included in this book, and some are open to trail vehicles. For safety and courtesy, a system of backcountry trail etiquette has evolved. All trail users yield to horses. Give horses and mules a wide right-of-way to avoid spooking them. Llamas should be treated as pack stock by hikers and bikers—yield to them. Those leading llamas should yield to horses and keep as far away if possible. Horses may be afraid of llamas, especially if they have never encountered them before. Trail bikes and mountain bikes yield to hikers.

You may encounter cattle on lower elevation trails, and sheep in the high country. The sheep are not usually on the main trails, but if they are, approach slowly and they will move off. Guard dogs may approach to investigate you; speak softly to them and keep walking. Once they see that you are not a coyote, they will usually leave you alone. If you have a dog with you, keep it on a leash if you are near livestock.

Underestimating time and energy

People tend to underestimate the time and energy needed for hikes that gain significant elevation. As a rule of thumb, add an "effort mile" to the overall mileage for every 500 feet gained. This will give you a more realistic approximation of how much energy the hike really takes. Give yourself enough time for your intended destination. If the hike is taking longer than you anticipated, don't push yourself to exhaustion; turn around. Mountain accidents are often the result of people becoming overly tired and losing their physical and mental acuity.

Hypothermia and Dehydration

Hypothermia is the plunging of your body's core temperature; if the condition is not arrested it can lead to death. It often develops in wet, windy weather at or above 50 degrees, when most people aren't concerned about their bodies losing heat faster than it can be produced. When clothes become wet from rain or sweat they lose as much as 90% of their insulating value. Wind-driven cool air refrigerates the wet clothing by evaporating moisture from its surface. The body reacts by shivering to try to generate heat, and later, shunting blood away from the extremities and brain to keep the core warm. This results in loss of coordination, memory lapses, poor judgment, unconsciousness and even death.

Treat initial symptoms seriously by getting out of the elements and into warm, dry clothes. After a long day of sweaty hiking, keep in mind that temperatures can plummet quickly when the sun sets. Change into dry, warm clothes before setting up camp or cooking dinner.

Dehydration is common at higher elevations. Every time you breathe, moisture is pulled from your lungs into the dry air. Sweat quickly evaporates in direct sunlight, making most people unaware of how much moisture they are losing. Make a conscious effort to regularly drink lots of fluids.

GENERAL FOREST REGULATIONS

▶ It is illegal anywhere in a national forest to fire a gun within 150 yards of a campground, or across a road or body of water next to the road. Safety is the reason for this regulation; no one wants to be responsible for hitting another visitor with a stray bullet. Be aware of others using the area if you are shooting, especially near trails. Make sure you are shooting in a safe place.

▶ Shortcutting a switchback in the trail is prohibited, to prevent soil erosion and protect the trail.

▶ Allowing free trailing of horses and mules is not allowed on forest trails, to minimize the number of stock taken by each party, and to keep the stock on the trail so multiple parallel tracks do not develop.

▶ Pelletized or certified weed-free feed is required, to reduce the spread of exotic weeds. Spotted knapweed is becoming an increasing problem in the region, as are several other invasive weeds that outcompete native plants and reduce the quality of forage for wildlife and livestock.

▶ Secure horses at least 200 feet from lakes and 100 feet from streams, to avoid damage to shoreline vegetation and soil.

▶ The stay limit for a single campsite, including campgrounds, is 16 days. After that you must move at least five miles, and cannot reoccupy the original campsite for seven days. This rule is intended to keep people from taking over a campsite for the entire season, so no one else can use it. In some high-use places such as the Snake River and Hoback Canyons, the stay limit is reduced. Notices are posted in the areas affected.

TREADING LIGHTLY

As more people visit and move into the region, preserving the pristine character of public lands becomes a challenge. Visitors can help maintain the wild character of the mountains ringing Jackson Hole by following a few simple practices in the backcountry:

▶ Use an established campsite rather than creating a new one. This avoids disturbing more ground, and the established camps are often in the most desirable places. In Grand Teton National Park, many backcountry camps are assigned.

▶ Leave your campsite cleaner than you found it, and pack out all trash.

▶ In the backcountry carry and use a backpacking stove. With the exception of designated lakeshore sites, backcountry fires are prohibited in Grand Teton National Park. If you build a fire on national forest land, use only dead, down material. Use an existing fire ring or firepan so you don't create another fire scar. Keep your fire small to reduce visual impact, wood consumption and forest fire danger. Never leave your fire unattended. Scatter unused firewood when you leave and make sure your fire is completely out—this means multiple trips to the creek with a bucket, much stirring with a stick, and cooling of any fire ring rocks. Many forest fires are started by people who neglect this important safety measure.

▶ Bury human waste at least 200 feet away from trails, campsites, waterways and other frequently used places. This prevents rain and snow run-off from carrying waste into lakes and streams, contaminating your source of drinking and cooking water. Dig a shallow hole 6-8 inches deep, make your deposit, and recover the hole. Carefully burn soiled toilet paper, or pack it out in a sealed plastic bag.

▶ To protect lakes and streams, minimize the use of biodegradable soap for bathing and dishes. Lather and rinse at least 200 feet away from the water source with water carried to your site in a pot. This allows the soap to break down as it filters through the soil before re-entering the water system. Some campers prefer using sand and gravel to clean their dishes.

▶ Walk in the middle of a path as much as possible, even if it is muddy. Walking on the edge of a trail to avoid a bog only makes the bog bigger by breaking down the trail edges and widening the mess. Similarly, snow patches on trails should be crossed rather than skirted to avoid creating small side trails.

▶ If you travel off-trail, spread out instead of walking single file to avoid creating a new trail. Even infrequent trampling can create an incipient trail that attracts additional use. Choose a route that crosses durable surfaces such as rock or hard ground.

▶ Avoid traveling on unsurfaced roads early season, when ground saturated from snowmelt deteriorates easily. Give the ground a chance to dry out.

▶ If you find rock barriers or fences placed along the river or creeks, leave them. They have been put there to allow plants to recover and to protect stream banks from erosion.

▶ Don't chase sheep or cattle if you encounter them. They are being distributed to avoid damage to the range, and if you chase them, they may end up in the very place the herders are trying to keep them out of.

▶ Obey posted travel restrictions. Most restrictions on vehicle travel in the area are intended to protect soil, vegetation, and wildlife. Your cooperation is needed.

In wilderness I sense the miracle of life and behind it our scientific accomplishments fade to trivia.

—Charles A. Lindbergh

HOW TO USE THIS BOOK

The hikes in this book have been arranged by geographical area. For each area, there is an introduction and a contact number for further information. Hike descriptions begin with an information capsule at the top of the page, followed by a written narrative intended to give you a general feeling of the route.

The first component in the information capsule is **distance**. This is just what the name implies: the number of miles covered on the hike. The mileage listed is either one-way or round-trip (RT), and has been digitally measured and/or verified by GPS waypoints. Be aware that most people think they have walked much farther than they actually have. Until you know your capabilities, it is recommended that you start with shorter distance hikes to see how you fare.

The next category in the information capsule is **elevation gain/change**, followed by maximum elevation reached on the hike. This information should help you determine how strenuous the hike will be, based upon the number of feet you ascend and top elevation. Elevation change is used for loop hikes. Elevation gain includes the number of feet you must re-ascend after a drop in the trail. If there is a significant amount of elevation lost en route, it is identified to let you know the route undulates, a consideration for the amount of energy you will need on your return to the trailhead. Elevation change and maximum elevation are both important in assessing time and energy needed for the trip. An average walking pace on level ground is 2-2.5 miles per hour. On steep terrain it drops to about 1.5 miles an hour. Altitude and uneven cross-country terrain further reduce speed.

The next capsule item is **maps**. Unless otherwise noted all maps listed are USGS 7.5', 1:24,000 scale topographic quadrangles. The U.S. Forest Service also publishes smaller-scale maps available at local visitor centers and area outdoor shops that are useful in finding trailheads. Line maps produced in this book are included only to show junctions. Reproduced topos included in this book show trails not plotted on existing maps, trails that have been significantly rerouted, or trailheads in potentially confusing areas. It is strongly suggested you purchase and use topo maps. Numerous trails in this book get low visitation and can be faint, and even clear paths can be obscured by bad weather conditions.

The information capsule also contains **use restrictions**. Because these may change to accommodate wildlife activity and trail conditions, it is suggested you check with the appropriate district office before embarking on a remote hike. Finally, the approximate **season** the trail is snow-free and/or will likely have only minimal snow is identified. Of all the information items, this is the most variable. The identified season reflects what is true of most years. Late spring snows may push forward the date a trail clears, and significant snowstorms can occur every month of the year at higher elevations. Use common sense and check with the appropriate district office for up-to-date conditions.

Mileage to trailheads is included in driving directions. Be aware that your odometer reading may be slightly different for short distances, more over long distances. Anyone who uses an oven knows not all 350 degree settings are 350 degrees. The same is true of odometer calibrations in different vehicles. If you treat the mileage as the best approximate available, and cross-check your travel progress with a smaller-scale U.S. Forest Service map, you should have no difficulty finding the trailhead.

Grand Teton National Park

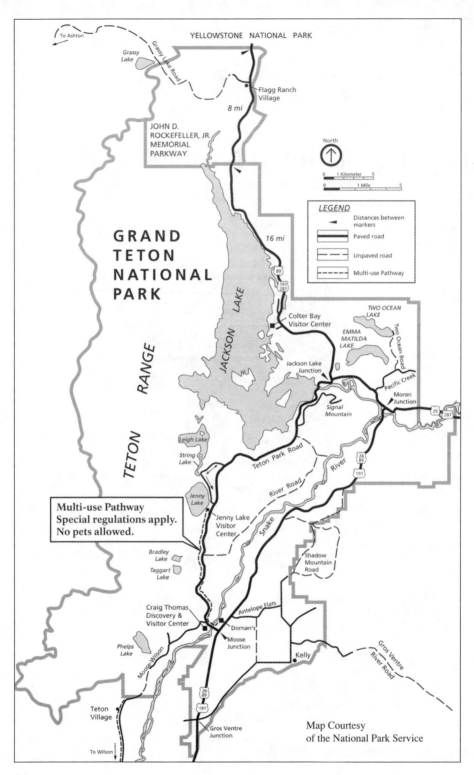

YELLOWSTONE NATIONAL PARK

To Ashton

Grassy Lake

Grassy Lake Road

Flagg Ranch Village

8 mi

JOHN D. ROCKEFELLER, JR. MEMORIAL PARKWAY

North

0   1 Kilometer   5
0   1 Mile   5

LEGEND

Distances between markers

Paved road

Unpaved road

Multi-use Pathway

GRAND TETON NATIONAL PARK

16 mi

JACKSON LAKE

89
191 287

Colter Bay Visitor Center

TWO OCEAN LAKE

EMMA MATILDA LAKE

Two Ocean Road

Jackson Lake Junction

Pacific Creek

Moran Junction

26 287

Signal Mountain

TETON RANGE

Leigh Lake

String Lake

Teton Park Road

River

26 89
191

River Road

Multi-use Pathway Special regulations apply. No pets allowed.

Jenny Lake

Snake

Jenny Lake Visitor Center

Bradley Lake

Taggart Lake

Shadow Mountain Road

Craig Thomas Discovery & Visitor Center

Antelope Flats

Dornan's

Moose Junction

Phelps Lake

Moose-Wilson

Kelly

Gros Ventre River Road

26 89
191

Teton Village

Gros Ventre Junction

To Wilson

Map Courtesy of the National Park Service

26

Introduction

G rand Teton National Park was established on February 26, 1929, by an act of Congress. It was only a third of its present size and excluded parts of the range and most of the valley floor. The park was expanded to its present size in 1950, with John D. Rockefeller, Jr. donating over a fifth of the 348 square miles added to the park. Appalled by the dance halls, saloons and other developments near Jenny Lake, Rockefeller had quietly been acquiring land to protect it from development.

His efforts began in 1927—two years before the park was initially created—with formation of the Snake River Land Company. The company was run by Harold Fabian; it was created to hide the Rockefeller name. Rockefeller correctly guessed that if valley residents knew his family was behind the land purchases, excessive speculation would limit his ability to buy sufficient acreage and defeat his purpose. Within three years, he had secured the core of over 33,000 acres eventually donated to the park.

In that time span, valley residents had grown increasingly suspicious of the company's activity. To quell rampant rumors, Rockefeller made the bold decision to unveil his intentions. Reaction was swift and often bitter, pitting long-time friends against each other on both the opinion that they had been hoodwinked (Rockefeller had actually paid fair market value for the land) and the hot-button issue of park expansion. Disliking the idea of the federal government limiting their use of the land for everything from hunting to grazing—and the specter of being forced off it entirely—led many valley residents to staunchly oppose park expansion. They communicated their opposition loudly and clearly to their elected representatives, and found allies in Wyoming's U.S. Senators Joseph Carey and John Kendrick. With Wyoming's own delegation opposed, park expansion efforts floundered.

Meanwhile, Rockefeller was saddled with paying taxes on his land purchases. By 1943—after repeated attempts to gift the land to the public had failed—he let President Franklin Roosevelt know that if the government wouldn't accept his gift, he would begin selling the land.

Roosevelt responded quickly. Citing the Antiquities Act of 1906, he issued an executive proclamation establishing Jackson Hole National Monument. Over 200,000 acres of federal land were placed in the newly created preserve. While Rockefeller's acreage was not included, the monument ultimately provided a means to gift his land to the public. The Secretary of Interior accepted Rockefeller's land on December 16, 1949. Less than a year later, Congress finally approved park expansion.

Josephine Fabian, wife of the man Rockefeller chose to run the Snake River Land

Company, remarked that the gift ended 25 years of "unlimited patience, effort and tenacity of purpose." She penned her reaction to the decision in 1951:

"No better proof of the vision of those early settlers can be found than to look across the open expanse of the valley toward the majestic Tetons, knowing this magnificent country will remain unspoiled forever."

It has been said that the Tetons look like mountains should: rugged, snow-capped peaks rising thousands of feet above the valley floor without foothills to lessen the impact. At 13,770 feet, the Grand Teton crowns the breathtaking range, annually drawing millions of sightseers, hikers, and climbers to admire it.

This, the youngest range in the Rocky Mountains, extends in a north-south direction for 40 miles. It forms the heart of Grand Teton National Park and the western boundary of Jackson Hole. The peaks rise 3,000 to 7,000 feet above the valley, soaring above treeline to craggy pinnacles and snowfields. They contain a dozen glaciers, remnants of the last ice age 10,000 years ago. Ten summits tower over 12,000 feet. An additional 18 top the 11,000 foot mark. Many of these giants are tightly grouped between Avalanche and Cascade Canyons, creating one of the most spectacular alpine vistas in the world.

The Tetons stunning appearance reflects the geologic forces that created the range. Approximately nine million years ago pressure deep within the Earth caused a zone of weakness on the crust to fracture, or fault. Continuing pressure along this break pushed the rock on the west side of the fault skyward—creating today's Tetons—while land east of the fault sank to form the valley floor we call Jackson Hole. Climatic cooling 250,000 years ago formed the first of many glaciers that sculpted these massive blocks of earth into the peaks and canyons we know today, chiseling the rugged peaks and gouging out deep U-shaped canyons.

Numerous periods of climatic warming and cooling followed the first glaciation. The last period cold enough to sustain large glaciers, the Pinedale Glaciation, ended approximately 10,000 years ago. As the glaciers began to recede, they dropped their load of rock and dirt scoured from the canyons, forming moraines that impounded the melting ice. In this manner, a chain of seven lakes was formed at the base of the range. From Phelps Lake northward they include Taggart, Bradley, Jenny, String, Leigh and Jackson lakes. These deep blue sapphires are ringed with lodgepole pine on their eastern shores and thick, shady forest of Engelmann spruce and Douglas fir to the west. The 24.5-mile Valley Trail skirts most of them, starting at Teton Village and crossing several glacial moraines while traveling north to Bearpaw Lake.

The valley floor is covered with sage and meadowlands comprised of over 100 species of grasses and wildflowers. Antelope, bison, moose, black bear, elk, coyotes and deer are all frequently seen in the park's lowlands and forest slopes. Among the smaller animals pikas, rabbits, marmots and ground squirrels are common. Trumpeter swans and bald eagles head the popularity list of more than 200 species of birds.

There are over 260 miles of hiking trails in the park. With the exception of those on the valley floor, most routes tend to gain elevation rapidly, switchbacking up steep slopes and canyons. The trail up Death Canyon is one of the steepest; the trail to the Forks of Cascade Canyon sports one of the easier grades. Low-lying trails are usually free of snow by mid-July. High trails can have patches of snow as late as early August. The highest point of maintained trail in the park is 10,800-ft. Static Peak Divide, closely followed by Paintbrush Divide at 10,720 feet.

BACKCOUNTRY REGULATIONS

▶ Permits are required for all overnight stays. The permit is valid only for the location and dates indicated. Permits are issued at the Moose Visitor Center on a first come, first serve basis one day before the start of a planned backcountry hike. Advance reservations can be secured before May 15th. See the following page for information.

▶ Backpackers are required to carry approved bear-proof canisters when camping below 10,000 feet. Bear-proof canisters are provided by the park or visitors may use their own hard-sided food storage canister if the item is approved by the National Park Service. See the appendix for a current listing. Hanging of food in park backcountry is no longer allowed.

▶ Campsite "improvements" such as the construction of rock walls, log benches, tree bough beds, new fire rings and trenches are prohibited.

▶ Fires are permitted only at designated lakeshore sites. Where permitted, fires must be confined to metal fire grates. Keep fires small and do not leave them unattended. Downed and dead wood may be collected. Gas stoves are encouraged.

▶ Pets, motorized equipment, wheeled conveyances, mountain bikes, firearms and explosives (including fireworks) are prohibited in the backcountry.

▶ Horse, mule and llama use is limited to established trails and stock camps. Use hitch rails where provided. Carry stock feed; grazing is not allowed.

▶ Cutting switchbacks is prohibited. Stay on established trails to prevent erosion.

▶ Keep a safe distance from wildlife. Feeding wildlife interferes with their natural diet and is harmful to their health. Feeding wildlife is prohibited.

▶ Carry out all trash and food scraps. When possible, carry out trash left by others. Never bury trash or burn aluminum.

▶ Do not pick wildflowers. It is permissible to gather berries and edible plants for personal consumption.

▶ It is illegal to remove rocks, antlers or bones.

▶ Anglers must have a Wyoming State fishing license in their possession.

▶ Prevent pollution by not washing dishes or bathing in or near streams or lakes.

For additional information on the above rules and regulations, call 307-739-3309 or 307-739-3397.

ADVANCE PERMIT RESERVATIONS

The park backcountry is very popular. Advance reservations are recommended. Requests are accepted by mail, fax, online, or in person from January 1st to May 15th. Advance permit requests are processed in the order received. Include your name, address, and daytime telephone number, the number of people, and your preferred campsites and dates. It is best to include alternate dates and campsites. Write to:

> Grand Teton National Park,
> Permits Office,
> P.O. Drawer 170,
> Moose, WY 83012
> or fax 307-739-3438

Reservations may be made in person at the Moose Visitor Center, open daily from 8 a.m. to 5 p.m. For online reservations go to: www.nps.gov/grte/planyourvisit/bcres. htm. Written confirmation will be made within two weeks. Phone reservations are not accepted. Call 307-739-3309 or 739-3397 for more information. **A non-refundable service fee of $25 will be charged for each reservation.**

Picking Up Your Permit

A reservation holds your permit but does not replace your permit. Obtain permits in person at the Moose and Colter Bay Visitor Centers or the Jenny Lake Ranger Station in the summer. During winter, permits may be picked up only at the Moose Visitor Center. You may get a permit as early as the day before your trip begins. Have alternate destinations and dates in mind in case your first choice is full. A reserved permit must be picked up by 10 a.m. the morning of your trip or it will become available to others. You may call to inform us if you will be late. If you know you will not be using your permit, please cancel your reservation as soon as possible.

1 Phelps Lake Overlook

2 Static Peak Divide & Static Peak

3 Death Canyon to Fox Creek Pass

Distance:
Phelps Lake Overlook: .9 mile one-way
Death Canyon/Open Canyon Junction: 1.6 miles one-way
Death Canyon Patrol Cabin: 3.7 miles one-way
Static Peak Divide: 7.7 miles one-way; 8 miles to Static Peak
Fox Creek Pass: 9.2 miles one-way

Elevation change:
Phelps Lake Overlook: Approx. 430 ft. gain
Death Canyon Patrol Cabin: Approx. 1,530 ft. gain, 460 ft. loss
Static Peak Divide: Approx. 4,460 ft. gain, 460 ft. loss
Static Peak: Approx. 4,960 ft. gain, 460 ft. loss
Fox Creek Pass: Approx. 3,315 ft. gain, 540 ft. loss

Maximum elevation:
Phelps Lake Overlook: 7,200 ft.
Patrol Cabin: 7,841 ft.
Static Peak Divide: 10,800 ft.
Static Peak: 11,303 ft.
Fox Creek Pass: 9,520 ft.

Maps: Grand Teton, Mount Bannon

With its broad upper expanse and nine-mile length from valley floor to the crest of the Teton Range, Death Canyon is second in size only to Webb Canyon at the northern end of the range. Phelps Lake, Static Peak Divide, Fox Creek Pass, Timberline Lake, the Valley Trail and Open Canyon Trail are all accessed from its trailhead. Hikers are drawn by lush wildflowers, the possibility of spying wildlife, superior berry picking, superb and varied alpine scenery and a notable display of the geologic forces that mold our planet. The vertical walls marking the entrance of lower Death Canyon are composed of some of the oldest exposed rock in the Tetons: Precambrian gneiss, schist and pegmatite scientifically dated to be at least 2.5 billion years old.

Switchbacks carry hikers through the narrow portals to the scenic mid-canyon floor where the trail divides. Hikers may access the crest of the range and spectacular Death Canyon Shelf by traveling west

31

to Fox Creek Pass. Or, they can ascend Static Peak Divide—the highest point of maintained trail in the park—and drop into famed Alaska Basin in adjacent Jedediah Smith Wilderness on Caribou-Targhee National Forest. Backpackers don't have to make the difficult choice. By joining Teton Crest Trail in Alaska Basin from either direction, it is possible to complete a long loop back to the trailhead.

With appealing trip options ranging from a two-hour jaunt to an extended, multi-day outing, it is not surprising that Death Canyon Trailhead draws heavy use. An early start increases your chance of enjoying wildlife and this memorable canyon in comparative solitude.

Driving Directions

To reach the trailhead, drive 12 miles north of Jackson on U.S. Hwy. 89/191 to Moose Junction. Turn left and drive over the bridge to the signed Moose-Wilson Road on your left a short distance farther. Turn in and drive three miles to the signed Death Canyon Trailhead access road on your right. This narrow paved road soon deteriorates into a potholed dirt artery that leads to a trailhead parking area at the end of the road, 1.6 miles beyond the turn-off. The signed trailhead is at the west end of the parking lot. You'll pass a large parking area shortly before reaching the end of the access road. If you are traveling in a low-clearance vehicle it is recommended that you park here to avoid the worst of the ruts just ahead. The trailhead has vault toilets and information signs, but no water.

Traveling north on the Moose-Wilson Road from Jackson Hole Mountain Resort, the trailhead access road is approximately 4 miles beyond the park entrance station.

Trail Description

Phelps Overlook and the entrance of Death Canyon beyond are reached by the Valley Trail. Towering lodgepole pine, Engelmann spruce and subalpine fir stretch high above you at the start of the well-trod path. Numerous small streams fed by snowmelt and springs above the trail contribute to the lushness of the forest floor. Magenta monkey flowers, mauve sticky geraniums, chocolate brown western coneflowers and fiery red Indian paintbrush grow in profusion well into the summer, gradually replaced by the lavender asters, goldenrod and deep pink fireweed of autumn.

The trail leaves the woods and enters open meadow as you gradually but steadily climb up the moraine. It drops slightly before entering a group of trees and cresting 7,200-ft. Phelps Lake Overlook. The viewpoint is perched 600 feet above the sparkling blue lake, formed by retreating Death Canyon Glacier 9,000 years ago. It provides a wonderful place to view the Gros Ventre Range across the valley floor to the east, the mouth of Death Canyon to the west and Phelps Lake below. At 1.5-miles long and 525 acres in size, Phelps is the fourth largest lake in Grand Teton National Park and the southernmost of seven glacially formed lakes at the base of the range. Its deepest point measures 161 feet. Phelps was a trapper who reported the lake's existence to members of the 1872 Hayden Expedition; expedition members subsequently named it in his honor. Historic JY Ranch, the first dude ranch in the valley built by Louis Joy in 1908, formerly stood at the east end of the lake. It was recently removed when the Laurance S. Rockefeller Estate, which owned the ranch and surrounding land, gifted its long held inholding to the National Park Service.

Two options at the overlook add enjoyment without extending the hike into an all-day affair. The first is to walk a short distance left (E) from the overlook along a

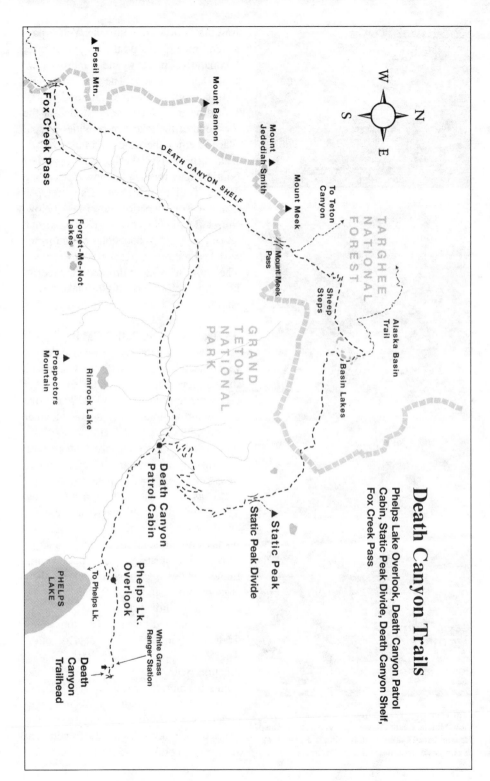

Death Canyon Trails

Phelps Lake Overlook, Death Canyon Patrol Cabin, Static Peak Divide, Death Canyon Shelf, Fox Creek Pass

▲ Fossil Mtn.

Fox Creek Pass

Mount Bannon ▲

Mount Jedediah Smith ▲

Mount Meek ▲

DEATH CANYON SHELF

To Teton Canyon

TARGHEE NATIONAL FOREST

/// Mount Meek Pass

Sheep Steps

Alaska Basin Trail

Basin Lakes

GRAND TETON NATIONAL PARK

Forget-Me-Not Lakes

Prospectors Mountain ▲

Rimrock Lake

Death Canyon Patrol Cabin ←

/// Static Peak Divide

▲ Static Peak

← To Phelps Lk.

Phelps Lk. Overlook ←

White Grass Ranger Station

PHELPS LAKE

Death Canyon Trailhead

W N E S

Top: Phelps Lake, seen from Phelps Canyon Overlook. Middle: Death Canyon opens up near the Death Canyon Patrol Cabin. Bottom: Hikers ascend rocky terrain just beyond the portal of the canyon.

trail that follows the moraine. You'll pass several nice places on the ridge that offer comparative privacy and superb views into Death Canyon. The second option is to commit to another mile and a 600-foot drop to reach a sandy stretch at the west end of the lake that provides a great place to enjoy the water and lunch before heading back. The lakeshore is accessed by continuing .7 mile on the now descending Valley Trail to the Death Canyon/Open Canyon Trail junction described below. Turn left at this junction and left again at a signed turn-off to backcountry campsites and the Laurance S. Rockefeller Preserve. The trail drops an additional 200 feet in elevation before reaching the lake's west shore.

To Death Canyon Patrol Cabin

Beyond Phelps Lake Overlook, the trail descends 400 feet in three switchbacks through forest and across talus slopes that are home to industrious pikas. Their size and coloring make this small member of the rabbit family difficult to spot, but they usually give themselves away with a shrill squeak or bark. Check for hay piles stuffed under the overhang of large rocks as your pass through the talus. These collections of herbs and grasses are frenetically gathered and stored by pikas from mid-summer until winter snow arrives. Biologists theorize pikas build tunnels under the snow to connect their storage rooms, and live off their collected food supply until spring.

The signed Death Canyon/Valley Trail Junction is reached at 1.6 miles. The Valley Trail continues left (E) to a junction with Open Canyon Trail and points beyond. Bear right to reach Death Canyon. The trail gradually ascends sage-covered slopes before entering a stretch of dense brush graced by gigantic Engelmann spruce and cottonwood trees. Laden with

Hikers work their way down a rocky, narrow section of scenic lower Death Canyon.

willows and berry bushes, both moose and black bear frequent this section of trail. Stay alert and make noise to avoid a surprise encounter.

The trail steepens as it enters the narrow mouth of the canyon, switchbacking eight times up its north side. It stays right of lively Death Canyon Creek, fed by snowmelt sufficient to support huge spruce, fir and lush understory liberally sprinkled with wild raspberry bushes.

At the switchback turns the trail passes beneath the steep rock walls of the canyon. Here, ancient schist and gneiss (pronounced "nice") are exposed in one of the most impressive geology displays in the park. These basement rocks of the planet—representing an estimated 7/8s of geologic time—metamorphosed over two billion years ago by pressure and heat deep within the Earth. The heat and pressure were great enough to soften and fold the sedimentary rock like pulled taffy, resulting in swirled and folded bands that reflect different concentrations of minerals. Quartz and feldspar form the white to light-gray swirls, hornblende and mica the dark green to blackish bands.

The fault that uplifted the Tetons, followed by glacial erosion of softer, overlying rock, exposed the banded gneiss, schist and pegmatite that form the canyon's narrow portal.

The canyon widens at the top of the switchbacks, reached at 3.5 miles. Here, the trail parallels the creek as it traverses forest and meadow for a quarter-mile to reach the Death Canyon Patrol Cabin. The small log structure was built in the 1930s by the Civilian Conservation Corp to provide shelter for the crews constructing the park trails. Rangers maintaining and patrolling the trails use it today.

A signed junction near the cabin indicates that the path continuing left (W) leads to Fox Creek Pass and Death Canyon Shelf. The trail to the right leads to Static Peak Divide and points beyond.

The view just beyond Death Canyon Patrol Cabin, looking north toward Static Peak Divide.

Those who wish to turn-around at the patrol cabin are well rewarded by traveling another half-mile toward Fox Creek Pass for wonderful views of the upper canyon.

To Static Peak Divide and Static Peak

Take the right fork at the signed junction near the patrol cabin. This steep trail gains almost 3,000 feet in four miles en route to Static Peak Divide, the highest point of maintained trail in the park. It is often snow-covered until late in the season. Check with the Jenny Lake Ranger Station or backcountry permit office for a report on current conditions before departing. Current trail condition reports are also posted online at http://www.tetonclimbingcany.blogspot.com/

Less than a quarter-mile from the patrol cabin the trail begins a steep, switchbacking ascent up open then wooded slopes. It stays left of a rushing run-off stream, crossing it 1.6 miles above the trail junction. A saddle between Horace Albright Peak to the south—shown by its former name of Peak 10,552 on the topo

map—and Static Peak is reached at 6.8 miles. The saddle offers great views of the valley floor.

The trail bears north at the saddle, and ascends a long, rocky ridge another .9 mile to the Divide. To climb Static Peak, leave the trail at the Divide and walk right (N) several yards. You'll soon see an unofficial trail winding through the talus of Static Peak's southern slopes. It gains roughly 500 feet in the .3 mile climb to the summit of the 11,303-foot peak, named for its propensity to attract lightning during storms. While the rubble covered southern slopes are a non-technical walk, Static Peak's northern side drops steeply into the chasm separating it from 11,938-ft. Buck Mountain. Mapmaker Thomas Bannon and his assistant George Buck, for whom the peak was named, first climbed this impressive peak in 1898. For many years it was called Mt. Alpenglow in recognition of its flanks catching and holding the last light of day. Prospectors Mountain to the south derives its name from the attempts to mine ore from Death Canyon in the late 1800s. In addition to these peaks, the magnificent panoramic view encompasses the valley floor, aquamarine Timberline Lake directly below you to the east, the Grand Teton farther north and the basin below Buck Mountain Pass to the west.

To Fox Creek Pass

Take the left branch of trail at the junction. It stays right of meandering Death Canyon Creek, lined with willow thickets that create prime moose habitat. At 4.2 miles, it crosses a bridge to the south side of the creek. Cascading down the canyon wall to your left is the outflow stream of Rimrock Lake. This enchanting alpine tarn is a favored destination for those with mountaineering skills; the difficult scramble, loose talus and late lingering snow place this destination out of reach for most hikers. Those who do visit the lake are reminded to treat this easily damaged alpine environment with exacting care and respect.

Beyond the bridge, the trail enters the signed Death Canyon Camping zone, steadily climbing the next mile through fir and spruce forest before reaching flowered meadows studded with slabs of granite. Just shy of six miles, the canyon begins to curve left (SW), opening up tremendous views of Death Canyon Shelf on the north wall of the canyon. This impressive limestone bench trends over three miles in a northeast/southwest direction. Unlike the lower stretches of Death Canyon, the scouring power of glaciers moving downhill did not strip the upper canyon of its sedimentary limestone and sandstone layers. The shelf is bordered to the west by a quartet of jagged 10,000-foot peaks. Mount Meek bounds the northern end of the shelf, followed by Mt. Jedediah Smith, Mount Bannon and Fossil Mountain.

At 6.6 miles, the trail crosses to the south side of Death Canyon Creek,

Top: Looking west across the open meadows near the head of Death Canyon. Bottom: The wall of Upper Death Canyon, below Death Canyon Shelf.

where it remains for the duration of the hike. Footbridges span several of the side creeks flowing into Death Canyon Creek as the trail continues its moderate ascent to the pass. The trail exits the permitted camping zone near the spectacularly flowered head of Death Canyon Creek at 8.0 miles. Beyond, it begins a steep switchbacking climb up open slopes to 9,560-ft. Fox Creek Pass and a signed intersection with Teton Crest Trail.

4 Death Canyon Shelf

Distance: 3.3 miles between Fox Creek Pass and Mount Meek Pass
Elevation change: Approx. 890 ft. gain, 700 ft. loss
Maximum elevation: 9,726 ft. at Mount Meek Pass
Maps: Mount Bannon
Season: Mid-July through mid-September

The impressive limestone bench between 9,560-ft. Fox Creek Pass and 9,726-ft. Mount Meek Pass seems ill named. "Death" does not come to mind when surveying the dramatic western slopes of Buck Mountain; the Grand, Middle and South Tetons; or the resplendent garden of subalpine wildflowers at your feet. But, death it is. The shelf bears the name of the canyon it heads. Its ominous moniker was reportedly applied after a member of an 1899 surveying party entered the canyon and was never seen again.

Teton Crest Trail traverses the length of Death Canyon Shelf, providing easy high country passage and the connecting link for a superb backpacking trip that circumnavigates the canyon. By traveling up Death Canyon, crossing the shelf, descending into Alaska Basin, then climbing to Static Peak Divide, one is able to descend the north side of Death Canyon and complete a memorable 26-mile loop.

Access

The shelf's southern end is reached by hiking 9.2 miles up Death Canyon to Fox Creek (see hike no. 3). It's northern terminus is accessed by the Devil's Stairs/Teton Shelf or Alaska Basin Trail in Jedediah Smith Wilderness.

Trail Description

Trending northeast beyond Fox Creek Pass, Death Canyon Shelf is a natural bench bound south to north by a string of 10,000-foot peaks: 10,916-ft. Fossil Mountain; an unnamed 10,612-foot summit; 10,966-ft. Mount Bannon; 10,610-ft. Mount Jedediah Smith and 10,681-ft. Mount Meek. Scattered trees and numerous seeps and springs make the shelf a hospitable place for an overnight stay. Views east of the surrounding Teton Peaks, into Death Canyon and across the valley are superb. The shelf is to be savored—not hurried through.

Sections of Death Canyon Shelf resemble a tiled floor, worn smooth and cracked by the forces of erosion and weather. The rock is predominantly dolomite and limestone, deposited by ancient seas 570 to 245 million years ago. A thick sedimentary layer once covered the entire Teton Range. Approximately nine million years ago geologic forces deep within our planet caused a zone of weakness in the Earth's crust to fracture, or fault. Continuing pressure along this break pushed the rock on the west side of the fault skyward—creating today's Tetons—while the east side of the break sank to form the valley floor we call Jackson Hole. Displacement of the valley floor was four times greater than the amount of uplift to the west, creating a far steeper eastern drop.

Climatic cooling 250,000 years ago formed glaciers that sculpted these mas-

Above: The alpine scenery of Death Canyon Shelf is unsurpassed, offering sweeping views of the heart of the Teton Range. Right: Wildflowers abound on the limestone shelf.

sive blocks of earth into the peaks and canyons we know today, chiseling the rugged peaks and gouging out deep U-shaped canyons as tongues of ice flowed to the valley floor. Most of the sedimentary layers on the steeper, eastern side of the fault were scoured away, but sedimentary rock at both ends of the fault and the gentler western slope of the Tetons still remain. The shelf is a prime example.

Mount Meek Pass marks the northern terminus of the bench. As the Teton Crest Trail drops north off the shelf at that pass, it leaves Grand Teton National Park and enters Jedediah Smith Wilderness on Targhee National Forest. The trail descends scree slopes to reach scenic Alaska Basin, intersecting trails to Teton Canyon Shelf, Buck Mountain and Hurricane Pass.

Pikas and marmots roam the bench, and bighorn sheep and black bear are oc-casionally sighted. Overnight campers are reminded that food and toiletry items must be stored in a park approved hard-sided bear canister.

39

5 Open Canyon to Mt. Hunt Divide

Distance: 7.3 miles one-way
Elevation gain: Approx. 3,530 ft.
Elevation loss: Approx. 620 ft.
Maximum elevation: 9,710 ft. at the divide
Maps: Grand Teton, Teton Village, Rendezvous Peak
Season: July through September

Like Webb and Berry Canyons at the northern end of the Teton Range, Open Canyon receives comparatively light use. This chasm near the range's southern extent lacks the scenic impact of its famous northern neighbors. Still, fine vistas are enjoyed in its lower reaches and the view near Mt. Hunt Divide is equal to better-known alpine panoramas to the north. There are picturesque places to camp in the meadows near the head of the canyon, and continuing on to Granite Canyon and Teton Crest Trail beyond offers numerous backpacking options. If you are looking for summer solitude in the Tetons, Open Canyon is a fine option.

The hike to Open Canyon begins on the Valley Trail, accessed by either Granite Canyon or Death Canyon trailheads. The Death Canyon entry point described here is shorter and the more scenic of the two. Follow the driving directions given for hike no. 1.

Trail Description

The first 1.6 miles of trail is described in detail in the write-up to Phelps Lake Overlook and Death Canyon Patrol Cabin. It climbs 400 feet through forest and meadow to Phelps Lake Overlook at .9 mile. It then drops via three long switchbacks to the signed Death Canyon/Valley Trail Junction at 1.6 miles. Bear left here to reach Open Canyon.

The trail descends to a bridged crossing of Death Canyon Creek, a luxuriant area carpeted by dense willow, shrubs and berry bushes. The understory provides cover and food for moose and black bears frequently seen near the mouth of the canyon and Phelps Lake. Stay alert and make noise to avoid surprising them.

Beyond the bridge, the path steadily ascends the wooded lateral moraine that impounds the lake to reach a signed junction with the Open Canyon Trail. The trail up Open makes a small semi-circle as it angles right into Open Canyon. Early summer, these slopes support a memorable wildflower garden.

You will reach a bridge over Open Canyon Creek at 3.9 miles. This is a nice turn-around spot for those seeking a shorter hike. As you approach the bridge, you'll see a cascade spilling down the rock wall above you to your right. If you are a seasoned Teton hiker, you may also notice that Open Canyon looks different than other canyons in the park. It lacks the broad U-shape of glacially formed Cascade or Paintbrush Canyons, and does not have a lake at its mouth. Both are clues to its origin. While glaciers played some role in carving this chasm, the canyon was mainly created by a fault than ran perpendicular to the Teton Fault. The rock on the south side of the canyon, like Death Canyon Shelf, is predominantly limestone.

Rugged terrain below Mt. Hunt Divide. Open Canyon is a fine option for those seeking Teton solitude.

Beyond the creek crossing, the trail hugs the south side of the canyon as it ascends dense forest. Snug below the trees and facing north, hikers encounter pockets of snow late into the season.

The trail emerges onto open slopes two miles up the canyon, revealing the meadowed canyon floor below. You'll pass a spur trail to your right that leads to a particularly attractive spot on the canyon floor where people obviously camp. From here, some scramble up the slopes at the head of the canyon, following Coyote Lake's outlet stream to that lake and Forget-Me-Not lakes considerably beyond. (Consult the Grand Teton topo map.) Pretty Forget-Me-Not Lakes offer good camping opportunities; rockbound Coyote Lake does not.

The final push to Mt. Hunt Divide is a series of tight, steep switchbacks that snake up the base of limestone slopes to the divide. Ahead is 10,783-ft. Mount Hunt, a nod of recognition to Wilson Price Hunt. Hunt led an 1811 expedition through Jackson Hole in an attempt to discover a route from the Missouri River to the west coast on behalf of his employer, John Jacob Astor. The party became known as the Astorians. Hunt's chief guide bore a familiar Jackson Hole name: John Hoback.

The 9,710-foot saddle provides a panoramic sweep bound by Prospectors Mountain to the north and Rendezvous Mountain to the south.

The trail drops 1,300 feet off the saddle to a signed intersection with Granite Canyon Trail in another 4.1 miles. Heading almost due west, that trail joins Teton Crest Trail 2.4 miles farther.

Mt. Hunt Divide can also be reached by hiking either the Lake Creek or Woodland trail in the Laurance S. Rockefeller Preserve to the Phelps Lake Trail, and following that path to its intersection with the trail up Open Canyon.

41

6 Stewart's Draw to Timberline Lake

Distance:
   To the former White Grass Campsite: Approx 2.7 miles
   To Timberline Lake: Approx. 4 miles
Elevation gain:
   White Grass campsite: Approx. 1,900 ft.
   To Timberline Lake: Approx, 3,900 ft.
Maximum elevation:
   White Grass campsite: Approx 8,600 ft.
   Timberline Lake: Approx. 10,400 ft.
Maps: Grand Teton
Season: Mid-July through early September

White Grass Ranch, presently a sad group of dilapidated log cabins at the foot of the Tetons, was once one of the largest dude operations in the valley. Wealthy Easterners stayed at the ranch for most of the summer. Dances and card playing, summer romances, cowboys and forays into the mountains provided the entertainment. White Grass wranglers led pack strings bearing equipment and dudes up Stewart Draw to an alpine camp at the head of the chasm. From there, they'd hike their charges to Timberline Lake, a glacial tarn at the base of Buck Mountain. Sweeping views encompassing adjacent Static Peak, Mount Wister, Nez Perce and Shadow Peak awaited the dudes. The trip was a highlight of the season.

The White Grass ceased operating in the mid-1980s, but horse trails up the draw and evidence of the ranch's high camp are still intact. Climbers en route to Buck Mountain and other destinations have forged a clearer path to the draw in recent years, making it easier to follow. While the path is obvious in the draw, there are potentially confusing horse trails in the lower sections of the hike—and steep route finding is required beyond

the head of the draw to reach the lake. Those lacking experience negotiating precipitous, rubblely terrain should consider ending their outing at the White Grass high camp. Timberline Lake is frozen much of the year, and the high, rocky terrain surrounding it is often snow-covered into July.

Driving Directions

To reach the trailhead, drive 12 miles north of Jackson on U.S. Hwy. 89/191 to Moose Junction. Turn left and drive over the bridge to the signed Moose-Wilson Road on your left a short distance farther. Turn in and drive south three miles to the signed Death Canyon Trailhead access road on your right.

The narrow paved access road soon deteriorates into a potholed dirt artery that terminates at a trailhead parking area 1.6 miles beyond the turn-off. The signed trailhead is at the west end of the parking lot. You'll pass a parking area shortly before reaching the end of the access road. If you are traveling in a low-clearance vehicle it is recommended that you park here to avoid the worst of the ruts just ahead. The trailhead has vault toilets and

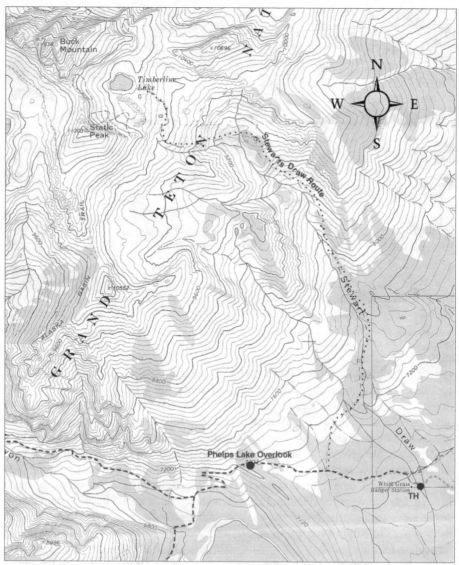

Approximate Timberline Lake Route. Inexperienced hikers should not attempt the final ascent to the lake.

information signs, but no water.

Traveling north on the Moose-Wilson Road from Jackson Hole Mountain Resort, the trailhead access road is approximately 4 miles beyond the park entrance station.

Trail Description

From the trailhead, hike west on the Valley Trail toward Phelps Overlook.

You'll cross two plank bridges. Just before the third bridge—roughly a half-mile beyond the trailhead—you'll see an unmarked trail to your right. This is the path you want. It bears generally north, climbing through open aspen forest to a large meadow. Here, it angles right across the flowered expanse toward a large glacial erratic, turning more directly north

A hiker surveys the terrain below Timberline Lake, nestled at the base of Buck Mountain and Static Peak.

upon reaching it. The path climbs then contours through open forest, crossing two small streambeds that are often dry by autumn. After dropping a short distance, it resumes its upward course at a moderate grade, staying left (S) of the draw's main stream, unseen but heard below you.

Numerous downed trees cover the path as you approach the draw and there are sections where it becomes less clear, but if you pay attention it is not particularly difficult to follow.

At approximately 1.3 miles the path reaches the main stream coursing down the draw and crosses to its north bank near a large glacial erratic. By heading slightly upstream, you can rock hop across the stream and keep your feet dry.

Beyond the crossing, the now clear path travels northwest up the draw, keeping right of the stream. As it nears the head of the draw it bears right and switchbacks up open slopes to a large boulder in a grove of whitebark pine. This is the former White Grass camp, a fine destination for a turn-around point.

To continue onward to Timberline Lake, follow the stream into the open meadow. Hop it above the point where it divides and follow its left branch up a very steep couloir on the southwest side of the cirque. Bear right when you reach a rocky ridge at the head of the couloir, soon passing a small pond. Angle left (W) above it to reach the lake. Timberline is framed by Static Peak to the immediate south, and is clearly seen from the top of that 11,303-foot summit.

The draw is named in honor of Henry Stewart, a Pennsylvanian who purchased the JY from Louis Joy in 1920. In his excellent history of Grand Teton National Park, *Crucible for Conservation*, historian Robert Righter reported that Stewart was paying alimony to four wives by the start of the 1930s. Perhaps strapped for cash, Stewart sold the ranch to the Rockefeller family for a reported $90,000.

7 Sawmill Ponds Bench

Distance: 1.2 miles RT
Elevation change: Negligible
Maximum elevation: 6,465 ft.
Maps: Moose
Season: April through November

A dawn or dusk walk along Sawmill Ponds Bench is a great way to start or end a summer day. The flat bench above the ponds offers a bird's-eye view into the riparian area below, frequented by moose, deer, muskrat, beaver and waterfowl. Panoramic views of the Teton Range and lush wildflowers add to the appeal.

The trail is an old roadbed that led to the Moose Bell, a small private ranch established circa 1925 when Bear Paw Ranch owner Coulter Huyler transferred land to friend Ed Pouch. Pouch built a summer home on the property. After enjoying it for many years, he sold the property to the Rob Cheek family in the early 1940s. The Cheeks greatly expanded Pouch's summer home, and either sold or gave neighbor Howard Ballew an acre or so of their land so he could create an airstrip to land his plane. The airstrip is still evident today. The Cheek family eventually sold its inholding to the National Park Service. The buildings were moved to C Bar V Ranch, a public school for the handicapped located on Moose-Wilson Road, in the 1980s. Scattered timber, concrete footings and log walls of outbuildings still remain on the old Moose Bell Ranch site.

Driving Directions

To reach the trailhead, drive 12 miles north of Jackson on U.S. Hwy. 89/191 to Moose Junction. Turn left and drive over the bridge to the signed Moose-Wilson Road on your left a short distance farther. Turn in and drive 1.2 miles to a gravel pullout on the left. Here, a sign describes moose habitat and you can view a portion of the ponds below. The start of the trail is the unsigned two-rack roadbed at the south end of the pullout. An anchored log across the track bars onward vehicle travel.

Approaching from Jackson Hole Mountain Resort in Teton Village, the trailhead access road is 5.8 miles beyond the park entrance station.

Trail Description

The old roadbed heads south, with numerous short paths skirting closer to the rim of the bench for views of the ponds below. The bench itself is a wildflower garden of wild parsley, long-leaf phlox, Oregon grape, lupine, woodland star, sticky geraniums, larkspur, Sitka valerian, chokecherry and dozens of other plants that will keep flower enthusiasts paging through their field guides. Blue spruce, cottonwoods and scattered aspens thrive on the bench as well. A powerline follows the roadbed for about a third of a mile before turning more directly west and visually melting into the background. Distinctive Buck Mountain dominates the western skyline, but the Grand Teton, Mt. Owen and Teewinot are also visible. Across the valley, the Gros Ventre Range rims the eastern horizon. Near the end of the old roadbed you'll find rusted metal

Above: Artifacts of the former Moose Bell Ranch can still be found along the bench above Sawmill Ponds. Right: The spring-fed ponds below Sawmill Ponds Bench are the source of Reserve Creek, which flows south near portions of the Moose-Wilson Road.

artifacts, old timber and foundations from the dismantled ranch. The track turns more directly west and ends at the abandoned airstrip. It is still discernible, but is slowly being reclaimed by sagebrush. Retrace your steps to return, or walk cross-country back to your vehicle.

Long dubbed Huckleberry Springs, valley old-timer Jack Huyler says the chain of spring-fed ponds became incorrectly known as Sawmill Ponds when a new Grand Teton National Park superintendent mistakenly believed the ponds were the location of Al Young's mill. In 1923, Young established a mill in the vicinity to produce lumber for the growing community of Moose. Before he ceased operating in 1929, he had cut and planed lumber for the now defunct Moose School and the Chapel of Transfiguration.

Huyler says Young's mill was not located at the ponds that exist today, but in the marshy area only a short distance from the Moose end of the Moose-Wilson Road. He adds that Young's sawmill pond was a popular fishing hole "before it sedged in." The spring-fed ponds below the bench are the source of Reserve Creek, which flows south near portions of the Moose-Wilson road. When bushes lining the creek are loaded with ripe fruit mid- to late August, visitors viewing black bears feasting on the berries often cause traffic jams on the narrow road.

Laurance S. Rockefeller Preserve

The 1,106-acre Laurance S. Rockefeller Preserve is located at the southern end of Phelps Lake on the site of the JY Ranch, a dude ranch established in the early 1900s by Louis Joy. The valley's first dude ranch was one of numerous properties at the base of the Tetons that John D. Rockefeller, Jr.—Laurance's father—bought during the 1920s and 30s with the intent of protecting and enlarging Grand Teton National Park. Over 33,000 acres purchased by Mr. Rockefeller eventually became part of the 1950 expansion of Grand Teton National Park. At the urging of some in the Park Service—who reasoned Mr. Rockefeller would remain interested in the area if he visited it frequently—the family retained the JY as a summer retreat. Laurance inherited the property after his father's death in 1960.

The Laurance S. Rockefeller Estate gave outlying portions of its 3,100-acre ranch inholding to the National Park Service in the 1990s. Laurance Rockefeller announced his intent to gift the remaining ranch land—the heart of the JY—to Grand Teton National Park in a May 26, 2001, ceremony held on the property. The gift carried maintenance and preservation stipulations designed to keep the future preserve a place where visitors could experience a renewed sense of nature and spiritual and emotional connection to Phelps Lake and the Teton Range.

A key stipulation was removal of the historic ranch structures to return the land to its natural state. Between July 2004 and May 2007, thirty buildings, roads, utilities and other structures were removed, and the developed areas were reclaimed to improve wildlife habitat, reduce non-native vegetation, and restore disjointed wetlands. Roughly half of the structures—including the oldest JY cabins and dining and recreation buildings—were moved to Rockefeller property outside Grand Teton National Park. The remaining structures were donated to the Park Service and relocated within the park to be used for housing and service facilities.

With the old ranch buildings removed, work began on a trail system and facilities required for public use of the preserve. The centerpiece of the latter is the 7,573-foot. visitor center designed by Carney Architects of Jackson, Wyoming. The design and construction of the center and outlying restrooms—funded by the Laurance S. Rockefeller Estate—incorporated sustainable, environmental technology that earned

Photos, top to bottom:
Preserve entrance. The center's use of sustainable technology and materials earned it Wyoming's first LEED certification. View of the Tetons from inside the center. The center's reading room. NPS photos.

the project the U.S. Green Building Council's first Leadership in Energy and Environmental Design (LEED) designation in Wyoming and only the fifty-second LEED platinum rating nationwide.

The innovative center features high definition nature videos, large-scale photography, and a soundscape room with nature recordings from the preserve. A resource room furnished with tables, chairs and a fireplace provides an inviting space for visitors to explore books, albums and maps.

The LSR Preserve Center is open annually on a daily basis from 8 a.m. to 5 p.m., May through September. Visitors can call 307-739-3654 for information on programs or facilities, road/parking lot access, and exact seasonal opening and closing dates.

Exploring the Preserve

Eight miles of trails wind throughout the preserve; several connect to existing trails within Grand Teton National Park. The popular new trail system opened in November of 2007 when the property was formally transferred to the National Park Service. Sagebrush and wildflower meadows, mixed conifer and aspen forest, and wetlands are among the natural communities hikers will encounter. The most heavily used, primary trail is the Lake Creek/Woodland Loop. It showcases Phelps Lake, Lake Creek and the Teton Range. Few short trails in Grand Teton National Park yield such big scenic rewards—but be prepared to share it with others. Secondary trails lead visitors to a series of overlooks along the glacial ridges.

Regulations and Guidelines

Horses are prohibited on internal trails on the preserve. Bicycles and pets are also prohibited on preserve trails, and visitors are required to pack out all trash. Parking is limited to roughly 50 cars at a time to control overuse of preserve trails; it is suggested that group size be limited to 10 people. Vehicles may not be parked in the lot overnight.

Preserve trails are open year-round. Visitors may utilize the preserve parking lot (weather dependent) after the center is closed for the season. The Moose-Wilson Road is seasonally closed to vehicles November 1. Preserve trails may then be accessed by hiking, biking or skiing on the closed Moose-Wilson Road to reach the preserve, located approximately 1.75 miles north of the

Granite Canyon trailhead and 3.7 miles south of the Moose-Wilson intersection with the inner Park Road. Bicyclists can lock their bikes to the racks located in the parking lot before setting out to hike.

Regrettably, some users illegally stop on the narrow Moose-Wilson Road, unload coolers, sun umbrellas and other paraphernalia, and haul them over preserve trails to set up a day camp along the shore of Phelps Lake. This is not the intent of the preserve and such use is discouraged. It negatively impacts the contemplative experience for other users, diminishes the chance of seeing wildlife, and is taxing on the resource. Visitors wishing to spend extended time by a lake should consider String Lake, which has road access, picnic tables and nearby bathroom facilities, or established picnic areas along the shore of Jackson Lake.

Driving Directions

To reach the preserve, drive 12 miles north of Jackson on U.S. Hwy. 89/191 to Moose Junction. Turn left and drive over the bridge to the signed Moose-Wilson Road on your left a short distance farther. Turn in and drive 3.7 miles to the signed entrance to the LSR Preserve off the left side of the road.

Approaching from the Jackson Hole Mountain Resort in Teton Village, the preserve entrance is located 3.3 miles beyond the park entrance station .

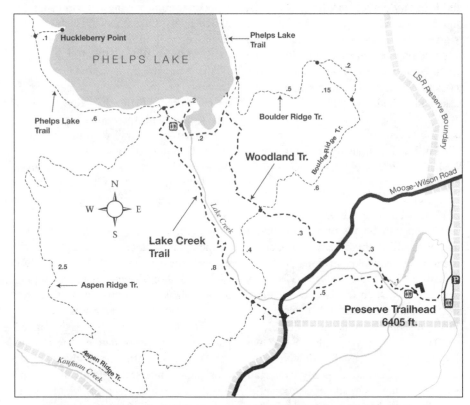

Laurance S. Rockefeller Preserve in Grand Teton National Park

8 Lake Creek/Woodland Trail Loop

Distance: 3 miles RT
Elevation gain: Approx. 300 feet
There is a 228 foot elevation gain from the preserve trailhead at 6,405 feet to Phelps Lake, nestled at 6,633 feet. Several small drops and climbs are encountered en route to the lake.
Maximum elevation: Approx. 6,640 ft.
Maps: Book map pg. 49
Season: May through October
Center opening date and parking lot access is weather dependent. Call 307-739-3654 for information.

Impressive views into Death Canyon and the high Teton Range, Phelps Lake and its pretty outflow stream, woodlands, and nominal elevation change combine to make the Lake Creek/Woodland Trail Loop a popular short outing in Grand Teton National Park. Log benches invite users to rest and relax en route to Phelps Lake and at the lake itself.

Driving Directions

Follow directions to the Laurance S. Rockefeller Preserve given on page 49.

Trail Description

The well-signed Lake Creek/Woodland Loop trail begins on the southwest side of the LSR Preserve Visitor Center. The loop can be walked in either direction. Perhaps because the Park Service lists Lake Creek first in the loop description, most people proceed in a clockwise direction. This option is described below.

The wide gravel path passes two limited mobility accessible viewing spots of Lake Creek and a pretty waterfall before reaching a signed intersection at .1 mile. Bear left here and cross the bridge to continue on Lake Creek Trail.

The path gently climbs through wooded terrain, staying left and generally above lively Lake Creek. It bends away from the creek to reach a signed crossing of the Moose-Wilson Road at .6 miles. It then travels through lodgepole and Douglas fir forest, soon descending at an easy grade, to reach a signed 4-way intersection with the Aspen Trail to your left, the Boulder Trail to your right at .7 miles. Continue straight. The trail closely parallels Lake Creek as it traverses wooded terrain. At 1.1 miles, it leaves the forest and enters a large, open meadow backdropped by 11,241-ft. Prospectors Mountain. The trail skirts the right edge of the opening, then bends right as it re-enters forested terrain. It moderately ascends a short distance before dropping to two plank bridge crossings in an area that can be quite wet early season.

At 1.4 miles, you'll reach the signed path to the comfort station. The trail to the lake travels straight another .1 mile, crossing an intersection with the Phelps Lake Trail, to reach an overlook of Phelps Lake and Death Canyon. Soak in the

Above: The view from the overlook along Phelps Lakeshore is a highlight of the Lake Creek/Woodland Trail loop. Left: Lake Creek plunges over a rock lip near the start of this loop hike. The creek is Phelps Lake outflow stream.

eat lunch and enjoy Lake Creek without impeding foot traffic.

Onward, the path wraps around Phelps Lake's southeast arm, then bends north to reach a signed intersection with the Woodland Trail. Turn right here to complete the loop in another 1.1 miles.

The Woodland Trail climbs gently uphill through open, wooded terrain for .4 miles to reach a signed intersection with the Boulder Ridge Trail to your left, the Aspen Ridge Trail to your right. Continue straight. The trail now gently descends to a crossing of the Moose-Wilson Road in another .3 mile. Beyond, it is an easy .4 miles back to the trailhead.

magnificent view before backtracking the short distance to the Phelps Lake Trail, and follow the directional signs to Woodland Trail to continue the loop. The trail follows a bend in the lakeshore and passes a trail to the comfort station before reaching a bridge over Lake Creek outlet. Stepped down benches on both sides of the bridge provide a wonderful place to

51

9 Aspen Ridge/Boulder Ridge Trail Loop

Distance: 5.8 miles round-trip
Elevation change: Approx. 800 ft.
> This loop was numerous ups-and-downs as it ascends glacial moraines surrounding Phelps Lake. The Park Service rates it moderate to strenuous.

Maximum elevation: Approx. 6,800 feet
Maps: Book map pg. 49
Season: May through October
> Center opening date and parking lot access is weather dependent. Call 307-739-3654 for information.

The Aspen Ridge/Boulder Ridge Trail Loop carries hikers to the same breathtaking overlook of Phelps Lake enjoyed on the shorter Lake Creek/Woodland Trail Loop. Because it is longer than the Lake Creek/Woodland Trail loop, far fewer preserve visitors elect to do this hike, making it a good choice for those seeking a quieter outing and the chance to see area wildlife. Beautiful aspen groves and large glacial erratics add to the appeal and variety of this loop hike.

Driving Directions

Follow directions to the Laurance S. Rockefeller Preserve given on page 49.

Trail Description

The loop, of course, can be hiked in either direction. This description travels clockwise by starting with the Aspen Ridge Trail, accessed off Lake Creek Trail. Follow the broad gravel path that begins on the southwest side of the LSR Preserve Visitor Center to a signed intersection at .1 mile. Turn left here and cross the bridge over Lake Creek.

The path gently climbs through wooded terrain, staying left and generally above lively Lake Creek. It bends away from the creek to reach a signed crossing of the Moose-Wilson Road at .6 mile. It

then travels through lodgepole and Douglas Fir forest, soon descending at an easy grade, to reach a signed 4-way intersection with the Aspen Trail to your left, the Boulder Trail to your right at .7 mile.

Turn left (W) onto the Aspen Trail. The trail ascends a hill, then drops via switchbacks to cross a service road. Beyond, it moderately ascends through young lodgepole then aspen forest, switchbacking as it climbs to the top of a rise where a sign indicates you have hiked 1.2 miles.

The trail drops off the rise, soon paralleling Kaufman Creek through a section of open forest. It then ascends a ridge that opens sweeping views of Granite and Open Canyons, and 10,783-ft. Mount Hunt. Aspen groves surround the trail as it climbs via switchbacks to reach the high point of the hike at the top of the moraine. 2.4 miles beyond the Visitor Center.

The trail leaves the aspen as it drops off the morainal ridge, crosses a grassy meadow and picks up an old ranch road that leads to the intersection with Lake Creek Trail at 3.2 miles and the Phelps Lake overlook just beyond. This is not country to hurry through—though you've intersected the popular Lake Creek/Woodland Trail loop, and will notice an increase in the number of visitors.

Returning from the overlook, turn left

Top: A hiker explores a glacial erratic along Boulder Ridge Trail. Right: Prospectors Mountain, viewed along the Aspen Ridge section of this loop hike.

onto the Phelps Lake Trail and follow the directional signs to the Woodland Trail. The path parallels a bend in the lakeshore and passes a trail to the comfort station before reaching a bridge over Lake Creek outlet. It then wraps around Phelps Lake's southeast arm and arcs north to reach a signed intersection with the Woodland Trail to your right at 3 miles. Continue straight another .1 mile to the signed intersection with the Boulder Ridge Trail.

The Boulder Trail immediately begins ascending above and away from the lakeshore. Like the Aspen Trail, it climbs and drops as it travels through openings and pretty pine and fir forest. You'll reach a split at 3.6 miles; both branches rejoin the main trail. Near the split and just after, you'll encounter the large boulders that give the trail its name. Glacial erratics are different in size or type from surrounding rocks, carried to their location by riding atop massive ice flows thousands of years ago. Erratics from the central Tetons have been found as far away as Mosquito Creek, 25 miles to the south.

Boulder Ridge Trail intersects the Woodland Trail at the 5.1 mile mark. Bear left here to return to the trailhead in .7 miles.

10 Phelps Lake Loop

Distance: 7.1 miles RT
Elevation change: Approx. 400 ft, gain and loss
Maximum elevation: Approx. 6,800 ft.
Maps: Book map opposite page.
Season: May through October
Center opening date and parking lot access is weather dependent.
Call 307-739-3654 for information.

The view across Jenny Lake into the steep portals of Cascade Canyon is justly one of the most photographed spots in Grand Teton National Park. In the fall of 2008, a new kid in town became an overnight rival: The view across Phelps Lake into Death Canyon. The priceless panorama is a lasting legacy of the Laurance S. Rockefeller Trust, which entrusted land along the east shore of the lake into the care of the National Park Service for people of the world to treasure.

Unlike Jenny, hikers circling Phelps enjoy sustained views of Death Canyon without paralleling a busy road. The loop travels through the preserve and the parklands surrounding it. Sagebrush meadows, wetlands, forest and lake environments are traversed along its 7.1-mile course.

While the loop can be walked in either direction, the Tetons are shown to best advantage by hiking counter-clockwise around Phelps. Mileage is calculated by hiking up Lake Creek Trail, hiking around Phelps, and returning either via Lake Creek or Woodland Trail.

Driving Directions

Follow directions to the Laurance S. Rockefeller Preserve given on page 49.

Trail Description

The trail begins as a wide gravel path on the southwest side of the LSR Preserve Visitor Center. Bear left at a signed intersection at .1 mile and cross the bridge to continue on Lake Creek Trail.

The path gently climbs through wooded terrain, staying left and generally above lively Lake Creek. It bends away from the creek to reach a signed crossing of the Moose-Wilson Road at .6 miles. It then travels through lodgepole and Douglas fir forest, soon descending at an easy grade, to reach a signed 4-way intersection with the Aspen Trail to your left, the Boulder Trail to your right at .7 miles. Continue straight. The trail closely parallels Lake Creek as it traverses wooded terrain. At 1.1 miles, it enters a large, open meadow backdropped by 11,241-ft. Prospectors Mountain. The trail skirts the right edge of the opening, then bends right as it re-enters forested terrain. It moderately ascends a short distance before dropping to two plank bridge crossings in an area that can be quite wet early season.

At 1.4 miles, you'll reach the signed path to the comfort station. The trail to the lake travels straight another .1 mile, crossing an intersection with the Phelps Lake Trail, to reach an overlook of Phelps Lake and Death Canyon. Soak in the magnificent view before backtracking the short distance to the Phelps Lake Trail, and follow the directional signs to

54

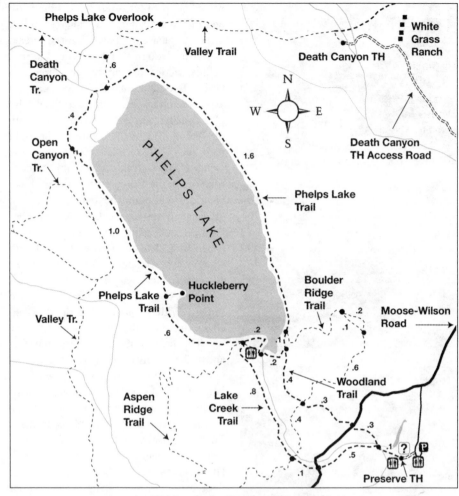

Phelps Lake Loop trail map

Woodland Trail to continue the loop. The trail follows a bend in the lakeshore and passes a trail to the comfort station before reaching a bridge over Lake Creek outlet. Stepped down benches on both sides of the bridge provide a wonderful place to eat lunch and enjoy Lake Creek without impeding foot traffic.

Onward, the path wraps around Phelps Lake's southeast arm, then bends north to reach a signed intersection with the Woodland Trail. Continue straight here and .1 mile farther, where the Boulder Ridge Trail comes in from the right.

The wooded trail travels north close to but above Phelp's eastern shoreline. You'll pass a section of buck-and-rail fence that marks the former Rockefeller property boundary and a signed junction near a horse trail before passing a large boulder often used by local swimmers to jump into Phelps. If swimmers haven't taken it over, it offers a great place to sit and enjoy the lake.

Trails to three backcountry campsites and a bear pole branch off the main trail

Top: The portal of Death Canyon is a highlight of the Phelps Lake Loop hike, both viewed across the lake and from the lake's north end. Middle: A young black bear roots for insects in a meadow on the west side of the lake. Bottom: Phelps Lake from the trail.

before the path turns left around the north end of the lake. Here, a sandy shoreline offers a pleasant "beach" for a break. Towering Douglas fir bordering the trail in this section are among the largest in Grand Teton National Park, and beautiful aspen march up the hillsides to the north.

You'll reach a signed junction with the Valley Trail at 3.6 miles. The right path leads to an intersection with the Death Canyon Trail above, and the continuance of the Valley Trail to Phelps Lake Overlook and points beyond. To complete the loop around Phelps Lake, keep left.

The path gently descends and enters an opening that provides views of Death Canyon's portal. Stay alert as you enter a wooded area near a bridged crossing of Death Canyon Creek a short distance farther. With an abundance of food and cover, this is black bear habitat.

The trail climbs the lateral moraine above the northwest corner of the lake to reach a signed junction with Open Canyon Trail at 4.0 miles, the high point of the hike. Bear left and descend steps to a meadow crossed by long plank bridges. The trail closely follows the western lakeshore for the next three-quarters of a mile. Huckleberry bushes abound on the forest floor in this section, their berries a treat that ripens mid- to late August.

You'll reach a signed intersection with Huckleberry Point to the left at 5.0 miles. Continue straight. The trail climbs then descends a small rise before leveling and traversing flat, open terrain around the south end of the lake. This is a wetlands area; grated metal walkways have been placed to prevent foot traffic damaging the sensitive terrain. At 5.6 miles, you'll reach a signed junction with Lake Creek Trail. Either return the way you came, or retrace your steps around the lakeshore to the Woodland Trail to hike back to the trailhead. The mileage is the same.

Taggart/Bradley Trailhead

Two popular lake loops and a rigorous trail/route hike up Avalanche Canyon depart from busy Taggart/Bradley Trailhead. The large paved parking lot provides easy driving access, and picnic tables are available on the opposite side of the road, just after the bridge spanning vigorous Cottonwood Creek. Vault toilets are located in both venues; drinking water is not available.

Taggart and Bradley Lakes are named after members of Hayden's 1872 expedition to this area. Frank Bradley, chief geologist for the expedition, drown while trying to find a ford across the Snake River. W.R. Taggart was an assistant geologist for the same expedition. He first visited Jackson Hole in 1860 as a member of a survey for the U.S. Army Engineers led by Capt. W. F. Raynolds.

Driving Directions

Drive 12 miles north of Jackson on U.S. Hwy. 89/191 to Moose Junction. Turn left and drive past park headquarters to the Moose Entrance of Grand Teton National Park. From the entrance it is three miles to the signed Taggart and Bradley Lake parking area on the left (W) side of the road.

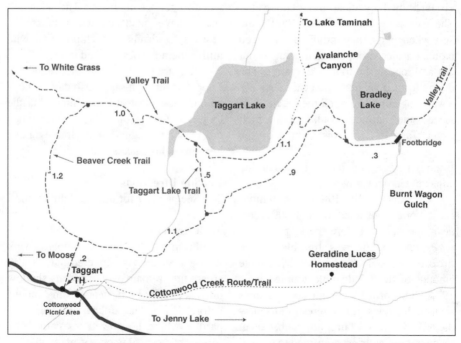

Taggart/Bradley Loop, Beaver Creek Loop, and Lucas Homestead Trails

57

11 Taggart/Bradley Lake Loop

12 Taggart Lake via Beaver Creek Loop

Distance:
    Taggart and Bradley Lake Loop: 5.1 miles RT
    Taggart Lake via Beaver Creek Loop: 4.0 miles RT
Elevation change:
    Taggart and Bradley Lake Loop: Approx. 620 ft. gain and loss
    Taggart Lake via Beaver Creek Loop: Approx. 420 ft. gain and loss
Maximum elevation:
    Taggart and Bradley Lake Loop: Approx. 7,140 ft.
    Taggart Lake via Beaver Creek Loop: 7050 ft.
Maps: Moose, Grand Teton. Book map pg. 57
Season: Mid-May through October

Bradley and Taggart Lakes rest at the base of the Tetons between Garnet and Avalanche Canyons, offering alpine vistas framed by clear mountain water. The pair were formed over 9,000 years ago when glaciers grinding down steep mountainsides dropped their gouged out dirt and rock at the foot of the range. The debris formed ridges called moraines. As a warming climate caused the ice flows to recede, the moraines contained the melt water. Taggart Lake was formed by the glacier that carved Avalanche Canyon, Bradley Lake by the mass of ice that dug adjacent Garnet Canyon.

On August 30, 1985, a lightning-caused fire consumed over 1,000 acres near the lakes before park personnel were able to suppress the blaze. The fire was intensely hot, fueled by a large amount of dead lodgepole toppled by a 1974 windstorm. Although charred trees scar the hillsides, it is interesting to view the effects of the fire and subsequent regeneration. Nutrients returned to the soil by the conflagration have created lush,

flower-filled terrain and the downed trees have drawn increased numbers of insects and birds that prey on them, particularly woodpeckers and owls. The standing snags have also attracted bluebirds, kestrels, squirrels and chipmunks, who utilize them for nesting and homes.

Taggart Lake via the Beaver Creek Loop cuts through sagebrush flats that can be quite hot most of the summer, but the loop is a good choice early season when the northern Taggart and Bradley Lake hike around the lakes still harbors snow.

Driving Directions
See page 57 for trailhead directions.

Trail Description
From the trailhead signboard, walk west across the sage-covered flats. You'll cross the remains of several shallow ditches dug by homesteader Jim Mangus before 1920. The ditches irrigated the pasture where he grazed his cattle. His former homestead is one of many that are now part of the park.

The footbridge over Bradley Lake's outlet stream is a scenic extension of the Taggart/Bradley Lake Loop.

You'll reach a trail junction at .2 mile. The left fork leads to Taggart Lake via Beaver Creek Trail. The path to the right is the start of the Taggart and Bradley Lake loop hike.

Taggart and Bradley Lake Loop

Bear right at the junction. The path skirts the base of the moraine and crosses a bridge over Taggart Creek before beginning a gradual ascent up a gully to the right of the creek. Lively Taggart Creek is fed by both Taggart Lake and snowmelt from Avalanche Canyon to the west. The Grand Teton—obscured by trees before the 1985 blaze—towers over charred trunks still standing on the forest floor. The floor itself is liberally covered with Ceanothus Velutinus, commonly called snowbrush. This aromatic member of the buckthorn family has shiny green leaves shaped like an egg and small, five-petaled white flowers that grow in clusters. Both its flowers and berries contain saponin, a substance used by Native Americans and homesteaders as an alternative to soap.

At 1.3 miles, the trail to Taggart and Bradley Lakes divides. You may head in either direction to complete the northern loop; for purpose of description bear left and walk among charred snags toward Taggart Lake. This is a good stretch to examine how the area is regenerating. Many people are surprised at the number of young lodgepole pine and ask park personnel if the area has been replanted. It has not. Lodgepole reseed themselves through a clever adaptation to fire. Some of the trees' cones are serotinous, a botanical term meaning "late opening." They remain closed on the tree for 10 or more years. Heat exceeding 112° melts the resin closing the cone and the seeds are dispersed. Studies have shown that 20-40 seeds per square foot are dropped when the cones open—a rather astonishing million seeds per acre.

A signed intersection with the Valley

59

Trail and the east shore of Taggart Lake is reached at 1.8 miles. Taggart's clear, blue-green waters sport good fishing (a Wyoming fishing license is required) and often reflect the 13,770-ft. Grand Teton. Particularly nice views of that signature peak are enjoyed on the bridge over Taggart's outlet stream, reached by walking a short distance to the left (S).

To continue to Bradley Lake, bear right onto the Valley Trail at the junction. The trail parallels Taggart's east shore then climbs a moraine separating the two bodies of water. After switchbacking to the top of the moraine, it drops 100 feet to a trail intersection near the southeast shore of Bradley Lake at 2.9 miles.

Here, the trail to your right climbs the moraine and curves south on its way back to the parking lot, reached in 2.2 miles. This completes the loop. It is highly recommended that those with time and energy continue left at the junction another .3 mile to a footbridge over the narrow neck of Bradley Lake. The view near the bridge is spectacular.

Taggart Lake via Beaver Creek

Bear left at the junction. In roughly 80 yards you'll reach a second junction. Keep left. The path follows a flat to slightly rolling course through open sagebrush-covered terrain. After about half a mile it bears right (W) and begins paralleling the north bank of Beaver Creek. Both moose and bear frequent this section. Stay alert.

The path gradually climbs to an intersection with the Valley Trail at 1.4 miles. Bear right here and ascend to the top of the lateral moraine impounding Taggart Lake—the high point of this hike. You'll enjoy nice views of the range and Taggart Lake below before descending to a long wooden bridge that spans Taggart's southern outlet. A memorable view from the bridge of the Grand Teton reflected in Taggart Lake is a highlight of this hike.

Beyond the bridge, the path hugs the southeastern shore of Taggart a short distance before reaching a signed junction at 2.4 miles. The Valley Trail you are on continues to Bradley Lake. To complete the loop, turn right onto the Taggart Lake Trail. The path travels north then east through a section of forest that burned in a 1985 lightning strike. The size of the new forest growth two decades later offers a vivid reminder both that nature regenerates, and that it is a slow process at this elevation and latitude. It takes a decade for lodgepole pine in Jackson Hole to grow an inch in diameter.

At 2.9 miles, you'll reach a junction with the Bradley Lake Trail. Keep right. The path climbs a short distance to the top of the moraine between the two lakes before steadily descending. You'll soon parallel spirited Taggart Creek to your right, and cross two small bridges over the creek before reaching the sagebrush flats and an intersection with the trail that returns you to the parking lot.

The Grand, reflected in Taggart Lake.

13 Avalanche Canyon

Distance:
> Lake Taminah: Approx. 10 miles RT
> Snowdrift Lake: Approx. 12 miles RT

Elevation gain:
> Lake Taminah: 2,455 ft.
> Snowdrift Lake: 3,460 ft.

Maximum elevation:
> Lake Taminah: 9,080 ft.
> Snowdrift Lake: 10,006 ft.

Maps: Moose, Grand Teton.
Season: July through mid-September.

Accessed only by game trails and a path forged by mountaineers, Avalanche Canyon is perhaps the least visited major canyon in the park. Climbers walk up it to approach routes up Buck Mountain, Mount Wister, Nez Perce, Cloudveil Dome and the South Teton. Hikers are drawn to Shoshoko Falls and high alpine lakes surrounded by snow-covered peaks. Pioneer Teton guide Paul Petzoldt called the canyon "one of the most beautiful in the entire United States."

The cross-country route up Avalanche Canyon is accessed by the popular trail to Taggart and Bradley Lakes. An unofficial, unmarked climbers trail between the two lakes heads west up the canyon. The path is not difficult to follow to the forks of Taggart Creek. Here hikers can enjoy views of 100-plus foot Shoshoko Falls. Travel beyond the forks to the lakes involves negotiating a route through brush, steep gullies, rock slabs and potentially snow-covered terrain. It is not recommended for inexperienced hikers or those who don't know how to travel safely on steep snow.

Driving Directions

See page 57 for trailhead directions.

Trail Description

Begin walking on the trail to Taggart Lake, crossing a broad meadow before reaching a trail junction at .2 mile. Bear right at the junction, soon crossing a bridge spanning Taggart Creek. At 1.3 miles you'll reach a second junction. Take the trail to the left to reach Taggart Lake a half-mile farther. This section of trail is described in detail in the write-up for hike no. 11.

Upon reaching Taggart Lake, bear right (N) onto the Valley Trail and walk toward Bradley Lake. The trail parallels Taggart's east shore, offering wonderful views across the lake into Avalanche Canyon. The broad, glacially carved chasm is bound by 11,490-ft. Mount Wister on the left (S) and 11,901-ft. Nez Perce on the right (N).

At approximately 2.6 miles, just before the trail begins to switchback up the glacial moraine separating the two

Shoshoko Falls in Avalanche Canyon

climbers trail follows this branch of the creek. Follow the path along the right (N) side of the creek through brush, willows and talus. It leads to Shoshoko Falls, a frothy 100-plus foot cascade that flows from the outlet of 9,080-ft. Lake Taminah. To reach the lake, walk right of the falls and ascend either the rock slabs or gullies until you reach somewhat flatter terrain. Carefully traverse left (S) to reach the rim of the lake.

If you wish to continue to Snowdrift Lake, an additional mile and almost 1,000 feet above Taminah, hike along the north shore to the rocky meadow at Lake Taminah's west end, then ascend the right side of the obvious drainage. Near the top of the drainage veer left (S) to gain access to the bench that circles the lake.

Following an average winter there is usually a significant amount of snow from the high, timberless country around the lakes all the way to the upper reaches of Avalanche Canyon. If you do not know how to safely negotiate steep snow it is best to stop below Shoshoko Falls.

Hikers attempting to reach the lakes should also be aware that, true to its name, avalanches frequently scour the canyon. During the winter of 1985-86 huge slides uprooted dozens of trees, making cross-country travel a slow proposition.

Allow yourself plenty of time to complete the trip. The rugged, rocky terrain takes much longer to negotiate than a maintained park trail.

lakes, you'll see a large, dead fallen tree to your left. The unofficial use trail up the canyon begins below the tree. This small but distinctive path heads west. Following the north side of Taggart Creek, it winds first through several boggy areas, then willow and brush as it gains elevation. Where the path looks like it splits, keep left closer to the stream. It splits again at the start of an extended rock field. Again, stay on the lower path closer to the creek.

Taggart Creek divides near several large boulders roughly 4.5 miles and 1,100 feet above the parking area. The left fork of the creek heads to the base of Buck Mountain. An intermittent

14 Geraldine Lucas Rock and Homestea

Distance: 1.2 miles one-way
Elevation gain: Negligible.
Maximum elevation: Approx. 6,700 ft.
Maps: Moose
Season: May through October

The short, cross-country walk along Cottonwood Creek to Geraldine Lucas Rock is an excellent half-day choice for fishermen, young families, history buffs and those who lack mountain lungs. It's also a serene place to observe bugling elk cutting across quiet meadows on frosty fall evenings.

Driving Directions

Drive 12 miles north of Jackson on U.S. Hwy. 89/191 to Moose Junction. Turn left and drive past park headquarters to the entrance of Grand Teton National Park. From the entrance it is 3.6 miles to the turnoff to the climbers ranch on your left. Turn in, drive across the bridge over Cottonwood Creek and park off the right side of the road in the obvious pull-off. An anglers use trail heads north along the west bank of Cottonwood Creek.

Trail Description

The trail parallels frothy Cottonwood Creek, aptly named for the lovely trees that grace its banks. Black and narrow-leafed cottonwoods grow in Grand Teton National Park. The seeds of these deciduous trees are attached to fluffy fiber, or "cotton," that carries them on the wind, helping the trees reproduce.

The beauty of the walk is heightened early to mid-summer, when sweet-smelling lupine reaches peak bloom and paints the surrounding terrain shades of indigo, periwinkle and lavender. Black bear, elk and mice consume various components of this hardy member of the pea family, from roots to seeds. Scarlet gilia, vanilla-colored wild buckwheat and sunny mule's ears add to the colorful palette.

Just under the halfway point, you'll reach a log bridge over a side tributary to Cottonwood Creek. The logs have a bit of "give" to them, so pay attention.

The path winds north through the trees along the creek, then bears slightly west and enters a meadow. A short distance ahead are the remains of Geraldine Lucas' homestead. Posted signs remind visitors not to enter the buildings or remove artifacts. Unless restrictions are put in place, it's presently okay to explore the outside of the buildings.

The path bends more directly left (W) before it reaches the homestead and enters sparse lodgepole forest. It soon reaches a second opening framed by the signature peaks of the range. The lone boulder ahead is known locally as Geraldine Lucas Rock. Cemented into the top of the boulder is a plaque noting her birth and death.

Geraldine Lucas began her homestead on Cottonwood Creek in 1913. The following year she filed a claim under the 1906 Forest Homestead Act. Lucas "proved up" her 160-acre parcel by living on in for five years and making required improvements.

Geraldine Lucas' homestead was so beautiful Rockefeller's land agent, Harold Fabian, chose to live in it.

Records show these included a five-room log cabin, an irrigation ditch, a storehouse, granary and buck-and-rail fence. In 1918, she filed for a certificate of land ownership. A series of bureaucratic problems delayed approval until 1922, nine years after the process was started.

Lucas was a feisty, independent woman intrigued by the small number of climbers scaling the Tetons in the 1920s. At the age of 58, she decided to have a crack at the high peaks herself. On August 19, 1924, she and three men—included famed mountaineer Paul Petzoldt—successfully climbed the Grand. She unfurled an American flag on the 13,770-foot summit and posed for the camera. Lucas was the first Jackson Hole woman to ascend the peak, the second overall. Eleanor Davis claimed first ascent honors for women less than a year earlier, when she and Albert Ellingwood successfully summited the Owen-Spalding route on August 27, 1923. Lucas' accomplishment was barely noted in the local papers. To put it mildly, she was a bit of a renegade. She had returned to college as a single mother, got divorced, wore knickers and built a homestead by herself. Now she was climbing mountains!

Lucas was one of many valley residents adamantly opposed to park expansion, perhaps stemming from her sour experience with the government in securing her homestead claim. She is on record stating that John D. Rockefeller—whose Snake River Land Company's acquisitions were later donated to the park—would not get her off her land. When she died without a will on August 12, 1938, her son Russell sold the property to neighbor J.D. Kimmel. Five years later, Kimmel ironically sold the property to Rockefeller.

But perhaps Geraldine Lucas was right: She remained on her land. Russell scattered his mother's ashes near the large boulder on her former property.

15 Surprise and Amphitheater Lakes
16 Delta Lake

Distance:
        Surprise Lake: 4.6 miles one-way
        Amphitheater Lake: 4.8 miles one-way
        Delta Lake: 4 miles one-way
Elevation gain:
        Surprise Lake: Approx. 2,840 ft.
        Amphitheater Lake: Approx. 3,000 ft.
        Delta Lake: 2,260 ft.
Maximum elevation:
        Surprise and Amphitheater Lakes: Approx. 9,720 ft.
        Delta Lake: Approx. 9,000 ft.
Maps: Moose, Grand Teton Book map pg. 69
Season: July through mid-September

A resplendent high cirque, alpine lakes and sweeping views of Jackson Hole on the ascent characterize the Glacier Trail to Surprise and Amphitheater Lakes. In a relatively short distance, hikers walk through the major plant zones in the park, beginning on the sage flats and ending with alpine cushion plants and whitebark pine at the lakes. Deer, elk and moose are frequently seen on the lower reaches of the trail, and wildflowers bloom throughout. These factors combine to make the path one of the most popular in the park. Since the first three miles to the lakes is also the approach for many climbing routes up the Grand Teton and surrounding peaks, expect to see lots of people on this well-traveled trail. An early start is advised to provide a measure of solitude and to beat the heat on the open, lower switchbacks to Garnet Canyon.

Delta Lake is reached by a route departing from the trail to Amphitheater and Surprise Lakes. It presents an alternative destination to that pair, or a nice loop hike option that encompasses all three lakes. Snug against the base of the east side of the 13,770-ft. Grand Teton and 12,928-ft. Mount Owen, Delta is a small alpine jewel framed by the two highest peaks in the Teton Range. Its striking turquoise color is created by minerals funneling into its west end from Teton Glacier above it, ground to fine flour by the moving ice.

Compared to Surprise and Amphitheater Lakes, Delta is lightly visited, its quietude fostered by lack of official trail access. Hikers must leave the Glacier Trail and pick a route through a steep boulder field to reach the lip of the lake. Those lacking route-finding ability, map reading skill and experience ascending boulder fields are advised to make Surprise and Amphitheater their goal. And regardless of experience, neither option is recommended if this is your first day in the area. Both destinations gain thousands of feet in a short distance. Give yourself several days to adjust to altitude before attempting to climb the 19 switchbacks to Surprise and Amphitheater, or the boulder field to Delta.

Driving Directions

Drive 12 miles north of Jackson on U.S. Hwy 89/191 to Moose Junction. Turn left and drive past park headquarters to the Moose Entrance Station of Grand Teton National Park. The signed junction to Lupine Meadows is roughly six miles north of the entrance station. Turn left (W) at Lupine Meadows and cross a bridge over Cottonwood Creek. Bear left just past the bridge; stay right where a side road shortly splits off to park employee housing. Follow the signs to the parking area, reached 1.6 miles beyond the park road turn-off. The trail begins at the far end of the lot.

The trailhead has vault toilets and information signs but no water.

Trail Description

It is immediately evident how this trailhead earned its moniker. Lavender-blue lupine thrives in the cobbled glacial outwash plain that comprises the valley floor. This drought-resistant member of the pea family poses a challenge to ranchers as summer turns to fall and its seeds ripen. Alkaloids poisonous to livestock are released during the ripening process, a threat that doesn't abate until the seeds are completely matured.

The trail travels south through the dry, lupine-dotted sage flats before entering forested terrain at the toe of a lateral moraine. Here, the unsorted soils and rocks dropped by the tongue of ice that flowed down Glacier Gulch hold moisture; unlike the outwash plain, moraines are hospitable to a variety of plants and trees.

The trail cuts through the sometimes boggy forest floor, crossing a bridge over a stream flowing from Teton Glacier above you at .6 mile. At one mile it bears right (W) and begins a sustained, moderate climb up the ridge separating Glacier Gulch to the right (N) and Burned Wagon Gulch to the left. Quiet parties may spy deer, elk or moose in the latter. The gulch was named after a Jackson game warden discovered a wagon and camp equipment in the gulch in 1911. Ensuing investigation disclosed that men named Reed and Arnett had left Butte, Montana, in a similar rig and Arnett had since disappeared. It has been speculated that Reed murdered Arnett, perhaps because a man also named Reed later served time in the Wyoming Penitentiary for killing two men.

At 1.7 miles and 700 feet higher than the trailhead, the trail to the lakes intersects the Valley Trail, which contours through forest before dropping to Bradley Lake. Continue straight to reach Amphitheater and Surprise.

The trail climbs at a steeper grade as it zigzags up the face between Glacier Gulch and Garnet Canyon in a series of long switchbacks. Monkey flowers, monkshood, Indian paintbrush and cow parsnip—wildflowers that thrive in moist environments—identify seeps .3 mile beyond the junction. If you fill your water bottle, treat it to avoid getting giardia or other unsavory intestinal hosts. There is no water available beyond this point until you reach the head of Garnet Canyon or the lakes. Carry plenty with you: the open slope ahead can be a cooker on hot days, with little shade to provide relief from the beating sun.

Surprise Lake

Amphitheater Lake

Beyond the seeps, superb views of Taggart and Bradley Lakes on the valley floor and pyramid-shaped 10,741-ft. Jackson Peak to the east unfold as you ascend to the signed Garnet Trail junction at the three-mile mark. The left fork heads into Garnet Canyon. The right fork carries you to Surprise and Amphitheater lakes via a series of 14 shorter, mostly wooded switchbacks.

To Surprise and Amphitheater Lakes

As the trail climbs 1,100-plus feet to the lakes, whitebark pine begins to replace subalpine and Douglas fir as the dominant species. Thin, light-gray bark and a contorted profile help identify this tree. Its needles grow in clusters of five and its closed cones are purplish and sticky. Squirrels and birds pry the gummy cones open to eat the seeds, an action that helps the tree survive through seed dispersal.

Surprise Lake is reached first, 1.6 miles past the Garnet Canyon junction. The 9,550-foot tarn is frozen much of the year and patches of snow may cover sections of trail well into July. A superb view of the terrain surrounding the lake is gained by carefully scrambling up the pinnacle southeast of its outlet. South to north, Nez Perce, Cloudveil Dome, South Teton, the Grand Teton and Mt. Owen stand in jagged relief against the skyline.

Amphitheater is .2 mile above Surprise Lake. It is reached by following the trail around the north side of Surprise. The lake nestles in a rugged cirque at the base of 11,618-ft. Disappointment Peak. The peak received its moniker after a 1925 climbing party thought they could reach the Grand by ascending a ridge above the lake, only to find a huge gap between the summit of "Disappointment" and the Grand.

Beyond Amphitheater, those skilled in snow and cross-country route finding may wish to explore Teton Glacier, reached in

The Grand Teton and Mt. Owen, the two highest peaks in the Teton Range, rise above Delta Lake.

an arduous two miles. Though receding, the glacier is the largest in the park. Unless you are traveling in the small window of time between maximum summer snowmelt and winter snows not-yet-begun, bring an ice axe for safety.

To reach the glacier, follow the trail angling north above Amphitheater to a low point on an obvious ridge. The ridge offers wonderful views of Delta Lake, Glacier Gulch and Teton Glacier cradled at its head. The trail bears left (W) around the flanks of Disappointment Peak. Very steep snowfields often bury the trail around Disappointment to the bowl between it and the Grand; this is not an endeavor to be entered into casually. Upon reaching the bowl, follow the moraine north, gradually cutting left (W) to a stagnant, flat area of dirty ice. The glacier's active ice falls and crevasses are ahead.

Gibb Scott and Homer Richards built the trail to the lakes in 1923 as a business

venture to get guided horseback trips and climbers up to Teton Glacier. It was widely used throughout the 1920s. Traffic leveled in the mid-1930s when the CCC completed the Garnet Canyon Trail, offering a viable alternative to the Grand Teton and opening access to other peaks.

To Reach Delta Lake

At Garnet Junction, walk right (N) toward Surprise and Amphitheater Lakes. At the end of the first switchback, leave the trail and drop steeply north through a short, wooded section, then contour northwest through the trees. Look back frequently so you have a mental picture of what your return route looks like. Stay high until you see large boulders straddling the lake's rocky outflow.

Angle right toward the boulder field. When you reach it, scramble up to the outflow, unseen until you are at the lip of the lake.

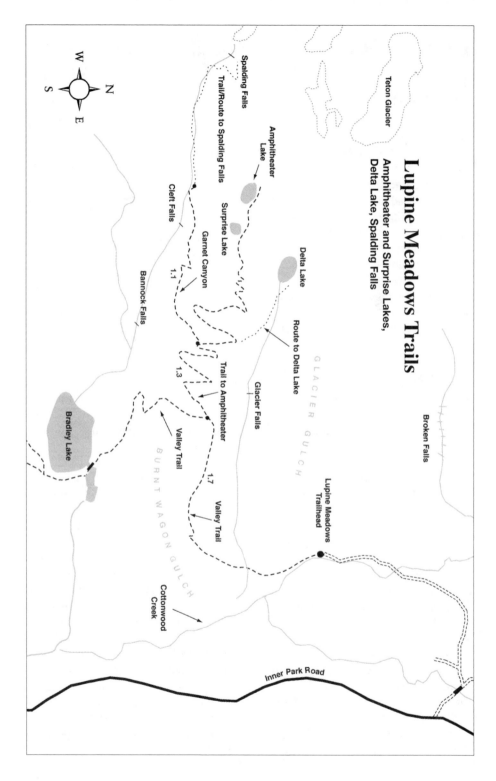

Lupine Meadows Trails
Amphitheater and Surprise Lakes,
Delta Lake, Spalding Falls

Teton Glacier

Spalding Falls

Trail/Route to Spalding Falls

Amphitheater
Lake

Surprise Lake

Cleft Falls

Garnet Canyon

1.1

Delta Lake

Bannock Falls

Route to Delta Lake

Glacier Falls

GLACIER GULCH

Broken Falls

1.3

Trail to Amphitheater

Bradley Lake

Valley Trail

BURNT WAGON GULCH

1.7

Valley Trail

Lupine Meadows
Trailhead

Cottonwood
Creek

Inner Park Road

N
W E
S

69

17 Garnet Canyon to Spalding Falls

18 Lower Saddle

Distance:
    The Meadows and Spalding Falls: 10 miles RT
    Lower Saddle: 14 miles RT
Elevation gain:
    To the head of the Meadows: 2,570 ft.
    To Top of Spalding Falls: 3,330 ft.
    To the Lower Saddle: Approx. 5,090 ft.
.Maximum elevation:
    The Meadows: Approx. 9,000 ft.
    Top of Spalding Falls: 10,000 ft.
    Lower Saddle: Approx. 11,600 ft.
Maps: Moose, Grand Teton. Book map pg. 69
Season: July through mid-September

A walk up Garnet Canyon to The Meadows takes you from the valley floor to a magnificent alpine vale that serves as the jumping-off point for climbs up the South, Middle, Grand and other Teton peaks. The Meadows is studded with boulders and alpine flowers. Graceful Spalding Falls arcs over a rock band near its head, dominated by the imposing 12,804-ft. Middle Teton. Ambitious, skilled hikers can continue beyond The Meadows to the Lower Saddle between the Middle and Grand Tetons. Dramatic views of the Grand, Idaho and Dartmouth Basin on the west slope of the range are enjoyed on the 11,600-foot divide.

Driving Directions

Follow directions to Lupine Meadows Trailhead on page 66.

Trail Description

The hike to Garnet Canyon shares the first three miles of trail to Surprise and Amphitheater Lakes, described in detail in hike no. 15. From the trailhead, the path travels south then west to a signed junction with the Valley Trail to your left at 1.7 miles. Continue past the junction and switchback up open slopes another 1.3 miles to the signed Garnet Trail junction at 8,400 feet—over 1,600 feet higher than Lupine Meadows trailhead.

Take the left fork at the junction to reach The Meadows and Lower Saddle. The trail climbs for a short distance beyond the junction, then levels out and drops as it bears right (W) and enters the canyon. Garnet Creek is seen far below. Early in the season the creek is an icy torrent fed by run-off from Nez Perce, Cloudveil Dome and the surrounding peaks. West, 11,901-ft. Nez Perce dominates the skyline. Viewed from the north, this mountain's distinctive profile has earned it the local nickname of "Howling Wolf."

Nez Perce (a French word pronounced Nay Pierce-say) is named for an Indian tribe based in Washington, Oregon and Idaho that futilely resisted attempts by the federal government to control key portions of its land. In a desperate bid to reach sanctuary in Canada, Chief Joseph led his people across the West before poignantly surrendering just 40 miles short of the border. Defeated and broken, his tribe suffering, Chief Joseph's reported capitulation speech to Colonel Miles of the U.S. Cavalry on September 30, 1877, is still haunting more than a decade later:

"…. The little children are all freezing to death. My people, some of them, have run away to the hills, and have no blankets, no food. No one knows where they are…I want to have time to look for my children and see how many I can find. Maybe I shall find them among the dead. Hear me my chiefs. I am tired; my heart is sick and sad. From where the sun now stands, I will fight no more forever."

After a brief descent entering the canyon, the trail resumes climbing, and the path becoming rocky as it switchbacks up talus slopes. It officially ends 1.1 miles beyond Garnet Trail junction near Cleft Falls. Returning to Lupine Meadows from here completes an 8.2-mile RT hike.

From the end of the trail a route marked by cairns heads west through a short boulder field to a rough path along Garnet Creek. The Meadows, a grassy alpine basin carpeted with flowers, is reached .6 mile from the end of the trail. The terrain was more reflective of its name before 1951, when a landslide tumbled east off the lower slopes of the Middle Teton and buried the vale's grassy slopes. Four decades later, vegetation is still fighting for a toehold among the rocks. At this elevation, plants have a tough go of it. If you have a permit to camp here, pitch your tent on spots that are already impacted—

Spalding Falls spills down a rocky slope at the west end of The Meadows.

and watch your feet. As veteran hiker and fellow guidebook writer Tom Carter puts it, "Try not to step on anything green."

The Meadows is a satisfying day hike destination. To the right, Spalding Falls gracefully spills over 80 feet to the grassy slope below. The falls carry the name of Bishop Frank Spalding, who accompanied William Owen on the official first ascent of the Grand Teton in 1898. The 12,804-ft. Middle Teton commands the western vista. Its east face is split by a prominent dike, formed when molten diabase—a dark igneous rock similar to basalt—intruded into fissures and cracks in older Precambrian rock an estimated 1.3 billion years ago. Dikes are a geologic feature repeated throughout the Tetons. The dike on the Middle is believed to be 20-40 feet thick, the one on the Grand 40-60 feet. The largest dike in the Tetons is the prominent

71

intrusion on Mount Moran. According to pre-eminent geologists David Love and John Reed, this dike is 150 feet thick near Moran's 12,605-foot summit. It has been traced west for over seven miles, and is still 100 feet thick as it exits the park near Green Lakes Mountain.

To the Lower Saddle

Strong, experienced parties with solid scrambling and route finding skills occasionally continue to the Lower Saddle beyond The Meadows. This is a long, arduous route that involves climbing a fixed rope below the Saddle's headwall. Those who lack sufficient experience should not attempt it. The route to the Saddle heads up the steep hillside toward the falls. The loose dirt and stone trail passes near its right side before switchbacking above it to a small level area dubbed Petzoldt's Caves. The "caves" are dirt camping spots under the overhang of several large boulders. In the 1930s and 40s mountain guide Paul Petzoldt dug space under the boulders to shelter overnight clients preparing to climb the Grand the next day.

Above the caves cairns mark the trail/route. It trends generally northwest to the morainal ridges that lead to the headwall. When in doubt, stay to the right. You'll cross a stream tumbling down from the base of Teepee Pillar just before entering the main moraine. Jackson Hole Mountain Guides' base camp is located above you. The route to the Saddle heads almost due west: If you start heading north you're likely on a trail to JHMG's camp.

The upper moraine ends at the steep, rocky headwall. The National Park Service maintains a heavy hemp fixed rope at the headwall to help climbers ascend the cliff band. Early season the bottom of the rope is often frozen in snow and ice, forcing a climb up the adjacent snowfields. Bring an ice axe and know how to use it. As

The Grand, viewed from the Lower Saddle.

the snow begins to melt you may find yourself showered by icy drops of water as you climb hand over hand up the slippery rope and rock. Hikers are advised to proceed carefully, as a fall here could be disastrous.

Above the rope the trail traverses south toward a potable spring, then west to the Lower Saddle. (The alpine vegetation is fragile; please stay on the paths to and from the spring and on the Lower Saddle.) Cresting its ridge, stalwart hikers are treated to a dramatic panorama. To the east and south, the view encompasses the valley floor, the Gros Ventres, Wind River and Wyoming Ranges. Pierre's Hole, the green and brown patchwork of Idaho farmland and the distant Lemhi Mountains are seen to the west. North, the Enclosure and the Grand Teton are close at hand.

The National Park Service and Exum Mountain Guides maintain huts on the divide. Although both are used for rescue operations, neither is open to the general public.

Return to the trailhead via the same route. Before hiking to the Lower Saddle hikers are advised to check in at Jenny Lake Ranger Station for current conditions and route information. Those wishing to camp overnight must obtain a permit in advance. Permits are limited.

19 Teewinot Apex

Distance:
    Waterfall: 1.8 miles RT
    Apex: Approx. 3.4 miles
Elevation gain:
    Waterfall: Approx. 420 ft.
    Apex: Approx. 2,860 ft.
Maximum elevation: Approx. 9,600 ft.
Maps: Grand Teton, Moose (not plotted)
Season:
    Late May through mid-October for the waterfall, late June through mid-October
    for Teewinot Apex

A steep climber's trail completed in 1980 zigzags up the east slope of 12,325-ft. Teewinot to the apex of a triangular fault scarp. Covered with trees, the apex is clearly viewed from the valley floor. The path passes an unnamed waterfall on its ascent. This extended series of drops over rock ledges—and up-close views of the upper flanks of the prominent "many pinnacled" peak—make the apex an intriguing outing. But, hikers pay a steep admission price. No less than 18 steep switchbacks are encountered from the parking area to the apex.

Early season, when the lower slopes are bare and the snowmelt-fed stream is at its maximum volume, is the best time to make the shorter hike up to the waterfall.

The unnamed waterfall near the lower Apex Trail.

Driving Directions

Follow directions to Lupine Meadows Trailhead on page 66.

Trail Description

From the boulders marking the west edge of the north end of the parking lot, walk about 30 feet west toward a young aspen grove; you'll soon see the trail. It continues west through terrain covered with serviceberry, chokecherry, elderberry, willow and wildflowers, on an initially flat then moderate grade. You'll soon see a section of the cascade to your left (S).

When the path reaches a rock band, it turns and travels up a number of rock slabs to a steeper rock band and divides. Go left here to reach the waterfall. For those seeking a leisurely day, the slabs

The upper slopes of Teewinot, viewed near the top of the Apex Trail.

offer a great place to enjoy a bite to eat and snooze in the sun. Those intent on ascending the apex should not pass up a closer view of the waterfall on the return.

To continue to the apex, bear right at the divide. The path travels north about a quarter-mile before turning left (S) and beginning its steep, switchbacking climb up Teewinot's flank. The path cuts in and out of Douglas fir and subalpine forest. As it turns right (N) on the eighth and tenth switchbacks, you'll enjoy tremendous views of Jenny and Jackson Lakes. Beginning with the thirteenth switchback's turn to the left (S), the summit and upper slopes of Teewinot pop into view. As you near the top of the apex, the length of trail between switchbacks increases and the trail cuts across grassy terrain at the base of rock slide areas. Bradley and Taggart Lakes are seen below.

The path ends at the edge of a whitebark pine forest at the base of the east face. Climbers head north of the Idol and Worshiper—the two obvious rock spires ahead of you—and ascend the snowfields that often cover the couloir well into the summer. If you are not a climber versed in proper use of an ice axe, stop at the end of the trail. There have been a number of very serious accidents—some fatal—resulting from inexperienced parties attempting to reach the summit via the snowfields.

The first recorded climb of Teewinot occurred August 14, 1929, when Fritiof Fryxell and Phil Smith reached the summit via the east face. Renny Jackson, coauthor of the landmark *A Climber's Guide to the Teton Range*, wrote in the same that Fryxell and Smith chose the Shoshone word for pinnacles, "Tee-Win-At, as it was originally spelled" for the peak. Visitors often confuse the prominent peak for the Grand, particularly from the Cathedral Group pullout on the Jenny Lake Loop Road.

South Jenny/Cascade Canyon

A magnificent, easy-to-access waterfall and the sheer beauty of Cascade Canyon draw more hikers to the southern end of Jenny Lake than perhaps any other area in the park. For many, Hidden Falls is the primary attraction. Thundering Cascade Creek plunges 200 feet down the lip of the canyon before flowing into Jenny Lake. The chasm is angled slightly south, making the falls truly hidden until you are upon it. The sheer, rugged walls for which the Tetons are famous frame the short wooded walk to the falls, and entertaining marmots are often seen basking in the sun or scurrying about on the surrounding rock slabs.

Famed Jenny Lake at the mouth of the canyon is also an undeniable calling card. Its deep blue waters reflect the soaring flanks of the Tetons rising almost magically from its western shoreline—a picture postcard scene that recently landed Jenny on a list of the top 10 "must see" destinations in the United States.

Above the lake, Cascade Canyon cuts far into the range just north of Teewinot, offering superb views of that mountain, Mt. Owen and the Grand Teton. The U-shaped glacial canyon extends due west 4.5 miles before branching north toward Lake Solitude and south toward Hurricane Pass and Alaska Basin—all destinations of striking beauty. Engelmann spruce and Douglas fir shade the forest floor of the lower canyon, carpeted by lush thimbleberry and huckleberry bushes and spreading willow. With plentiful food and cover, it is not surprising that moose and black bear are frequently seen in the lower to mid-section of the canyon. Regrettably, in recent years some black bears have learned to associate humans with food. For the safety of the animals and park visitors, it is now prohibited to eat near Hidden Falls or at Inspiration Point above the falls. And, because of its popularity, the area around Lake Solitude has been closed to camping since 1972 and the number of overnight backcountry travelers in the upper forks limited. Current camping sites are located about a mile below the lake.

Though heavily visited, the reason people flock to this region remains intact. An early start still provides a welcome degree of solitude on the trail. This author doesn't let a hiking season go by without returning to Cascade Canyon.

Driving Directions

To reach South Jenny Lake/Cascade Canyon trails, drive approximately 12 miles north of Jackson on US Hwy 89/191 to Moose Junction. Turn left and drive past park headquarters to the Moose Entrance Station. Roughly seven miles past the entrance station turn left at the signed South Jenny Lake Junction and park in the large lot. Follow directional signs to the East Shore Boat Dock. All trails in this section begin by crossing the bridge over Cottonwood Creek at the boat dock, or taking the boat across the lake to the west shore.

20 Moose Ponds Loop
21 Hidden Falls Loop

Distance:
Moose Ponds: 3 miles RT
Hidden Falls Loop: 4.9 miles RT
Elevation change:
Moose Ponds: Approx. 90 ft.
Hidden Falls Loop: Approx. 530 ft.
.Maximum elevation:
Moose Ponds: 6,860 ft.
Hidden Falls: 7,180 ft.
Maps: Jenny Lake, Moose. Map opposite page.
Season: May through October
Use Restrictions:
Eating prohibited in vicinity of Hidden Falls and at Inspiration Point for bear control

Moose Ponds and the Hidden Falls Loop hikes share the first .6 mile of trail. The scenic Moose Ponds Loop lies below 12,325-ft. Teewinot Mountain. It curves through a lush wetlands area just south of Jenny Lake. Moose, elk, deer and waterfowl frequent the three small ponds you pass on this pleasant hike. The Hidden Falls/Inspiration Point Loop traverses forest and rocky slopes above Jenny Lake's western shoreline and returns along the lakeshore. The magnificent 200-foot waterfall, views of the lake and chance of seeing moose, black bear, marmots and energetic pikas make this one of the favorite hikes in the park. Plan on an early start if you appreciate solitude.

Driving Directions
Follow directions on page 75.

Trail Description
At the East Shore Boat Dock, cross the bridge over Jenny Lake outlet and bear left. The wide path parallels Jenny's southeast shore, opening superb views of Cascade Canyon, St. John's and Teewinot rising above Jenny's western shoreline. Twinberry, huckleberry and serviceberry bushes line portions of the path, intermittently shaded by an open forest of Engelmann spruce, subalpine fir, lodgepole pine and aspen.

At .4 mile, you'll reach a signed junction with the Valley Trail to your left. That path travels south to Bradley and Taggart Lakes and points beyond. Continue straight (W).

The path ascends the lateral moraine containing Jenny Lake to reach a junction with the Moose Ponds Loop Trail at .6

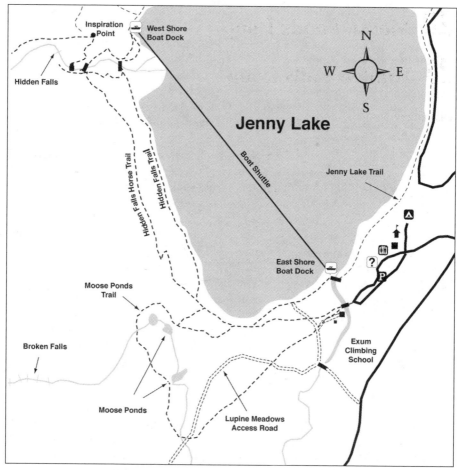

Moose Ponds and Hidden Falls loop hikes

mile. To complete the Moose Ponds Loop, turn left. To reach Hidden Falls, continue straight.

Moose Ponds Loop

Beyond the junction the Moose Ponds Trail leads south a short distance, then bends on a more westerly course and ascends to the edge of the moraine separating Jenny Lake from the trio of ponds below. It descends via moderate switchbacks through young aspen and willow to the lush terrain surrounding the first two ponds. Cow parsnip, woodland

star, buttercups, bluebells, groundsel, Indian paintbrush, Utah honeysuckle, meadowrue and stickseed forget-me-not were all in bloom one early June day.

The path gently climbs as it heads west. It soon curls left (S) and crosses a plank bridge over a run-off stream tumbling down Teewinot's flank. An effortless ascent through a stand of young aspen clones brings you to a second run-off stream, easily negotiated by judicious rock hopping. Beyond, the trail descends to a pretty wildflower meadow watered by a third easily-spanned run-off stream and enters a pleasant subalpine fir and Engelmann spruce forest. A hop over yet another stream brings you to a bridged crossing of a more substantial waterway.

As the path bends left (E), you leave the forest for open terrain and great views of Teewinot. Beyond the final moose pond, the trail bends right (S/SE) and travels through flat, open forest to an intersection with the Lupine Meadows Trailhead access road at 1.8 miles. Cross the road and angle right toward the north end of a buck-and-rail fence and you'll regain the trail through Lupine Meadows. Despite road traffic, the superb views of Teewinot and an arresting sweep of lupine that gives the meadow its name make this an enjoyable amble. Western dock, scarlet gilia, sorrel and yellow paintbrush intersperse splashes of red and yellow into the lavender blue and silvery green palette at your feet.

The trail intersects the access road again near a Y road junction. Walk up the right fork of the road toward the building that now houses Exum Climbing School. (The building was formerly the bath and shower house for the CCC camp.) You'll pick up a faint trail behind the building that curves left to a bridged crossing of Cottonwood Creek and the South Jenny Lake parking lot.

Hidden Falls Loop

From the junction with the Moose Ponds trail, the path ascends to the top of the moraine, turns right (N) and levels out. Follow the wide, well-used path until you reach a metal sign at .8 mile that directs you straight to Jenny Lake, Hidden Falls and Cascade Canyon. An unsigned, smaller trail angles left up the slope near the sign. This is the path you want. It is the old commercial horse trail to Hidden Falls. The rocky tread climbs at an easy to moderate grade above the west shore

of Jenny Lake. It soon switchbacks left (S) and travels a short distance before doglegging north again. Look for deer, elk and moose in the willowed terrain below you at the turn.

Mid-way above Jenny's west shore the forested trail opens up to nice views of the lake, valley floor and the distance Gros Ventre Range to the east. Beyond, it climbs before gently descending and contouring across a large rock slide area. This section is one of the prettiest of the hike, offering grand views of Jenny Lake, boats ferrying across her deep blue water and the sentinel peaks on the north side of Cascade Canyon. Listen for pikas that live among the boulders. Pine martens and yellow-bellied marmots are also spied among the rocks.

Stay left where the path splits. The trail switchbacks to the top of a large, flat boulder overlooking the lake, a perfect spot to soak in the scenery. Wood hitching poles left of the trail are remnants of a commercial trail riding operation phased out by the park in the early 1990s, when it was determined that the volume of hikers and horses on Cascade Canyon trails was a potentially unsafe mix for both hikers and riders.

Beyond the overlook, the trail drops through a heavily shaded section of forest. This short section may harbor patches of snow through mid-June. At 2.1 miles, it intersects the trail to the falls from the West Shore Boat Dock. Bear left here; continue straight a short distance farther when a path to the right leads to a bridge over Cascade Creek. (This leads to Inspiration Point and Cascade Canyon beyond.) Hidden Falls is but a short distance farther.

After enjoying the falls, backtrack to the junction with the trail to Inspiration Point—a worthwhile scenic overlook of Jenny Lake and Jackson Hole. (For a description of the trail, see hike no. 22.)

Above: Approaching Cascade Canyon and Hidden Falls via the old Jenny Lake Horse Trail. Left: Teewinot is showcased on the Moose Ponds loop hike.

Keep right and walk a short distance to a second signed junction. Continue straight here, following the sign to the Jenny Lake parking area rather than taking the trail to the left signed "boat dock." Both trails will get you back to your vehicle, but the direct path ahead bypasses the hubbub at the West Shore Boat Dock.

The path descends to a signed intersection with a trail traveling left (N) to the boat dock and String Lake Parking Area. Continue straight, descending at an easy to moderate grade through forest to the lakeshore, reached at the bottom of the rock slide. The trail skinnies between the toe of the slide and the lake. Clematis, columbine, bluebells, monkshood and Indian paintbrush line the lush, forested path. It gradually climbs above the lake to the intersection with the old horse trail at 4.1 miles. Retrace your steps to return.

22 Hidden Falls/Inspiration Pt. via Boat

23 Forks of Cascade Canyon

24 Lake Solitude

25 Hurricane Pass/Alaska Basin

Hidden Falls/Inspiration Point
Distance: .9 miles one-way
Elevation gain: Approx. 410 ft.
Maximum elevation: Approx. 7,200 ft.
Maps: Book map pg. 82
Use restrictions: Eating prohibited in vicinity of falls and at Inspiration Point for bear control
Season: May through October (call 734-9227 for boat operation dates)

Forks of Cascade Canyon
Distance: *6.5 miles one-way
Elevation gain: Approx. 1,050 ft.
Maximum elevation: 7,800 ft.
Maps: Jenny, Mount Moran.
Season: June through October

Lake Solitude
Distance: *9.2 miles one-way
Elevation gain: Approx. 2,300 ft.
Maximum elevation: Approx. 9,050 ft.
Maps: Jenny, Mount Moran.
Season: July through early October

Hurricane Pass
Distance: *11.6 miles one-way
Elevation gain: Approx. 3,640 ft.
Maximum elevation: 10,372 ft.
Maps: Jenny Lake, Mount Moran, Grand Teton.
Season: July through September

* Note: If starting from the West Shore Boat Dock, deduct 2 miles from the listed mileages.

80

Scenic Cascade Canyon offers numerous hiking options, from a short outing to Hidden Falls and Inspiration Point to multi-day backpacking trips. From its mouth at Jenny Lake, the canyon leads west 4.5 miles to the Forks of Cascade Canyon, a nice day hike turnaround option. At the forks, hikers and backpackers may take the South Fork of Cascade Canyon to Hurricane Pass and renowned Alaska Basin in Jedediah Wilderness on the west slope of the Tetons. Traveling up the North Fork of Cascade Canyon accesses Lake Solitude, one of the prettiest backcountry lakes in the range. From there, many backpackers and strong, ambitious day hikers hike up Paintbrush Divide and down Paintbrush Canyon, where it is possible to return to their vehicle at South Jenny via the Valley Trail. Backpackers are reminded that they need a free permit to camp overnight in the park's backcountry. Because of its popularity, Lake Solitude has been closed to camping since 1972 and the number of overnight backcountry travelers in the upper forks of the canyon is limited. Camping sites are located about a mile below the lake.

Hidden Falls drops 200 feet.

Driving Directions

Follow directions on page 75.

To Hidden Falls/Inspiration Point via boat shuttle

During the summer season, shuttle boats leave from the East Shore Boat Dock approximately every 20 minutes. The boats cross to Jenny Lake's west shore, a pretty ride that offers wonderful views of Cascade Canyon and surrounding peaks. Left (S) is 11,901-ft. Nez Perce, soon slipping out of view behind 12,325-ft. Teewinot, a jagged peak people often mistake for the Grand Teton. Numerous peaks and spires that attract climbers—including 10,054-ft. Storm Point, 9,920-ft. Ice Point and 10,560-ft. Symmetry Spire—form the right (N) flank of the canyon. Farther north is 11,430-ft. Mount St. John. When snow hugs its undulating summit ridge, this long peak resembles a stack of French toast sprinkled with powdered sugar. It is named in honor of Orestes St. John, a geologist who was a member of the 1877 Hayden Survey.

From the West Shore Boat Dock, hike left (S) on the well marked, .5-mile trail to Hidden Falls. Take the middle of three trails at the next signed intersection. The path travels west as it parallels Cascade Creek. It crosses a bridge over the same at .3 mile and splits. Turn left. You'll shortly reach a junction near another bridge over Cascade Creek. This path leads to Inspiration Point. Continue straight and walk a short distance to reach a viewpoint of the falls. The 200-foot drop is truly hidden until you are almost upon it. Hidden Falls thunders early season, when

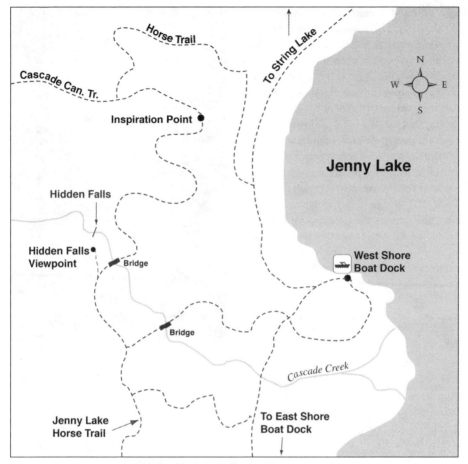

Hidden Falls/Inspiration Point detail

heavy snowmelt turns Cascade Creek into a white torrent.

To continue to Inspiration Point, backtrack the short distance to the trail junction. Cross the bridge over Cascade Creek and continue straight to yet another bridge over the creek. Beyond, the trail climbs .4 mile to the well-known overlook. The steep path cuts through an imposing granite wall. It drops off abruptly on first the right then the left side as it switchbacks its way to 7,200-ft. Inspiration Point.

Civilian Conservation Corp crews constructed this impressive segment of trail in the 1930s. The CCC program was initiated during the depression as a means to provide employment for young men and complete needed facilities in our national parks and forests. CCC boys constructed roads, bridges, cabins and most of the trails in the park.

Inspiration Point rises almost 500 feet above Jenny Lake and provides good views of it, the valley floor and the Gros Ventre Range east of Jackson Hole. Particularly noticeable is the light colored slash running down Sheep Mountain across the valley. This is the Gros Ventre Slide, one of the largest landslides ever recorded. The Forest Service has constructed an interpretative walk through a segment of the slide. (See hike no. 66.)

A glacier that gouged out Cascade Canyon over 9,000 years ago formed Jenny Lake. As the glacier began to melt at the canyon's base, it dropped rock debris it had carried down from Cascade's upper reaches. The earth and rock formed a terminal moraine that subsequently held in the glacier's melt water. Jackson, Leigh, Bradley, Taggart and Phelps lakes were all formed in the same manner.

Jenny is 1.5 miles wide and 2.5 miles long. It's deepest point measures 236 feet. The lake is named for the Shoshone Indian wife of trapper Beaver Dick Leigh.

To Forks of Cascade Canyon

Beyond Inspiration Point, the trail up Cascade Canyon ascends at a much gentler grade, gaining only 640 feet on its way to the Forks 3.6 miles farther. The steep north side of Mt. Owen, the second highest peak in the park at 12,928 feet, rises over a mile above you to the left (S). Right, talus slopes periodically slice through the forest. The slopes are home to often unseen but heard pikas.

Two-and-a-half miles above Inspiration Point, Cascade Creek widens considerably at a spot known as Perch's Pond. Rockfall from the lower slopes of Storm Point dammed the creek. The "pond" is a good place to take a break and look for climbers on Guides' Wall, the sheer, rocky southwest ridge of Storm Point on the north side of the canyon. Climbers can be seen testing their skill on difficult routes named Blobular Oscillations, Bat Attack Crack, Hot Dogs, Bum's Wall and Picnic and Paranoia.

Numerous tributaries from the flanks of Teewinot and Mt. Owen to the south and Rock of Ages and The Jaw to the north flow into Cascade Creek as you walk up the canyon. Roughly a mile before the

Cascade Canyon below the Forks.

canyon divides you'll see a thin, silvery cascade tumbling down its south wall. A hard scramble up either side of this steep cascade leads to Valhalla Canyon over 2,200 feet above the creek floor. This high, hanging canyon—nestled between Mt. Owen and the Grand—is an ambitious goal for day hikers skilled in cross-country travel. It is quite difficult to reach, as it involves a tricky crossing of Cascade Creek and steep brushy scrambling. Check with the Jenny Lake Range station before attempting it.

Cascade Creek forks .3 mile before the trail splits. Cross the bridge and continue west to the marked junction, a well-worn spot on the forest floor 4.5 miles beyond the West Shore Boat Dock that offers a good turn-around point.

To Lake Solitude

Many day hikers continue beyond the Forks to Lake Solitude, 2.7 miles farther and almost 1,200 feet higher. The 9,035-foot glacial tarn is often snowbound into July. Ringed by rocky cliffs on three sides and framed by wildflowers mid- to late summer, the lake and surrounding terrain form one of the most breathtaking spots in the range. To reach it, bear right at the Forks. The trail steadily ascends another mile through spruce and fir forest before entering the high, grassy alpine zone. Paintbrush Divide is clearly seen to your right. Left, the pointy Wigwam Peaks define the skyline. The grade steepens considerably as it climbs up the last stretch to the lake. Continue a bit farther to Solitude's far shore for spectacular down-canyon views of Teewinot, Mt. Owen and the Grand.

A scramble up the northwest side of the cirque containing Lake Solitude brings you to the high basin below Little's Peak and the head of South Leigh Creek, offering a fine cross-country hike down the west side of the range on South Leigh Canyon Trail. For most people, this is a multi-day backpacking trip. Another popular backpacking option from Lake Solitude is continuing north 2.4 miles to Paintbrush Divide and returning to the valley floor via Paintbrush Canyon, a strenuous 19.2-mile trip.

To Hurricane Pass and Alaska Basin

By turning left at the Forks of Cascade Canyon, hikers can follow the South Fork of Cascade Creek to Hurricane Pass and Alaska Basin. Not as heavily used as the North Fork Trail, the path climbs just over 2,500 feet in 5.1 miles before cresting the 10,372-foot pass and dropping into the famed alpine basin on the west side of the Tetons.

Beyond the Fork, the path begins the first of three steep switchbacks—opening up fine views of the steep buttresses of Table Mountain—before entering a forest of impressive whitebark pine, many exceeding five feet in diameter. It passes through this magnificent stand of trees for the next two miles, reaching treeline 10 miles beyond the start of the trail. Four short but steep switchbacks lead to a trail junction in .3 mile. The left trail, no longer maintained by the Park Service, leads to Avalanche Canyon Divide.

Take the right fork of the trail and climb switchbacks through talus 1.3 miles to the top of Hurricane Pass, passing above Schoolroom Glacier to your left (S). Of the dozen glaciers in Grand Teton National Park, this permanent snowfield is marked by textbook examples of lateral and terminal moraines, crevasses and a lake clouded by glacial flour (powdered rock) at its toe; thus, its name. The trail

Above: A hiker soaks in amazing views of the Grand and surrounding terrain from Hurricane Pass A trail drops into Alaska Basin on the west slope of the range. Opposite page, top to bottom: Lake Solitude is a popular destination; looking south of Lake Solitude down the North Fork of Cascade Canyon; the upper South fork of Cascade; Sunset Lake.

tops out at Hurricane Pass just below 10,400 feet, offering views of the Grand, Middle and South Tetons, Avalanche Divide and The Wall. From here it drops steeply west into rock-studded Alaska Basin and Sunset Lake 2.7 miles below.

Guide Paul Petzoldt named the basin in 1924 after he and a horse party crossed the snow-covered alpine meadows early season. Its beauty and accessibility from both sides of the range has led to heavy use of the area.

Targhee National Forest presently does not require an overnight permit to camp in the basin.

26 Hanging Canyon

Distance:
String Lake to Lake of the Crags: Approx 7.3 miles RT
West Shore Boat Dock to Lake of the Crags: Approx. 5.5 miles RT
Elevation gain: Approx. 2,800 ft.
Maximum elevation: Approx. 9,590 ft.
Maps: Jenny Lake. Mt. Moran
Season: Mid-July through mid-September

Surrounded on all but the east side by towering pinnacles and virtually hidden from the valley below, this magnificent canyon leads to an impressive cirque and a trio of lakes. The view from the highest, Lake of the Crags, is one of the most spectacular vistas in the Tetons—in many ways surpassing the beauty of the signature peaks for which the range is known.

While the canyon does not have an official trail, hikers and climbers heading to Cube Point, Symmetry Spire, The Jaw and other destinations have worn a path to the lakes. The trail is extremely steep. It gains almost 1,000 feet per mile and requires route finding and scrambling to reach the upper lakes. Hanging Canyon is not a good choice for inexperienced hikers, young children or early season outings. Its upper reaches are typically snowbound well into July.

Driving Directions

The most common approach to the canyon is via the West Shore Boat Dock on Jenny Lake. Follow the directions on page 75. During the summer months Jenny Lake Boating ferries customers across the lake for a small fee. The trip across the lake takes about 20 minutes.

Alternately, one can continue driving past the South Jenny Lake Junction to signs marking the North Jenny Lake Junction and String Lake. Turn left at the junction and drive to the String Lake turn-off. Park at the first parking area at String Lake and cross the hiker's bridge near the outlet. Bear left at the String Lake/ Jenny Lake trail junction at .3 mile and walk along the west side of the creek then southwest along the shore of Jenny Lake to the unmarked trail up Hanging Canyon on your right, reached approximately 1.4 miles beyond the trailhead.

Trail Description

From the West Shore Boat Dock follow the trail signs to String Lake. The trail passes the old horse trail up Cascade Canyon and crosses two bridges spanning a marshy area fed in part by Hanging Canyon Creek tumbling down from the canyon above you. Shortly after the second bridge, an unmarked path heads left (W) through the trees. This is the path you want. It steeply ascends the east flank of Mount St. John, staying on the right (N) side of Hanging Canyon Creek as it travels through pines and open slopes to rock slabs above. To help prevent further erosion of the steep slopes, stay on the unofficial trail/route marked by cairns.

Shortly before you reach Arrowhead

Rock of Ages dominates the backdrop at Lake of the Crags, nestled at the head of Hanging Canyon.

Pool the trail swings close to Ribbon Cascade. Columbine, monkshood, and forget-me-not thrive in the mid-summer mountain run-off, making this a beautiful place for a rest stop. Parties interested in scrambling up Cube Point, the 9,000-foot peak at the end of Symmetry Spire's east ridge, should cross the stream here and head left (S) to its base. To continue on to Ramshead Lake and Lake of the Crags, stay right of the stream and follow the cairns. The route ends in the talus slopes on the west side of Ramshead. A short scramble up and over these brings you to the head of the canyon and the final lake. Jagged, perpendicular peaks and pinnacles surround this alpine jewel. The impressive flat-topped peak to the southwest is Rock of Ages. Ayres' Crags extend from the Rock northward to The Jaw, the highest pinnacle due west. Mount St. John dominates the northern skyline. Hikers with sufficient mountaineering skill may want to consider scrambling up the non-technical east face of The Jaw by following the canyon's western benches and talus slopes to the summit. The summit offers impressive views of the north and northwest faces of Teewinot, Mt. Owen and the Grand Teton.

There is space for a party of two to camp near the trees by Lake of the Crags' north shore. Much more desirable sites, however, are located due east of Ramshead Lake. Those wishing to camp in Hanging Canyon are reminded that a permit must be secured in advance.

Hanging Canyon's name is derived from the forces that created it. Geologists believe smaller glaciers flowing into larger sheets of ice create canyons carved high above the valley floor. When the glaciers recede, the canyon is left "hanging" on the mountainside, the slopes below it scraped away by the larger glacier scouring the valley floor.

NORTH JENNY/PAINTBRUSH CANYON TRAILHEAD

North Jenny/Paintbrush Canyon

Some of the most popular hiking trails in Grand Teton National Park originate from the Jenny Lake/String Lake/Leigh Lake area. Their sparkling blue waters reflect the rocky spires of Teewinot, the Grand Teton, Mt. Owen and Mt. Moran. Grouse whortleberry, honeysuckle, huckleberries and a garden of wildflowers thrive in the shade along their wooded shores. Shallow String Lake is an ideal swimming spot, and Leigh Lake provides some of the nicest views of Mount Moran anywhere in the park. Jenny Lake offers access to Hidden Falls and superb views into Cascade Canyon from its eastern shore. There is no better destination for picnickers or families with young children to enjoy a sunny afternoon in the Tetons.

Exploring this area it is sobering to realize its beauty was almost lost forever. On the heels of a severe drought in 1919, Wyoming State Engineer Frank Emerson proposed impounding Jenny and Leigh Lake for irrigation purposes by constructing a dam at the outlet of Jenny Lake. The project would have raised the level of Jenny 20 feet, Leigh Lake 10 feet. Intense pressure from the newly formed National Park Service eventually forced the Department of the Interior and Emerson to back down. Realizing the ongoing threat of development that would irreparably damage the environment, the incident was one of many that motivated Struthers Burt and other prominent Jackson Hole citizens to begin a campaign to have the Teton Range be designated a national park.

Holly Lake in scenic Paintbrush Canyon is a favored destination for hikers looking for a full day outing. The trail to it and Paintbrush Divide beyond are part of the Paintbrush/Cascade Canyon Loop, perhaps the premier two-day backpacking trip in the park.

Trailhead Directions
The trio of lakes and Paintbrush Canyon are accessed from the String Lake Parking Area. To reach it drive 12 miles north of Jackson on US Hwy. 89/191 to Moose Junction. Turn left (N) and drive past park headquarters to the Moose Entrance of Grand Teton National Park. Ten miles beyond the entrance station, turn left at signed North Jenny Lake Junction and drive 1.5 miles to the String Lake Parking Area on the right. The parking area itself is .4 mile long. Mileage for the hike around Jenny Lake is calculated from the String Lake outlet bridge at the south end of the lot. Mileage for the String, Leigh Lake and Holly Lake/Paintbrush Canyon hikes is calculated from the north end of the lot.

27 Jenny Lake Loop

Distance: 6.6 miles RT
Elevation change: Approx. 300 ft. gain and loss
Maximum elevation: Approx. 6,880 ft.
Maps: Jenny Lake, Mt. Moran. Book map pg. 91
Season: Mid-May through October

The pleasant trail around Jenny Lake provides access to Hidden Falls and offers wonderful views into Cascade Canyon from its eastern shore. Meadows, lodgepole forest and mixed conifer stretches are encountered on this varied hike. Black bear are occasionally seen cooling off in the lake on a hot summer day and gorging themselves in stretches of huckleberry bushes when the berries ripen in August.

Driving Directions

See preceding page.

Trail Description

The trail begins at the near (S) end of String Lake Parking Lot. Cross the bridge over the outlet between String and Jenny Lakes and follow the trail .3 mile to a signed junction. Bear left. The trail travels southwest above Jenny Lake through an area burned in a 1999 blaze.

On September 2nd of that year, lightning ignited the Alder Fire. As specified in Grand Teton National Park's Fire Management Plan, the fire was allowed to take its natural course in order to benefit plants and wildlife habitat, and reduce years of accumulated fuels. Some areas burned hot, while others were only slightly scorched.

The monitored fire burned for six weeks with no problems until October 14, when high winds resulted in the fire jumping String and Jenny Lakes and

spreading rapidly in the direction of historic Jenny Lake Lodge, forcing fire managers to take emergency suppression action. Over four dozen firefighters, two helicopters dropping water and three air drops of fire retardant from aerial tankers were utilized to prevent the then 77-year-old lodge from going up in flames.

After the fire was contained, interior areas were allowed to smolder until November snowfall, as the fire posed no risk to people or property. It eventually burned 312 acres. From String Lake and North Jenny Lake trails, you can see the varying degrees of the Alder Fire's intensity and the positive effects of fire in terms of forest health and new plant growth. Fire creates nutrient-rich soils fertilized by ash, a favorable environment for wind-borne seeds or plants sprouting from roots. It opens up space for grasses and food favored by browsing ungulates such as elk and deer. Studies show that forests are at their peak diversity and health 25 years after a blaze.

At 1.5 miles the slightly rolling trail drops to the lakeshore and crosses a stream rushing down Hanging Canyon. The Cathedral Group looms ahead of you, named because this vantage point makes three of the major Teton Peaks look like one mountain, a "cathedral" with dozens of spires. Craggy Teewinot is in the forefront, the Grand Teton is in the middle background and Mt. Owen is to the right.

At 1.7 miles, the trail passes busy

West Shore Boat Dock. From here, it is .5 miles up a marked side trail to 200-foot Hidden Falls. Many hikers take the boat shuttle across the lake, making the falls a one-mile round-trip venture (see hike no. 22). Though crowded, it is heavily-visited for a reason and well-worth the extra time and distance to visit.

Continue hiking past the junction along the southwest shore to reach Moose Ponds Overlook in another mile. Early morning and late afternoon visitors may see elk, deer or the ponds namesake moose from this vantage point.

The trail leaves the woods as it turns east beyond the overlook and drops toward the East Shore Boat Dock and footbridge crossing south Jenny Lake outlet at 3.7 miles. From here, it is a 2.9-mile walk in-and-out of lodgepole forest back to the String Lake parking area. The trail closely follows the lakeshore, offering spectacular views up Cascade Canyon. Unfortunately, at places it is very close to the one-way scenic drive above the lake's east shore.

You will both see and hear vehicles on your return to the trailhead.

Jenny Lake is named in honor of trapper Beaver Dick Leigh's Shoshone Indian wife. Tragically, she and the couple's six children died of smallpox during Christmas week of 1876. Jenny, their newborn son, and daughter Ann Jane died on Christmas Eve. William died on Christmas. Dick Junior succumbed on the 26th, John on the 27th, Elizabeth on the 28th. In a touching letter to a friend after their deaths, heartbroken Leigh wrote,

"i shall improve the place and live and die near my family but I shall not be able to do eny thing for a few months for my mind is disturbed at the sight that I see around me…

Leigh was not to remain a widower. Several years later, already past 50, he married a 14-year-old Bannock girl.

The scenic lake is one of the largest in Grand Teton National Park, second only to Jackson Lake in size.

The still waters of Jenny Lake mirror the mouth of Cascade Canyon .

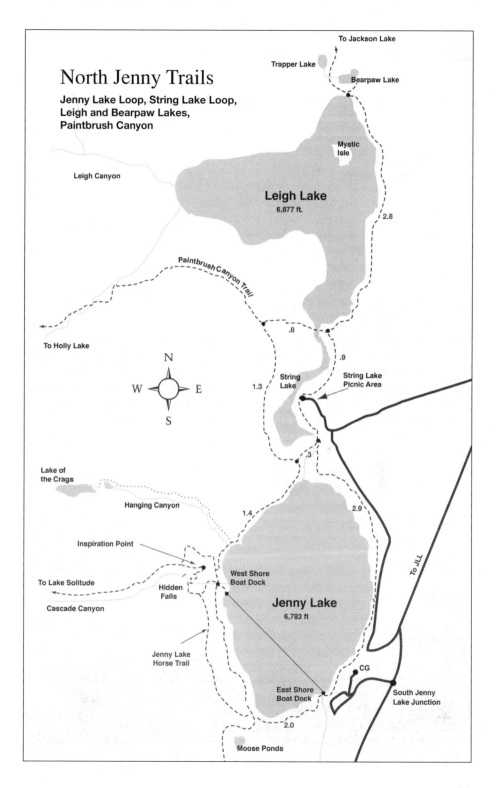

North Jenny Trails

**Jenny Lake Loop, String Lake Loop,
Leigh and Bearpaw Lakes,
Paintbrush Canyon**

To Jackson Lake

Trapper Lake

Bearpaw Lake

Leigh Canyon

Mystic
Isle

Leigh Lake
6,877 ft.

2.8

Paintbrush Canyon Trail

.8

To Holly Lake

.9

N
W E
S

String
Lake

String Lake
Picnic Area

1.3

.3

Lake of
the Crags

Hanging Canyon

1.4

2.9

Inspiration Point

To Lake Solitude

West Shore
Boat Dock

To JLL

Hidden
Falls

Cascade Canyon

Jenny Lake
6,783 ft

Jenny Lake
Horse Trail

CG

East Shore
Boat Dock

South Jenny
Lake Junction

2.0

Moose Ponds

28 String Lake Loop

29 Leigh, Bearpaw and Trapper Lakes

String Lake Loop
Distance: 3.6 miles RT
Elevation gain: Approx. 310 ft.
Maximum elevation: Approx. 7,120 ft.
Maps: Mount Moran, Jenny Lake

Leigh, Bearpaw and Trapper Lakes
Distance:
Leigh Lake: 7.4 miles RT
Bearpaw Lake: 7.8 miles RT
Trapper Lake: 8.6 miles RT
Elevation gain: Approx. 90 ft.
Maximum elevation: Approx. 6,900 ft.
Maps: Mount Moran, Jenny Lake
Season: May through October

String, Leigh, Bearpaw and Trapper Lakes rest at the base of the Tetons, offering wonderful, easy strolls along their shores and memorable views of the peaks soaring above them. The pair of hikes share almost a mile of trail, and are thus presented together.

Driving Directions
Follow the directions on page 88.

String Lake Loop
Barely 10 feet deep and just over a football field in width, String Lake is one of the few lakes in the Tetons sufficiently warmed by the sun to make swimming more than a jump in-jump out proposition. Mount St. John and Rockchuck Peak rise almost a mile above its western shore, forming an exceptionally pretty background for swimmers, picnickers and canoeists enjoying its waters. The narrow

lake is believed to be an old river channel. It connects Jenny Lake to the south with Leigh Lake to the north. The trail around String Lake can be easily walked in a couple of hours. The path crosses a bridge over the outlet between it and Leigh Lake and climbs a short distance up the eastern slopes of Rockchuck Peak, opening views of the Gros Ventre Range across the valley floor. It then drops to a bridge over the outlet connecting String with Jenny Lake and turns north to complete the loop.

While this hike can be done in either direction, the description that follows begins at the trailhead at the north end of the parking area. Here the trail winds through lodgepole along the northeast shore of String Lake. At .9 mile it crosses the bridge over the outlet connecting String and Leigh Lakes and forks at a signed junction near a large glacial erratic. The trail to the right follows the west shore

of Leigh Lake a short distance to several lakeshore campsites. Leigh Lake once had a trail circling its shores. It has long been abandoned and is now quite difficult to follow. Those with time may want to browse the huckleberry bushes near the glacial erratic before hiking around String, continued by bearing left at the junction.

The trail gently climbs the east slope of 11,144-ft. Rockchuck Peak and travels above the lake through thick lodgepole forest alive with bird song and the chatter of squirrels. It reaches a signed intersection with the trail to Paintbrush Canyon to your right at 1.7 miles. Continue straight ahead.

The trail leaves the forest and descends at an easy grade through open slopes and sparse stands of aspen and ash. At dawn or dusk, moose may be seen feeding in the wet terrain bordering String Lake below.

A mile past the junction with Paintbrush Canyon Trail you'll pass an unmarked trail on the right (W) that cuts steeply up open slopes. This leads to Laurel Lake, nestled at the bottom of the drainage between Rockchuck to the north and Mount St. John to the south. Laurel is a nice half-mile side trip that offers a quiet place to eat lunch.

Three miles around the lake you'll intersect the Jenny Lake Trail to your right. Bear left and walk .3 mile to a bridge crossing the outlet between String and Jenny Lake, an exceptionally scenic spot framed by the Cathedral grouping of peaks. From here it is .3 mile back to the south end of the parking area. The path intersects a canoe launch site and parking areas as it follows the lakeshore back to your starting point.

Leigh, Bearpaw and Trapper Lakes

Leigh Lake is named after "Beaver Dick" Leigh, a colorful mountain man who made his living trapping in canyons on the west side of the Tetons. He forayed onto the east side of the range often enough to be hired as a guide for the 1872 Hayden expedition to Yellowstone and Jackson Hole. When he died in 1899, Leigh was buried on a bluff in Idaho that overlooks the Teton River. By all accounts, this uneducated but intelligent man was well-liked, honorable and courageous. His name is carried by a canyon and group of lakes on the west slope of the Tetons as well as on the jewel described here.

The shores of Leigh Lake offer some of the best views of Mount Moran in the park. The massive peak towers over 3,000 feet above the lakeshore, its rocky slopes calmly reflected in the still waters. Falling Ice Glacier, a field of ice over 100 feet thick that hangs between Moran's East and West Horns, discharges glacial flour into the lake, giving Leigh its distinctive green hue. Two miles long and almost 250 feet deep, run-off streams tumbling down both Leigh and Paintbrush Canyons feed the lake. In 1963, famed Jackson Hole naturalist Olaus Murie wrote that to him and his family,

"Leigh Lake has always seemed the most beautiful lake we know. At its head there are some white sand beaches and old drift logs to sit upon while you gaze across the blue-green water to the mouth of Leigh Canyon and to Mt. Moran ...All this beauty just 45 minutes walk from your car. How good it is that the Park Service has kept this gem without a road. Here is peace and quiet, the country itself, and yet open to any who will come quietly, under his own power."

Murie's observations five decades ago still ring true today.

The first .9 mile of this trail is the same as that described for String Lake above. Begin at the north end of the parking lot and follow the path around String's northeast side to a bridged crossing of the outlet between String and Leigh Lakes at .9 mile. Do not cross the bridge; instead, continue straight along Leigh's east lakeshore. There are several abandoned trails in the area as well as paths used by those portaging canoes. Stay on the trail closest to the lake. This follows a level course around Leigh's shore. Whortleberry, huckleberry bushes and wildflowers cover the forest floor, shaded by fir and lodgepole pine.

At 3.1 miles, you'll reach a series of sand and gravel beaches that provide ideal lunch spots. There are also numerous backcountry campsites located here. (These beaches are appealing, but since the sites are relatively close to a heavily trafficked trail, a nicer alternative for overnight campers and canoeists is to secure a site on the quiet west side of the lake.) Mystic Isle is the large island near Leigh's north end. Keep a sharp eye out for osprey that nest in dead snags on its south side.

The trail follows the lake to its north end and a trail junction at 3.7 miles. The trail to Bearpaw Lake heads north (R), reaching the lake in .2 mile. To reach Trapper, stay left. That lake is reached .6 mile farther. North of Trapper an abandoned trail connects with Moran Bay on Jackson Lake. It is hard to follow, particularly near Moran Creek, but does offer good access to a nice backcountry site that otherwise requires an approach by boat.

30 Holly Lake and Paintbrush Divide

Distance:
   Holly Lake: 6.2 miles one-way
   Paintbrush Divide: 7.9 miles one-way
Elevation gain:
   Holly Lake: Approx. 2,650 ft.
   Paintbrush Divide: Approx. 3,870 ft.
Maximum elevation:
   Holly Lake: 9,410 ft.
   Paintbrush Divide: 10,700.
Maps: Jenny Lake, Moran.
Season: July through September

Holly Lake lies at the bottom of a glacial cirque below 11,555-ft. Mount Woodring. This beautiful glacial tarn is reached by a steep trail up Paintbrush Canyon that travels through coniferous forest and rocky terrain. It switchbacks up three distinct glacial benches as it climbs over 2,500 feet to the lake.

Striking views of the north side of 11,144-ft. Rockchuck Peak and permanent snowfields beneath The Jaw and Mount St. John—and the fiery red wildflower that gives the canyon its name—lend to this hike's appeal. It is part of one of the most popular backpacking trips in the park, the 19.2 mile Paintbrush/Cascade Canyon loop.

Driving Directions
   See page 88.

Trail Description
   The trail winds through lodgepole pine at a level to easy grade, following the east side of String Lake. From late June through August, you may see laurel, a low-branching shrub with striking rose-colored flowers. This member of the heath family

Mount Woodring rises above Holly Lake.

grows in wet soils, typically at treeline in the Rockies. The last several years it has bloomed near the shore of both String and Leigh Lakes.

95

The path crosses a wooden bridge over Leigh Lake outlet at .9 mile and divides at a junction. The unmaintained trail to the right follows the west shore of Leigh Lake to the mouth of Leigh Canyon. That is often wet and Leigh Canyon itself is not trailed. Follow the left fork as it gently climbs above String Lake, hugging the slope of Rockchuck Peak. (Several large, glacial erratics near the junction attract climbers practicing bouldering moves. The berry patches beyond them attract bears as the fruit ripens early to mid-August.)

The trail intersects the signed path to Paintbrush Canyon at 1.7 miles. Turn right at this junction. The trail ascending lower Paintbrush bears steadily west through the densely forested slopes of lower Paintbrush Canyon until it reaches Paintbrush Canyon Creek, roughly 3.2 miles and a thousand feet above the trailhead. It soon crosses a bridge over the creek to its north side, following it through scattered trees and rocky slopes. After numerous small crossings of side streams tumbling down Rockchuck, Mount Woodring and Mount St. John's, the trail ascends several wooded switchbacks. It then travels due west up a long, straight stretch to a trail junction at 5.7 miles. The left trail leads to the camping zone below Paintbrush Divide. Take the right trail and climb two short, steep switchbacks to a crossing of the outlet of a small lake on your left. This is not Holly Lake, which lies another .3 mile up the trail.

Holly Lake is nestled in a classically beautiful alpine setting. Looking down the canyon from the lake, the permanent snowfields and sheer north side of The Jaw dominate the view to the right, while the valley floor can be seen far below. Around it rise the rocky slopes of Mount Woodring. When a party of six climbers ascended its southeast slope on July 24, 1929—believing they were the first to climb the peak—they discovered a cairn on top. In his landmark *Climbers Guide to the Teton Range*, Renny Jackson speculates that the U.S. Forest Service crew that constructed the trail in the 1920s likely built the cairn.

From the southeast slopes it is a Class II scramble to the summit, a 2,100-foot gain in elevation that unveils extraordinary views of Mount Moran and Thor Peak.

A return via the same route to the trailhead completes a full hiking day. Those skilled in off-trail, cross-country travel could ascend the slopes west of the lake, just above the obvious saddle, and drop into Grizzly Bear Lake in upper Leigh Canyon. Walk down that trailless canyon to the west shore of Leigh Lake, and then return via String Lake. This is a beautiful, rugged trip of several days duration.

Alternatively, one could continue west on the trail past the lake and rejoin the main trail to Paintbrush Divide, reached in another 1.7 miles. From the divide the trail drops into the upper reaches of the North Fork of Cascade Canyon and travels south to Lake Solitude. It then descends Cascade Canyon to Jenny Lake. This is one of the most popular backpacking trips in the park. While it is occasionally done as a long day hike, taking two or three days is recommended. Due to heavy use both Holly Lake and Lake Solitude have been closed to camping since 1972. Permitted camping is allowed in zones below both lakes.

Holly Lake is named after Holly Leek, the son of one of the valley's earliest residents, rancher Stephen Leek. Leek's photographs of elk starving during severe Jackson Hole winters were instrumental in efforts to establish the National Elk Refuge north of Jackson.

31 Snake River Trail

Distance: Variable 1-2 miles RT
Elevation gain/loss: Negligible
Maximum elevation: Approx. 6,720 ft.
Maps: Moran.
Season: May through October
Use restrictions: No camping or fires. Wyoming fishing license required to fish.

Anglers plying the Snake River have created a pleasant, level trail along its banks. The chance to catch fish, picnic, spy osprey, eagles and wildlife and enjoy magnificent Teton views in relative solitude puts this outing on the top of the list of short, easy hikes.

Driving Directions

Drive 12 miles north of Jackson on U.S. Highway 89/291 to the signed Moose Junction. Turn left and drive past park headquarters to the Moose Entrance of Grand Teton National Park. From the entrance, drive 14.8 miles to an unsigned dirt road on your right. Alternately, drive to Moran Junction, turn left, and continue to the junction with the inner park road. Turn left here and drive 4.2 miles to the unsigned dirt road on your left.

The glacial cobble and dirt road splits at 2.1 miles; continue straight. Bison and antelope are often spied in the sage grasslands. The road travels through a willowed riparian area and conifer forest before ending at a parking area 3.6 miles from the paved road.

Anglers need a Wyoming fishing

An anglers path along the Snake River provides easy access for both fishing and hiking.

It is not unusual to see or hear sandhill cranes when hiking the Snake River Trail.

wildflowers of every size and description paint the ground. The path hugs the top of a bench about 15 feet above the river. Plentiful moose, elk and deer tracks lead down the bench to the water. If you are quiet and walking near dawn or dusk, chances are good you'll see the natives.

The path drops down the bench and crosses a small tributary at approximately .5 mile. It soon disappears in the sage.

Continue walking north and you'll regain the main channel of the braided river and path. The trail travels through a comely stand of cottonwoods before bearing left (W) and ascending a hill above the steeply dropping bank. It then re-enters open sage grasslands. Bear left (S) here and walk cross country to return to your vehicle or retrace your steps.

Sandhill cranes have frequently been spotted in the sage grasslands along the return route. They require a river or other body of water and undisturbed habitat, both abundant in this area.

Sandhills typically nest on a mound of aquatic vegetation found in still water or along a shoreline. The female produces two olive-brown, spotted eggs that the pair incubate for about a month before the young hatch. Their offspring grow quickly, fledging in under two months.

It would be unusual to surprise a sandhill on its nest. It is more probable that the ever-attentive parents will announce your approach with their unmistakable, loud rattling call.

Mature adult sandhills stand 40-50 inches tall and have an impressive 6-7 foot wingspan. Their light gray plumage is frequently stained rusty brown from oxides present in water, and their heads sport a red crown and long, straight bill. Immature cranes lack the red crown and are reddish-brown in color. Sandhills are often observed gleaning the ground for seeds, grass shoots, insects and worms.

license and may only use artificial flies and lures. The section of river between the gauging station downstream to the Wilson Bridge is open to trout fishing from April 1 through October 31. Anglers may keep three trout, but only one may exceed 18 inches. All trout between 12-18 inches must be released immediately.

Trail Description

A path leads from the sign through a short stretch of forest to the west bank of the Snake River. Bearing right at the bank yields great views of the Tetons. This author's preferred option is to angle left from the sign until you intersect the path along the bank. Turn left (N). Mount Moran dominates the western skyline and

32 Signal Mt. Summit Loop

Distance: 5.5 miles RT
Elevation gain: Approx. 700 ft.
Maximum elevation: 7,593 ft.
Maps: Moran. Book map pg. 101
 Season: Late May though mid-October

The undulating trail to the crown of 7,593-ft. Signal Mountain packs a lot into a relatively short hike. Waterfowl and wildlife congregate on or near various ponds passed on the way to the top. Surprisingly good views of Jackson Lake and the Teton Range—especially Mt. Moran—are enjoyed after climbing only a minor ridge. The summit offers one of the finest geology overviews in the valley, clearly explained by park service interpretative displays. In autumn golden aspens framing the cobalt blue water of the lake makes the lower loop doubly appealing, and elk are often heard bugling in the peaceful meadows.

Because a paved road leads to the overlook, most people drive rather than walk to the top, leaving this worthwhile excursion wonderfully uncrowded during busy summer months. While this hike is enjoyable the entire hiking season, it is recommended in late May and early June, when many of the higher elevations are still clothed in snow, and late summer when the leaves begin to turn.

Those who desire a shorter outing can easily pare two miles and the major elevation gain off this hike by simply walking the loop and not taking the one-mile spur to the summit.

Driving Directions

The trail to the summit begins off the signed Signal Mountain Summit Road, located four miles south of the Jackson Lake Lodge Junction on the inner park road. Turn in and drive approximately one mile to the small trailhead sign and pullout on the right side of the road. If this is full, drive .1 mile farther to a larger pullout on the right and walk back to the trailhead. People staying at the campground or lodge may wish to take the cut-off trail. This crosses the highway (be careful!) and gently climbs through the woods, intersecting the summit road near the signed trailhead. Consult the book map.

Trail Description

The path travels through lodgepole forest as it skirts a lily pad-covered pond to your left. Moose are often seen browsing here and the pond is a good place to bird watch. At a quarter-mile you'll reach a signed intersection that indicates it is 2.5 miles to the summit via the ridge to the left, or 2.5 miles to the summit via the ponds to the right. This loop hike encompasses both. The trail can be walked in either direction; the description below begins by bearing right toward the ponds.

The level path soon leaves the forest, entering a flower-filled meadow overshadowed by magnificent views west of Mount Moran. This 12,605-foot summit is one of the most distinctive in the park. Its large summit is capped by Flathead sandstone, a vestige of the sedimentary rock that buried the valley floor before the

Mount Moran rises dramatically above Oxbow Bend, seen here along a segment of the Signal Mtn. Loop.

Tetons were uplifted. Similar sandstone found deep below the valley surface indicates a vertical displacement of over 24,000 feet. The peak bears the name of Thomas Moran, a landscape artist on the 1870 Washburn Doane Expedition to Yellowstone. Moran's paintings helped persuade Congress to designate Yellowstone a national park. Ironically, he never traveled through Jackson Hole.

The trail stays left of two small ponds then moderately climbs up a small draw and enters open lodgepole and aspen forest. At 1.75 miles it reaches a signed intersection. Bear left if you wish to forego the hike to the summit; the ridge trail loops back to your starting point. To reach the summit, continue right. The path climbs at a moderate, steady grade through stands of Douglas fir. The grade eases as it enters a pleasant meadow colored by penstemon, gilia, buckwheat, hyssop, salsify and sticky geraniums.

Beyond the meadow, the trail re-enters the forest and begins a steady, switchbacking climb to the summit, reached 2.75 miles beyond the trailhead. Those who have driven to the top will join you in soaking in the view. From gray-green sagebrush covered flats to the forested moraines and kettled area to the east, the handiwork created by glaciers thousands of years ago is spread out on the valley floor below. The summit affords a bird's-eye view of most of the range and the meandering Snake River at its foot.

A tragedy the summer of 1890 gave this low peak its name. An owner of a nearby ranch, Robert Hamilton, embarked on a hunting trip near the end of August. When he failed to return, his worried business partner organized search parties to look for him. They agreed to climb a high point and build a signal fire when Hamilton was located to terminate the search.

Hamilton's body was discovered below the outlet to Jackson Lake a week

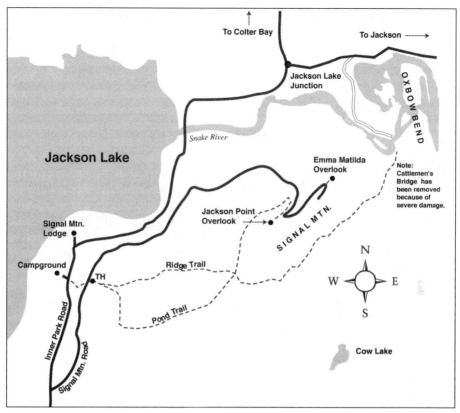

Signal Mountain Loop

later. He apparently drowned while trying to ford the powerful Snake River. As agreed upon, the party who found him ascended a nearby hill and built a smoky fire. The hill, of course, is now called Signal Mountain.

Signal Mountain was formerly the site of a forest service fire lookout. A CCC crew built the lookout in the 1930s, one of six on the northern portion of Teton National Forest. Its lower portion was constructed of stone while its upper section was ringed up multi-paned windows. The National Park Service dismantled the lookout in 1943.

To return to the trailhead, backtrack one mile to the signed intersection with the ridge trail and bear right (W). The trail crosses open meadows studded with large Douglas fir. It ascends three small ridges before turning south, opening excellent views of the Tetons. North to south you see Eagles Peak, Rolling Thunder Mountain, Bivouac Peak, Mount Moran, Rockchuck, St. John's, Mount Owen and the Grand.

The path climbs a gentle rise then drops through lodgepole forest before ascending the final low ridge. Here, the Grand and Mount Moran are framed by quaking aspen in a classic postcard snapshot. A short distance farther, the trail drops down to the signed junction with the pond side of the loop.

The parking lot is reached in a quarter-mile, completing this pleasant 5.5-mile hike.

Colter Bay Trails

The sagebrush meadows, lodgepole pine forest, thick willows and marshy areas along Jackson Lake's eastern shoreline near Colter Bay provide ideal habitat for wildlife. Muskrat, otter and beaver thrive in the still inlets. Moose, elk and deer often browse on the plentiful vegetation, while cranes, ducks and trumpeter swans frequent the bay and nearby small bodies of water. Nature's inhabitants are most active in the soft light of dawn and dusk, when the Grand and Mount Moran's reflections color Jackson Lake with delicate shades of gold, rose and peach.

A number of trails crisscross this peaceful area. All are virtually flat, winding over occasional rises as they follow the lakeshore and loop to Swan Lake and Heron Pond. The trail network offers numerous possibilities; three are presented here.

Colter Bay is a shallow harbor formed in 1916, when completion of a dam at the south end of Jackson Lake raised its water level nine feet. When the water was lowered in the mid-1980s to repair and rebuild the old dam, archeologists unearthed interesting Native American artifacts near this end of the lake. It is recommended that those with time visit Colter Bay Indian Arts Museum, housed in the visitor's center. The free museum is open daily from mid-May through September. Its extensive Plains Indian collection includes shields, ceremonial pipes, masks, clothing, moccasins, warbonnets, decorated hides and other items.

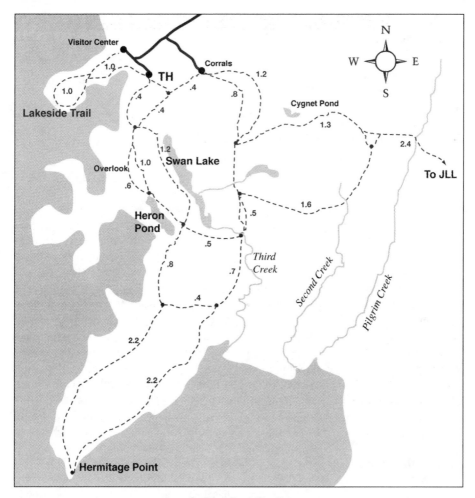

Colter Bay Trails

The bay is named in honor of John Colter, a member of the 1804 Lewis and Clark Expedition who was granted permission to leave the expedition to explore the region. It is believed Colter's travels carried him through what is now Yellowstone and Grand Teton National Parks in 1807-1808. He is thought to be the first European to visit today's parks.

Driving Directions

Drive north out of Jackson 30 miles on U.S. Hwy 89/191 to Moran Junction. Turn left onto U.S. Hwy 89/287 and drive 10 miles to the signed Colter Bay turn-off on the left-hand side of the road, passing the turn-off to Jackson Lake Lodge. (From the Inner Park Road junction with the highway, it is 5.5 miles to Colter Bay.) Turn in and follow Colter Bay Road to its western terminus near the visitor center. The signed trail to Hermitage Point and Swan and Heron Ponds starts at the far south end of the parking lot near the marina. The Lakeshore Trail begins right (N) of the visitor's center.

33 Lakeshore Trail

Distance: 2 miles RT
Elevation gain: Negligible. No climb greater than 150 ft.
Maximum elevation: Approx. 8,000 ft.
Maps: Colter Bay. Book map pg. 103
Season: Late May though mid-October

The short but rewarding Lakeside Trail circles a forested peninsula jutting into Jackson Lake. An interpretive brochure of the trail is available at the visitor's center and is well worth its modest cost. In addition to wonderful views of the Tetons and Jackson Lake at the west end of the peninsula, hikers can clearly see the effects of forest fire near the mouths of Moran and Waterfall Canyons.

Driving Directions

See page 103.

Trail Description

The blacktop trail starts immediately north of the visitors' center. It travels west onto the spit of land for .3 mile. Here, the pavement ends and the trail becomes a dirt track. This continues west, reaching a narrow isthmus .2 mile farther that leads to the loop around the peninsula. You may walk either direction around the loop. Near the west end of the peninsula, the trail dips to the lakeshore. This is a delightful place to enjoy Jackson Lake, the largest in Grand Teton National Park.

Jackson Lake was formed an esti-

mated 12,000 years ago when glaciers flowing down the northern canyons of the Teton Range merged with a large glacier flowing south from Yellowstone at the base of the range. This gargantuan sheet of ice raked the valley floor as it flowed south, digging a basin and dropping churned up soil and rocks along its edges. As the climate warmed, the ice receded and meltwater filled the basin, forming the lake. An 1814 map drawn by Capt. William Clark of the famed Lewis and Clark expedition identified it as Lake Biddle, and at various times it has been called Teton Lake and Lewis Lake. Its present moniker was conferred by trapper William Sublette in honor of David Jackson, who trapped this region in the mid 1800s.

In its natural state, Jackson Lake was 17,000 acres in size, reaching a depth of 386 feet. Pressured by Jackson Hole residents who desired flood control and Idaho farmers who wanted irrigation water, the State of Wyoming granted water rights to Idaho in exchange for Idaho farmers paying to dam the lake—a decision that has wide-ranging consequences for today's national park.

The first of four succeeding dams

Mount Moran, reflected in Jackson Lake. The distinctive peak is viewed from the Lakeshore Trail.

over its outlet was completed in 1906, the last in 1988. The present dam raised the lake level 39 feet, bringing its high-water size to almost 26,000 acres and 52 miles of shoreline. In dry conditions, Idaho farmers exercise their water rights, significantly decreasing the lake's size. This yearly fluctuation has prevented establishment of vegetation around the lakeshore. It also poses grave challenges for aquatic and amphibian species, and periodically closes marinas and recreation sites on the lake.

Controversial today, it must be remembered that the dam preceded initial formation of Grand Teton National Park by almost two decades. Without guaranteeing its continued existence, the park may not have attained the political support needed to include the valley floor in its 1950 expansion.

Mount Moran dominates the view across the lake. To its right (N) are 10,825-ft. Bivouac Peak, 11,258-ft. Eagles Rest Peak and 11,355-ft. Ranger Peak. Moran Canyon is nestled between Mt. Moran and Bivouac Peak, Waterfall Canyon between Eagles Rest and Ranger Peak.

In 1932, a blaze consumed 115 acres near the mouth of Moran Canyon before crews put it out. Forty-two years later, a lightning-caused fire near Waterfall Canyon was allowed to burn, consuming 3,500 acres before naturally extinguishing itself.

The difference reflects recognition of the importance of fire to an ecosystem. Fires return nutrients to the soil, help control natural diseases, and improve wildlife habitat. They are a part of nature's cycle of death and rebirth.

Beyond the lake, the trail loops back to the isthmus through predominantly lodgepole forest.

105

34 Swan Lake/Heron Pond Loop

35 Hermitage Point

Swan Lake/Heron Pond Loop
> Distance: 3 miles
> Elevation gain: Negligible. No climb greater than 150 ft..
> Maximum elevation: Approx. 6,800 ft.
> Maps: Colter Bay. Book map pg. 103
> Season: Late May through October

Hermitage Point
> Distance: 9.4 miles RT
> Elevation gain: Approx. 440 ft. No climb greater than 150 ft..
> Maximum elevation: Approx. 6.890 ft.
> Maps: Colter Bay. Book map pg. 103
> Season: Late May through October

The Swan Lake/Heron Pond Loop is one of the best wildlife excursions in the park. Moose, elk and deer are often seen and birds and waterfowl abound. Herons, cranes and trumpeter swans are among the showier species of the latter. The best time to view wildlife is at dawn and dusk, when many species feed and move about. Those with patience and binoculars are usually well rewarded with generous wildlife sightings. The lofty summits bordering the west shores of Jackson Lake provide a stunning backdrop for Heron Pond, while the wide-open expanse of adjacent Bridger-Teton National Forest is viewed from larger Swan Lake.

The hike to Hermitage Point is an extension of the Swan Lake/Heron Pond Loop. This onward trail circumnavigates a peninsula of Jackson Lake. Views of that lake and the Teton Range, wildlife, wildflowers and the likelihood of seeing few other people are in the plus column

of this hike. As it gains the peninsula, the terrain is quite open—something to consider if it is a hot day; little shade is available on much of the upper stretches.

There are numerous paths in this area, both official ones and informal paths created by horse users and recreationists. When in doubt, confer with the map in this book or pick up a Colter Bay trail map at the visitor's center.

Driving Directions

See page 103. The description for the start of both trails begins near the south end of the parking lot by the marina, at a trail sign posted by a service road.

Trail Description

Walk up the road paralleling the bay's east shore to a signed trail junction at .4 mile. Bear left. You'll soon pass concrete pads and pipes, the remains of Colter Bay's old sewage disposal ponds.

Top: The Tetons, reflected in Heron Pond. Right: Magnificent trumpeter swans and other waterfowl are among the attractions of the Swan/Heron Pond loop hike.

The trail traverses flat terrain through stretches of open sagebrush and lodgepole forest before reaching the north end of long, shallow Swan Lake. Here, lily pads almost completely cover the water. Rocky Mountain pond lilies' favored environment is small lakes and beaver ponds. This appealing aquatic plant sports a sunny yellow, 3-5" flower that blooms late June through August. Indians roast and ate the plant's seeds, that reportedly taste like popcorn. Ducks also eat the plant's seeds

and muskrats use its roots to construct their lodges. Look for waterfowl, muskrat and beaver when you see pond lilies. Barrows' Goldeneye, cinnamon teal, buffalohead, mallards, mergansers and muskrats were all viewed near the lake's north end on a hike one summer, as were a pair of elegant sandhill cranes on the pond's far shore. These stately birds stand up to four feet high. Adults are grayish in color with a red crown, juveniles light brown.

As you follow the trail south it veers away from the pond and travels briefly through forest. This section of trail was rerouted to direct human presence away from a large trumpeter swan nest. This magnificent white bird was hunted and poached almost to extinction in the 1930s and 40s. Valiant efforts by wildlife managers have nursed the population back

107

to an estimated 400 swans, but recent research indicates that both the number of cygnets born and their survival rate are on the decline. Earth may yet lose its largest of North American waterfowl. Please don't try to approach swans you may see on the lake or nest. Trumpeters are sensitive to intrusion, and your presence may negatively impact breeding or nesting activity

The trail reaches a three-way signed junction at 1.6 miles. The trails ahead and to your left lead to Hermitage Point. Right leads you to Heron Pond.

To complete the
Swan Lake/Heron Pond Loop

Take the path that travels right at the junction. It traverses lodgepole forest the next half-mile as it parallels the pretty pond, named for the great blue herons that ply its waters. Look for them and the more commonly sighted Canada geese and kingfishers.

As the trail reaches the end of Heron Pond at 2.1 miles, you'll intersect a spur trail to the left that climbs a ridge for views of Jackson Lake. It rejoins the trail in .4 mile. (If you climb to the ridge, bear left onto the main trail to return to the trailhead.) The main trail continues its northwest direction through a forest floor covered with grouse whortleberry. This low-growing member of the heath family favors the shade provided by lodgepole pine. Its tiny egg-shaped leaves, typically under a half-inch long, are attached to green branches resembling broom straws. The shrub produces a small tasty berry as summer progresses. (While it is illegal to pick wildflowers in the park, it is legal to pick berries for personal consumption.)

At 2.6 miles, you reach the Swan Lake trail junction. Stay right and retrace your steps .4 mile to the trailhead and end of this hike.

To complete the Hermitage Point Loop

At the three-way trail junction, you may proceed left or straight to reach the point. This description describes the fork of trail that proceeds straight. It wraps around the southern end of Heron Pond, then heads south .8 mile to another junction. Bear right here and ascend a small hill guarded by massive Douglas fir. The top of the rise is graced by views of Mt. Moran.

The trail weaves in and out of forest for another mile before crossing sagebrush flats to reach Hermitage Point at 4.6 miles. There are several nice spots at the end of the peninsula and along its upper west side to take a break and soak in views of Moran and the Grand across the lake.

The end of the peninsula was named Hermitage Point following a developer's plans to build an inn, or hermitage, there. He procured a large quantity of logs for the project then decided not to build. After completion of Jackson Lake Dam in 1916, he floated the logs down the Snake and sold them off. While the lodge was never built, the point retained its name.

To complete the loop, continue around the point. The trail ascends a small rise before it bears left (N). It parallels the lakeshore for a mile or so, then bends left and re-enters the woods before reaching a trail junction at 6.8 miles. Stay right here. You'll soon see meandering Third Creek east of the trail; it flows out of Swan Lake into Jackson Lake. The marshy terrain is prime moose habitat—an animal you don't want to surprise. Stay alert.

Near the southeast finger of Swan Lake, you'll reach a signed intersection at 7.5 miles. Bear left. The trail arcs around Swan's southern shore to reach the Heron Pond intersection a half-mile farther. Continue straight here, paralleling Heron Pond on your return to the parking lot in 1.4 more miles.

36 Jackson Lake Lodge to Colter Bay

Distance: 4.5 miles one-way
Elevation gain: Negligible.
Maximum elevation: Approx. 6,800 ft.
Maps: Moran, Colter Bay.
Season: May though October
Use restrictions: Mountain biking prohibited

An often overlooked but pleasant trail is the old roadbed between Jackson Lake Lodge and Colter Bay. This flat, 4.5-mile hike may be started from Willow Flats Overlook or, as described here, from an asphalt walk at the south end of Jackson Lake Lodge. It ends at the horse corrals at Colter Bay. In addition to views of Jackson Lake and the Teton Range north of the Grand, hikers enjoy a variety of wildlife and forest environments en route. These are described in-depth in an inexpensive trail pamphlet published by the Grand Teton Association, available for purchase in the lodge.

While the closed roadbed seems a perfect venue for mountain biking, visitors are reminded that biking is prohibited.

Willowed wetlands characterize segments of the hike between Jackson Lake Lodge and Colter Bay.

Driving Directions

To reach the lodge and trailhead, drive 30 miles north of Jackson on U.S. Hwy. 89/191 to Moran Junction. Turn left onto U.S. Hwy. 89/287 and drive through the Buffalo Entrance Station to Grand Teton National Park. Four miles north of the entrance, drive straight past the turn-off to Jackson Lake and Signal Mountain. It is another .8 mile to the well-signed turn-off to Jackson Lake Lodge on your left. Park in the back lot and walk to the south end of the lodge (left of the building's main entrance). A paved asphalt trail quickly drops to the old road.

Trail Description

The road/trail cuts through Willow Flats, the large freshwater marsh sand-

Beaver, above, and mallards are two of the area inhabitants hikers may see on this outing. Numerous creeks and towering cottonwoods provide favorable habitat for dozens of bird species.

wiched between the lodge and Jackson Lake. Here, ponds, willows and small grassy openings provide ideal protection and food for beaver, moose, elk, cranes and a host of other winged friends— including woodpeckers, yellow-headed blackbirds, soras, barn swallows, fly-catchers, and sparrows. It is a great area to make yourself comfortable and wildlife watch. Remember to bring the binoculars you've used as a bookend the last five years and forgotten about. This outing has the potential to delight even the most casual of birders.

As you walk north beyond Willow Flats, the road travels through stands of spruce and fir before crossing a bridge over Pilgrim Creek at 1.8 miles. Shortly beyond the bridge the terrain opens up to reveal views of Mount Moran framed by conifers and stately cottonwoods. This section is spectacular in fall, when the trees are dressed in gold and the low-angle light paints the silhouettes of the jagged Tetons soldier blue.

A junction is reached at 2.4 miles. The triangle of trails in this vicinity is a bit confusing. Stay right to continue on to Colter Bay, left to reach Second Creek and/or Hermitage Point. The trail to Colter Bay skirts the south side of Cygnet Pond, where moose can often be seen browsing and feeding on aquatic vegetation in the pond. A variety of waterfowl is attracted to the pond as well.

At 3.6 miles, you'll reach a second junction. Two routes here lead to Colter Bay. The shorter .8-mile path travels past the sewage holding ponds to reach the corrals. The longer option travels east of the ponds to reach the corrals in 1.2 miles. If you have shuttled a car in advance, your hike is done at the corrals.

A number of longer loops departing from Jackson Lake Lodge or the corrals are also possible. Consult the book map.

37 Christian Pond
38 Emma Matilda Lake

Christian Pond
> Distance: 3.7 mile RT
> Elevation gain: Approx 140 ft.
> Maximum elevation: Approx. 6,970 ft.
> Maps: Moran, Two Ocean. Book map pg. 115
> Season: May though October

Emma Matilda Lake
> Distance via Christian Pond: 11 miles RT
> Elevation gain: Approx 920 ft.
> Maximum elevation: Approx. 7,300 ft.
> Maps: Two Ocean. Book map pg. 115
> Season: Mid-May though October

The short walk around Christian Pond offers some of the best opportunities in the valley to enjoy trumpeter swans, a variety of birds, wildflowers, moose and views of the Tetons—without lung-searing or knee-busting climbs and drops. Not surprisingly the trail receives a fair amount of use, including horse traffic from Jackson Lake Lodge. If you start early, however, you'll likely have this delightful hike to yourself.

The loop around Emma Matilda Lake shares the first 1.2 miles of trail as the hike around Christian Pond before diverging. It climbs several hundred feet to a ridge above the lake's north shore, a vantage point that provides panoramic views of Jackson Lake and the Tetons.

Driving Directions
The trail begins at a small parking area just north of Jackson Lake Lodge, reached by driving north of Jackson on U.S. Hwy. 89/191. You may either turn left at Moose Junction and take the inner park road to its junction with U.S. Hwy. 89/287—turning left there to reach the lodge—or continue straight and drive another 18 miles to Moran Junction. Turn left at this junction, pass through the Buffalo Entrance Station, and drive four miles north to the signed turn-off.

Park north of the bridge in the small parking area off the right (E) side of the highway. If this is full, park in the back lot for Jackson Lake Lodge. From the lodge, the trail begins near the horse corrals and travels under the highway bridge to join the loop around Christian Pond.

Trail Description
The trail dips to a willow-filled basin, crosses Christian Creek and climbs a small knoll to a signed trail junction at .4 mile. Either direction takes you around Christian Pond. For purpose of description for this pair of hikes, turn right.

The trail gently ascends an overlook

above the pond. This is a superb place to view waterfowl, particularly a pair of nesting trumpeter swans. Trumpeters are the largest of all North American waterfowl, weighing up to 30 pounds. With a wingspan of seven to eight feet, these magnificent white birds can reach air speeds of 50 mph.

Once ranging over most of the United States and Canada, the swans reached near extinction in the 1940s. Severely hunted for their eggs, feathers and flesh, their population dipped to less than 20 birds in the continental US. Concerted efforts by wildlife managers have improved their status, but they are not out of danger. Please do not leave the trail for a closer look: You may disturb their nest site. Bring a pair of binoculars or spotting scope to observe the swans, coots, teals, yellow-headed blackbirds and splashy blue-billed ruddy ducks that inhabit the pond.

Past the overlook, the trail parallels the west side of the pond, its track seasonally lined with a colorful garden of flowering balsamroot, scarlet gilia, lupine and sulphur buckwheat. As you near the south end of the pond at one mile you'll reach a signed junction. The right fork leads to a scenic overlook of Oxbow Bend. (See hike no. 41.) Bear left here and again at 1.2 miles.

This section of the hike climbs at an easy grade through Douglas fir, Engelmann spruce and aspen forest to a ridge, gaining just enough elevation to unveil views of the pond, Jackson Lake and the Tetons. The trail then descends to a three-way junction at 2.2 miles. Straight, the path heading north leads to Grand View Point and Two Ocean Lake (hikes no. 39 and 40). Right, the path continues its circumnavigation around Emma Matilda.

Turn left at the three-way junction to complete the Christian Pond Loop. The trail drops then levels as it travels through willowed lowland. Moose frequent this area and can be hidden in the foliage. Travel carefully. After turning west the path ascends the short distance to the parking lot.

Christian Pond bears the name of Charles A. "Tex" Christian, who managed one of the first lodges in the area.

Emma Matilda Lake

Bear right at the three-way junction. The trail travels east as it ascends 320 feet to a ridge above the north side of Emma Matilda. The long, crescent-shaped body of water is cradled between two ridges, almost 100 feet higher than Jackson Lake. The path travels the length of the ridge, gradually dropping to an intersection with a trail leading to Two Ocean Lake at 4.7 miles. Stay right here to continue around Emma Matilda.

The trail bends south around Emma's east end, staying 100 feet above the lake until it descends to cross a footbridge over its outlet at 6.6 miles. (You will pass two spur trails en route. These lead to an access road to the lakes off Pacific Creek Road. Stay right at both of these junctions.) Beyond the footbridge, the path hugs the lakeshore for over a mile then gently climbs 200 feet above it through thick forest. It swings close to the shore again at 8.4 miles, traversing southwest through huge Douglas and subalpine fir and stately Engelmann spruce forest. Stay right at 8.8 miles and again at 9.4 miles, where trails lead south to the Oxbow Bend area. At 9.8 miles, the Emma Matilda trail rejoins the trail around Christian Pond. Bear left at this junction, retracing the first 1.2 miles of the hike to return to your vehicle.

Emma Matilda Lake is named in honor of William Owen's wife. Emma attempted to climb the Grand Teton with him in 1891; he successfully scaled the peak seven years later with Frank Spalding. Although

Christian Pond, above, is a wonderful place to watch birds and other area wildlife. One species commonly seen is the yellow-headed blackbird, pictured left.

some controversy exists in regards to the Grand's mountaineering history, many believe his climb was the first ascent.

Both Emma Matilda and Two Ocean Lakes were threatened by irrigation projects in the 1920s, when District Forester R. H. Rutledge granted water storage rights to the Utah-Idaho Sugar Company and Osgood Land and Livestock Company following the severe drought of 1919. Though Grand Teton National Park had not yet been created, Yellowstone National Park Superintendent Horace Albright—who had long felt the Tetons should be included in the national park system—applied political pressure to halt construction of the water projects. Wood headgates at the outlets of both lakes were in place until 1950, when the former Forest Service land was added to Grand Teton National Park.

An obsidian knife estimated to be 8,000 years old was found near Emma Matilda a number of years ago, and a quartzite projectile point of the same age was unearthed near Two Ocean. Anthropologists believe early hunters living near Yellowstone migrated south in late spring to hunt for animals and gather food. There is no evidence these nomadic peoples wintered in the valley.

39 Grand View Point

Distance: 1.1 miles one-way
Elevation gain: Approx. 460 ft.
Maximum elevation: 7,594 ft.
Maps: Two Ocean. Book map opposite page
Season: Late May though October

The short but surprisingly steep hike up Grand View Point yields some of the nicest views of the northern reaches of Grand Teton National Park to be found. Looking west, Jackson Lake on the valley floor and the Tetons beyond are showcased. East, the Gros Ventre Range frames portions of Emma Matilda and Two Ocean Lakes.

In mid-June, the display of arrow-leafed balsamroot dotting the open slopes leading to the point is particularly memorable. This ubiquitous Jackson Hole wildflower thrives in dry soils at elevations up to 8,000 feet. Both elk and deer eat its young shoots, which appear as early as late April on sunny hillsides.

This hike can easily be extended by starting from Jackson Lake Lodge or by descending the overlook and walking around Two Ocean Lake. Consult the book map. It is a favored early morning destination for employees and guests of the lodge hoping to catch the rosy glow of sunrise on the Tetons' eastern slopes.

Driving Directions

Drive north .9 mile beyond the Jackson Lake Lodge turn-off on US Hwy. 89 to an unmarked dirt road on the right (E) side of the highway. Turn in, keeping right where an unsigned fork leads left a short distance farther. Stay on the obvious main road until its terminus at the trailhead, roughly a mile beyond the highway.

The track is often badly rutted but still negotiable in a low-clearance vehicle if driven slowly. In wet weather, deep ruts and mud may render the track impassable for most—if not all—vehicles.

Trail Description

The clear trail ascends lodgepole forest to a signed intersection with the trail circumnavigating Emma Matilda and Two Ocean Lakes at .2 mile. Bear left (N) at the junction. The path climbs the nose of the hillock leading to the point, steadily gaining elevation as it travels through lodgepole and subalpine fir forest. As it nears the top of the ridge, Douglas fir becomes more dominant, with several large trees framing the first glimpses of Emma Matilda and Two Ocean lakes at .8 mile. A short distance farther you reach the crest of the point, an obvious bald promontory that offers views both east and west.

The point is composed of reddish volcanic rock called andesite, common around the Mt. Washburn area of Yellowstone.

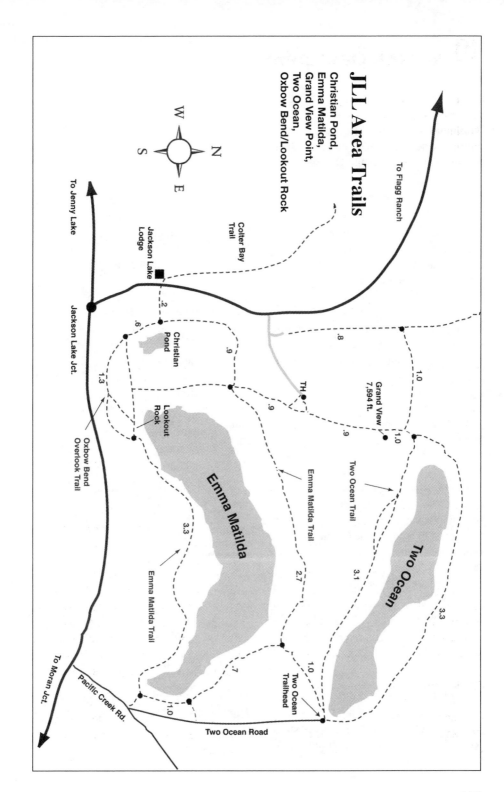

JLL Area Trails

Christian Pond,
Emma Matilda,
Grand View Point,
Two Ocean,
Oxbow Bend/Lookout Rock

To Flagg Ranch

To Jenny Lake

Jackson Lake Jct.

To Moran Jct.

Jackson Lake Lodge

Colter Bay Trail

Christian Pond

.2

.6

.9

1.3

Oxbow Bend Overlook Trail

Lookout Rock

.9

.9

TH

Grand View 7,594 ft.

.8

1.0

1.0

1.0

Two Ocean Trail

Emma Matilda Trail

Emma Matilda

3.3

Emma Matilda Trail

2.7

3.1

Two Ocean

3.3

1.0

.7

11.0

Two Ocean Trailhead

1.0

Two Ocean Road

Pacific Creek Rd.

N
W   E
S

40 Two Ocean Lake

Distance: 6.4 miles RT
Elevation gain: Approx. 340 ft.
Maximum elevation: 7,130 ft.
Maps: Two Ocean. Book map pg. 115
Season: Late May though October

Two Ocean Lake lies just north of Emma Matilda. Conifer forest, flowered meadows, wildlife viewing opportunities and appealing Teton Views make both lakes a nice choice early summer, when many of the higher trails are still engulfed in snow.

Glaciers scouring out hollows created Two Ocean and Emma Matilda, pushing earth and rock ridges around each depression. Around 15,000 years ago, the glaciers began to retreat and the swales filled with meltwater. Two Ocean Lake derives its name from the erroneous belief that water from its outlet flows to both the Atlantic and Pacific Oceans. While this is true of nearby Two Ocean Plateau—which straddles the Continental Divide—the lake lies west of that hydrologic landmark. Its outlet joins the Snake and eventually the Columbia River, draining into the Pacific. Water from the lake does not flow into the Atlantic.

The lake tempts fewer hikers than other park trails, perhaps because of a recent increase in bear sightings, particularly grizzly bears. Travel with companions and make noise should you choose this outing.

Driving Directions

Two Ocean Lake can be accessed by a number of roads: the trailhead for Grand View Point, the primary trailhead for Christian Pond, or trailheads along Pacific Creek Road. The description given below begins at the Pacific Creek Road trailhead, Drive north of Jackson for approximately 30 miles on U.S. Hwy. 89/191 to Moran Junction. Turn left at this junction, pass through the Buffalo Entrance Station and drive .9 mile to signed Pacific Creek Road on your right. Turn in. The road divides in two miles; bear left onto the graded dirt road and drive another 2.4 miles to the signed trailhead. There is a vault toilet, picnic tables, grills and trash cans, but no water. This trailhead is a popular launching spot for people choosing to canoe the lake.

Trail Description

The trail around Two Ocean Lake can be walked in either direction. This description begins on the north shore of the lake. The path descends a short distance and crosses a bridge over the lake's outlet. Here, a sign indicates it is 4.3 miles to Grand View Point. Head north through shady aspen and lodgepole pine forest that initially obscures views of the lake. The Tetons and lake soon pop into view, with particularly nice vistas of Mt. Moran. As it proceeds north the trail climbs at a gentle grade near the lake, crossing open, sage-covered slopes spiked with green gentian. This lanky herbaceous plant grows to heights of five feet. From a distance its flowers aren't impressive, but a close look reveals striking greenish, four-petaled blossoms flecked with purple. Also called deer tongue and monument plant, elk dine on its young basal leaves in the spring. Native Americans ate the plant's fleshy roots.

After a half-mile or so, the path begins angling north away from the shore of the lake. Below, banks of willow frequented by moose line Two Ocean's shore. Make noise so you don't surprise this unpredictable, aquatic browser.

The trail hops a creek lined with tall cottonwood trees and crosses a flowered meadow before entering a pleasant aspen forest. Here it gently climbs, gaining enough height to enjoy beautiful reflections of the Grand Teton in the lake.

After traversing open meadows, the path drops to cross the lake's inlet. The creek is shin-deep but the crossing is not broad or swift.

Beyond it, the path continues its easy climb around the open west end of Two Ocean Lake to a trail sign. The trail divides just beyond the sign. To continue around Two Ocean Lake, stay right on the clearer path through shady forest, soon reaching

a second signed junction at 3.3 miles. Walking straight here leads you to the top of Grand View Point and/or the Emma Matilda Lake Trail, options for extending this hike. To continue circumnavigating Two Ocean, keep left at the junction. The sign indicates it is 3.1 miles to return to the parking lot. The trail beyond the junction gently descends through lodgepole forest to two bridged crossings of small streams that flow into Two Ocean Lake. After a short uphill climb, it levels and views of the lake open up.

The trail follows a gentle undulating course along Two Ocean's south shore, skirting a large meadow before reaching another bridged stream crossing. Beyond, it climbs through lodgepole and fir forest above the lake, traversing a flower-filled meadow before re-entering the woods.

Several more clearings are passed before the trail crosses a small plank bridge spanning a bog and reaches a signed intersection with the Emma Matilda Lake Trail to your right.

Stay left to return to the parking lot a short distance farther.

Two Ocean Lake, seen from Grand View Point. Bear activity in recent years has curtailed trail visitors.

41 Oxbow Bend Overlook/Lookout Rock

Distance: 3.6 miles RT via cut-off trail. Add .2 mile if you opt not to take the cut-off
Elevation change: Approx. 340 ft.
Maximum elevation: 6,920 ft.
Maps: Moose, Two Ocean. Book map pg. 115
Season: Mid-May though October

Tremendous views of the Oxbow, Mt. Moran, Jackson and Emma Matilda Lakes—plus the opportunity to see waterfowl and moose—make this a favored loop hike in the northern reaches of Grand Teton National Park. It is typically snow-free early in the season, when sunny yellow balsamroot is at its peak.

Driving Directions

Travel north out of Jackson approximately 30 miles on U.S. Hwy. 89/191 to signed Moran Junction. Turn left, pass through the Buffalo Entrance Station and drive four miles north to the signed turn-off for Jackson Lake Lodge. Turn in, drive .2 mile, and turn left toward the horse corrals. The lodge asks that you park in the parking area to the right. A path begins at the east end of the lot, skirting the horse corrals to the right before passing under the highway bridge and emerging at the official trailhead. (Note: Just north of the highway bridge is a small parking area off the right (E) side of the highway with room for about three cars. You may want to check this before turning into the lodge access road.)

Trail Description

From the trailhead, the path dips to a willow-filled basin, crosses Christian Creek and climbs a small knoll to a signed trail junction at .4 mile. Bear right and ascend at a moderate grade to an overlook marked by a sign that reads, "Do Not Disturb: Trumpeter Swans nesting." These magnificent white swans, among the largest waterfowl in the United States, are struggling to survive. Please do not leave the trail for a closer look. Bring a pair of binoculars or spotting scope to observe the swans, coots, teals, yellow-headed blackbirds and splashy blue-billed ruddy ducks that inhabit the pond.

The trail bears right and ascends a knoll dressed in balsamroot early summer to reach a signed junction at the one-mile mark. At this junction, it is possible to hike in either direction to complete the Oxbow Bend/Lookout Rock Loop. This description takes the left fork. The well-used path descends a short hill then climbs back up, passing close to a massive Douglas fir. Look carefully for leopard lilies in this area, a wonderful wildflower that is easy to miss. After reaching the top of the second small rise, the trail bends left (N) and descends slightly before leveling. To your left (W), panoramic views of the Tetons unfold, particularly appealing early season when winter snow still blankets the peaks. Keep left when you reach an unsigned split in the trail. Shortly, you'll reach a signed junction at 1.2 miles. Here, the trail to the left continues around Christian Pond, the west end of Emma

Oxbow Bend, above and Mount Moran, right, viewed along the Oxbow Bend/Lookout Rock Trail.

Matilda Lake and/or on to Grand View Point. Continue straight toward Lookout Rock. The level trail travels through open forest before descending into a short stretch of dense lodgepole forest that soon opens to views of Emma Matilda Lake. The path parallels the lakeshore to reach a wooden bridge spanning a wet area and a signed split in the trail. Go left to reach Lookout Rock, a total of 1.5 miles

beyond your vehicle. To complete the loop, backtrack from Lookout Rock to the junction and bear left.

The path skirts a willowed expanse to your right. It then turns left and gently climbs through open forest before curving right and leveling out. Here, the top of the Grand and Mount Moran poke above a line of lodgepole ahead to your right. The path traverses open sagebrush to reach vistas of Oxbow Bend below you and to your left (E), framed by Mt. Leidy on the horizon.

Descend to a signed junction at 2.1 miles and continue walking straight to complete the loop.

The trail shortly curves more directly northwest and climbs a small rise that offers superlative views of the Tetons and Jackson Lake Dam. It stays on this undulating ridge before descending to the junction that closes the loop. Bear left here to retrace the final mile to your vehicle.

42 Schwabacher's Landing

Distance: Varies. Not more than 4.5 miles RT
Elevation change: Negligible
Maximum elevation: Check
Maps: None needed
Season: April though October

Schwabacher's Landing is a popular destination for anglers. The access road leads to the banks of the Snake River, where wader-clad piscators ply its waters from April 1 to October 31. Complete rules and regulations are given to anglers when they buy a required Wyoming license.

Both amateur and professional photographers stalk not the wily trout, but the perfect shot. Many of the famed pictures of the Tetons reflected in a still body of water are shot at dawn or dusk along the quiet side channels of the river. That same peaceful environment is home to moose, elk, otter, eagles and waterfowl—most commonly seen by visitors to the riverbanks.

The Snake River begins as a small stream near the southern boundary of Yellowstone National Park. As tributaries flow into it, it swells into a major river that curves west then south through Jackson, exiting the valley through the Snake River Canyon on its way to Idaho. The Snake is the tenth largest river in the United States, carrying two-and-a-half times the volume of the Colorado River on its 1,056-mile course to the Columbia River in Washington.

Schwabacher's Landing provides an intimate look at a small portion of this mighty river, and should not be missed.

Driving Directions

The landing is easily accessed by driving north out of Jackson on U.S. Hwy. 89/191. Pass Moose Junction at 12 miles, continuing north another four miles to signed Schwabacher's Landing road on your left (W). Turn in. The steep gravel road divides in .6 mile. The left fork leads to a parking area. The right travels north another .4 mile to the lower landing. Either one is a fine jumping-off point.

Trail Description

With the river on one side and the road on the other, it is difficult to get lost. Wander at will, but exercise caution if you decide to step into the river: The current is often stronger than it appears. Those interested in viewing a series of beaver dams and lodges, both abandoned and active, should walk on the well-defined angler's trail heading upstream (N) from the lower parking area. While evidence of their handiwork is abundant along the river, the nocturnal beaver is not often

Quiet channels of the Snake River near Schwabacher's Landing are a favorite haunt for photographers.

seen out and about. Beaver live in families of two adults, yearlings and newborn kits. Several families band together to form a colony, that lives in bank dens or lodges. Dams are constructed to protect the lodges from predators, by forming a moat around the lodge, and to create a swimming area deep enough for lodge access under winter ice. As ponds are formed behind the dams, the surrounding soil becomes saturated, killing plants not adapted to moist soils. The type of plants and trees that thrive in waterlogged soil are coincidentally beavers' staple food: Alder, willows, aspen and cottonwoods. Thus, dams create both protection and a food source.

The large dams and lodges are testament to this tenacious rodent's survival. When top hats made from beaver pelts became the fashion rage in the 1800s, the animal was over-trapped to the verge of extinction. Fashion taste changed and beaver rebounded.

Shutterbugs will find placid side channels and pools by walking upstream from the dams and downstream from the upper parking lot. These still bodies of water frame some of the most famous shots taken of the Tetons, and offer particularly beautiful reflections of the peaks at dawn. Expect Canon and Nikon-toting company: This is one of those magic places.

In the fall, elk bugle poignantly as they crash through the cottonwoods seeking hormonal relief. Moose also reside in the willows and cottonwoods. Both can be quite testy during rut. Make noise and give them a wide berth if you are visiting the Snake from late summer on to avoid an unpleasant encounter. The river bottom is closed to winter use to protect sensitive habitat.

Schwabacher's Landing was once a favorite haunt of its namesake, Albert Schwabacher. Schwabacher was a San Francisco-based financier who loved to flyfish. He owned numerous properties in the valley to indulge his passion, including Lost Creek Ranch across the highway.

43 Blacktail Butte Traverse

Distance: 3.8 miles
Elevation change: Approx. 900 ft.
Maximum elevation: 7,440 ft.
Maps: Moose. Book page pg.
Season: Late May though October

Blacktail Butte rises a thousand feet above the valley floor, providing sweeping views of the Teton Range. The vantage gained from the summit prompted the US Forest Service to construct a fire lookout on its apex in the 1930s. The National Park Service dismantled the lookout in 1943 when the butte was transferred from Teton National Forest into the newly created Jackson Hole National Monument. The views, of course, remain.

Sinkholes in limestone rock near Blacktail's north summit hold water throughout the summer, attracting elk, moose and other animals. Shady, moist ravines en route and sunny open slopes on the butte's crest allow one to enjoy the whole spectrum of wildflowers. This pleasant hike is free of snow comparatively early, offering a nice first outing when higher destinations remain inaccessible.

Geologists are uncertain how Blacktail and East and West Gros Ventre Buttes were formed. One theory is that these isolated, steep hills were created by a separate uplift independent of the Teton fault. Fault lines have been identified at the base of Blacktail's east and west slopes.

Driving Directions

Drive five miles north out of Jackson on U.S. Hwy. 89/187 to Gros Ventre Junction. Turn right (E) at the junction toward Kelly and drive 4.9 miles to an unmarked dirt and gravel artery off the left side of the road. This is the southern end of Mormon Row. Turn in and drive .4 mile to a metal gate off the left side of the road. Park off road here.

The traverse begins just beyond the gate and ends at the parking area for Blacktail Butte. If you wish to shuttle a car in advance, that parking area is located .9 mile north of Moose Junction off the east side U.S. Hwy 89/187. Drop a vehicle here first, then backtrack 7.9 miles to Gros Ventre Junction and the east end of the traverse.

For those who are unable to shuttle a car, it is recommended that you walk up the trail starting at the west end, and return by the same route.

Trail Description

Walk up the closed road beyond the gate. The trail is a wide swath that travels west through sagebrush toward the Tetons, passing numerous north-south trails formed by bison that graze the valley floor. The track narrows to trail width and heads toward a pretty aspen grove as it climbs a small rise, soon intersecting a path to the right that ascends the butte. This is the trail you want. It steeply climbs the butte's east slope, dotted with blooming lupine and balsamroot early to midsummer. As you gain elevation, expansive views of the old

Top: Blacktail Butte, once the site of a fire lookout tower, offers panoramic Teton vistas.

hayfields and resident bison herd below open up. On a hike one August, over 100 animals were grazing the flat expanse.

Rabbitbrush, brittlebrush and sage cling to the butte's steep slopes. The path follows a line of aspen and Douglas fir as it ascends to an obvious north-south ridge reached at one mile. Here the path turns right and descends slightly before resuming its upward course toward a group of limber pine.

The trail becomes indistinct near the trees. Keep right, walking around several large, downed pines. Beyond, you'll regain a good tread. The path bears east and enters a brief but welcome stretch of shady fir forest before popping into the open and turning north up the ridge.

Keep right when you intersect a game trial, soon reaching a flat meadow covered with harebell and sticky geranium. The path descends slightly to a small pond on your left, then enters Douglas fir and lodgepole pine forest. It begins bearing gradually but noticeably left in a semi-circle as it gently ascends open slopes. Here, the path is lined with giant hyssop, a member of the mint family. A square stem, opposing leaves and spicy aroma easily distinguish mint.

The best views of the Teton Range are off a low rock ledge that outlines the left side of the crest. Jackson Hole—from the meandering Snake River to the top of the Grand—is spread before you. Prominent peaks of the southern Tetons, including Prospector and Buck Mountain, stand out against the western horizon. Sleeping Indian and Jackson Peak dominate the eastern skyline.

To continue the traverse, drop left off the west side of the knoll. The path descends a wooded drainage at a moderately steep grade, eventually meeting and paralleling a small stream as it drops to open tremendous views of the Tetons.

As you near the valley floor, you'll pass the base of talus slopes and an imposing rock wall. This is part of a vertical

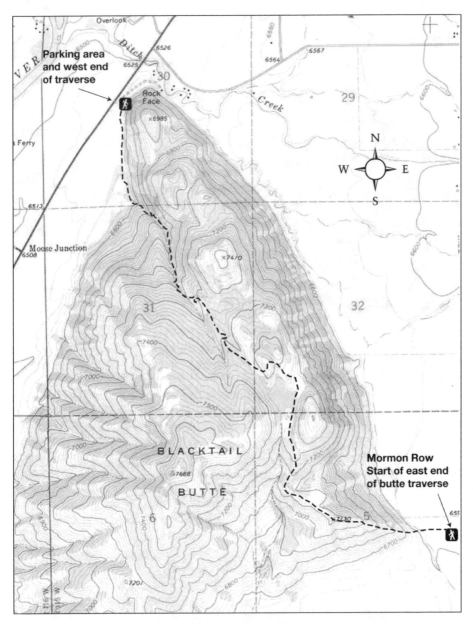

Blacktail Butte Traverse

limestone formation on the northwest end of the butte. Climbers test their skill on short but challenging routes up the wall. A number of years ago, a staircase was built to provide easy access for top-roping.

Now descending at an easier grade, the trail passes through pleasant aspen and fir forest, hops the stream and bears right, skirting the base of the butte as it travels north to the Blacktail Butte parking area.

44 Teton Crest Trail

Distance:

	South to North	North to South
Ski Lake TH	0.0	39.4
Moose Creek Divide Via Phillips Pass	8.0	31.4
Middle Fork Cut-off	8.6	30.8
Granite Canyon Trail Junction.	10.1	29.3
Marion Lake	10.7	28.7
Fox Creek Pass	13.0	26.4
Basin Lakes	18.7	20.7
Hurricane Pass	21.3	18.1
Forks of Cascade Canyon	26.4	13.0
Lake Solitude	29.1	10.3
Paintbrush Divide	31.5	7.9
Holly Lake	33.2	6.2
String Lake Picnic Area	39.4	0.0

Approx. Elevation Change: South to North
Ski Lake TH to Moose Creek Divide: +2780/ -1,390 ft.
Moose Creek Divide to Fox Creek Pass: +1,410/ -910 ft.
Fox Creek Pass to Basin Lakes: +1,080/ - 1,180 ft.
Basin Lakes to Hurricane Pass: +1,260/ -430 ft.
Hurricane Pass to Forks of Cascade: - 2,550 ft.
Forks of Cascade Canyon to Paintbrush Divide: + 2,880 ft.
Paintbrush Divide to String Lake parking area: +80 / -3,870 ft.

Maximum elevation: Paintbrush Divide, 10,720 ft.

Maps: South to North
Teton Pass
Rendezvous Peak
Mount Bannon
Grand Teton
Mount Moran
Jenny Lake

Season: Mid-July through mid-September

Teton Crest Trail runs along the spine of the range, beginning at Moose Creek Divide at the park's southern boundary and heading north to Hurricane Pass at the head of the South Fork of Cascade Canyon. By walking up either Coal Creek Canyon or Phillips Pass to reach Moose Creek Divide, hiking the heart of the range along its crest to Paintbrush Divide and descending the canyon of the same name, you complete one of the most spectacular mountain walks in the United States. The trail weaves in and out of Grand Teton National Park and the Jedediah Smith

Top to Bottom: Sunset Lake in Alaska Basin; Upper Paintbrush Canyon; dropping into Marian Lake; Upper South Fork of Cascade Canyon.

Wilderness Area of Caribou-Targhee National Forest as it crosses from the east to the west side of the range. It skirts numerous small alpine lakes, traverses the dramatic Death Canyon Shelf and crosses five passes or divides along its course. Wildflowers are plentiful from mid-July to mid-August and chances of spying moose, mountain sheep and possibly black bears are good.

The time the trip takes depends on personal preference. Fit and speedy souls blitz it in as little as two long days. Those with lots of time, who enjoy dallying in beautiful camping spots or striking out on side trips, might easily spend a week for more on the trail. In general, four nights and five days will allow a comfortable pace of eight miles a day (remember, you're at high altitude and carrying weight on your back).

As many segments of this trail are described elsewhere in this book, the description below is given for general directions only. Please consult individual write-ups for more detail. The elevation changes register the numerous drops and gains along the way for each segment to give you a feel for the route.

You may begin the trail by hiking up Coal Creek Canyon and over Mesquite Pass to reach Moose Creek Divide, or hiking from the Ski Lake Trailhead on the east side of Teton Pass to Phillips Pass and the Divide. The latter is slightly shorter, and since you are starting at a higher elevation on the Pass, it saves you about 500 feet of initial ascent.

From 9,085-ft. Moose Creek Divide, Teton Crest Trail drops to the junction with the Middle Fork Cut-off Trail to your right, 8.6 miles from the start of the trail's southern end. This area is an appealing place to camp the first evening. The subalpine meadows offer a nice view, water from intermittent streams,

126

lots of wildflowers and a good chance of spotting moose and deer.

Beyond the Middle Fork Cutoff, the trail follows a 2.7-mile up-and-down course to pretty Marion Lake, skirts its east side, and then climbs 2.3 miles up a steep slope toward a high bench and 9,600-ft. Fox Creek Pass. From there it heads north, dropping onto Death Canyon Shelf. This 3.5-mile limestone bench is a classic example of Karst topography. Slightly acidic rainwater has eaten through cracks and crevices of the soft dolomite and limestone rock, forming underground passages and caverns. It is one of the prettiest places in the Tetons and an excellent place to camp. Above it to the west tower four peaks over 10,600 feet: Fossil Mountain, Mount Bannon, Mount Jedediah Smith and Mount Meek. To the east, the shelf cliffs down to the upper reaches of Death Canyon. A spot near the bench's northern end is a suggested destination for the second evening.

From the northern end of Death Canyon Shelf, the Teton Crest Trail ascends 9,726-ft. Mount Meek Pass and leaves Grand Teton National Park, descending to Basin Lakes in the Jedediah Smith Wilderness Area of Caribou-Targhee National Forest, 18.7 miles from the start of the trail. Passing this exquisite cluster of eight lakes, the trail then steeply climbs 2.6 miles north to 10,382-ft. Hurricane Pass.

Dropping east off the pass, the path re-enters Grand Teton National Park and passes Schoolroom Glacier as it descends the South Fork of Cascade Canyon. The South Fork features an impressive forest of whitebark pine, some estimated to be over 400 years old. Here one enjoys wonderful views of the south faces of the Middle and Grand Tetons. The lower reach of the South Fork is a good area to camp the third evening.

Continuing its descent, the Crest Trail reaches the Forks of Cascade Canyon 26.4 miles beyond the Ski Lake trailhead. Bear left at the Forks (N) toward Lake Solitude. A steady climb takes you past the lake and over 10,720-ft. Paintbrush Divide. This 5.1-mile segment gains 2,880 feet and brings you to the highest elevation of the trip. The Divide can harbor snow late into the season. It is advised that you check with Jenny Lake Ranger Station for a trail condition report and safety recommendations before departing on this trip.

From the top of the Divide, the trail drops very steeply into upper Paintbrush Canyon. Camp for the night in the marked upper camping zone. Other sites may be found near Holly Lake, 1.7 miles below the Divide and 33.2 miles from the start of the trail.

From upper Paintbrush it is an easy cruise down the canyon to String Lake parking area. The downhill hike crosses three glacial benches that offer good views of Jackson, Leigh and String Lakes below you.

The Teton Crest Trail can, of course, be walked in either direction. The main advantage of walking south to north is a more gradual start. As you head north, the hiking becomes more rugged and the scenery intensifies. Conversely, traveling north to south lets one deal with the most strenuous sections early in the trip.

Granite, Death and Cascade Canyons to the east and Teton Canyon to the west provide conveniently spaced exit routes along the course of the hike. These offer several options for shorter variations of this classic trip. Time permitting, the entire trail is recommended.

A free permit, available at the Moose Visitor Center, is required to camp overnight in the backcountry in Grand Teton National Park.

45 Valley Trail

Distance:

	South to North	North to South
Teton Village	0.0	15.8
Granite Canyon Trail Junction	2.5	13.3
Open Canyon Trail Junction	4.4	11.4
Death Canyon Trail Junction	5.9	9.9
Phelps Lake Overlook	6.6	9.2
Death Canyon Traihead (White Grass)	7.5	8.3
Beaver Creek Junction	10.9	4.9
Taggart Trail Junction (North Loop)	11.6	4.2
Bradley Lake Junction	12.8	3.0
Amphitheater Lake Junction	14.1	1.7
Lupine Meadows Parking Area	15.8	0.0

Elevation Change:
Numerous small but steep climbs and drops over lateral moraines that impound the Lakes. Don't let the name "Valley Trail" deceive: This trail is not flat. The trail generally gains elevation south to north. The trailhead at Teton Village is 6,440 feet; the elevation at Lupine Meadows Trailhead is 6,760 feet.

Maximum elevation: 7,400 feet at Amphitheater Lake Junction

Maps: South to North
Teton Pass
Rendezvous Peak
Mount Bannon
Grand Teton
Mount Moran
Jenny Lake

Season: Late May through October

In the early to mid-1900s Jackson Hole visitors stayed at a string of lodges and dude ranches nestled at the foot of the Tetons. The Amoretti Inn and Teton Lodge near Moran and the JY, Bar BC, Double Diamond, White Grass and STS dude ranches were in their heyday. Guests often rode horses between the facilities, both to socialize and to enjoy the breathtaking scenery. When Grand Teton National Park was created in 1929, the existing horse trails were among the first trails in the park.

Civilian Conservation Corp crews improved the horse routes in the 1930s and built connecting links. The portion between Phelps Lake north to Taggart and Bradley Lakes was named the Lakes Trail. Eventually the path extended from Teton Village north to Trapper Lake—a distance of over 24 miles. It traversed the eastern toe of the Tetons, traveling through small meadows, groves of aspen and coniferous forest as it climbed and dropped over the morainal ridges containing Phelps, Taggart and Bradley and Jenny Lakes.

Top: Hikers head toward Bradley Lake. Bottom: Approaching Death Canyon on the Valley Trail.

This is today's Valley Trail. Because the trail follows a portion of the Lupine Meadows Road to connect with the path network around Jenny Lake, most people walk the portion between the Village and Lupine Meadows, or the northern end of the Valley Trail to Trapper Lake. This avoids hiking on dusty road.

The longer, southern end is described in this general write-up. Most of the trail is covered in greater detail in individual trail descriptions to Open and Death Canyons, Bradley and Taggart Lakes and the lower portion of trail to Amphitheater Lake. Intersecting the trail at Granite, Death Canyon or Taggart Lake trailheads provides shorter options of this hike.

Driving Directions

Drive south out of Jackson on U.S. Hwy. 89/191, turning right onto Wyoming Hwy. 22 at the traffic light by Albertsons. Head west five miles to a bridge over the Snake River. Just over the bridge turn right onto Wyoming Hwy. 390 and drive seven

Talus slopes below Phelps Overlook.

miles to Jackson Hole Mountain Resort in Teton Village. The turn-off to the Village is well marked. Park in the large lot and head toward the Teewinot chairlift on Après Vous Mountain at the resort's north end. Follow the directional signs to the trailhead.

Trail Description

After gently climbing through conifer forest the trail enters open slopes dotted with aspen groves. Early summer, balsamroot and lupine grow in profusion along this section of trail, and elk are often seen.

The trail re-enters coniferous forest and travels north to its intersection with the Granite Canyon Trail at 2.4 miles. The next mile or so is an almost level course through pleasant forest and small clearings. You'll climb several hundred feet to the first of two intersections to Open Canyon Trail before dropping to Phelps Lake and reaching a signed intersection with the trail heading west up Death Canyon at 5.9

miles. En route you'll cross a bridge over Death Canyon Creek and travel through lush understory. Moose and occasionally black bear are seen in this area.

Beyond Phelps Lake, the trail climbs via switchbacks to Phelps Lake Overlook at 7,200 feet. It then travels at an easy to slightly downhill grade to Death Canyon Trailhead near White Grass Ranger Station, approaching the half-way mark of this hike at 7.5 miles.

The trail continues traveling north at an easy grade through sunny, open meadows and predominantly aspen and lodgepole forest to an intersection with the Beaver Creek Trail near Taggart Lake. Beyond a bridged crossing of the creek, the path hugs the edge of a forest that escaped the Beaver Creek Fire, the results of which are before you.

The path eventually crosses the burn and climbs the moraine above Taggart Lake before dropping off the ridge to a bridged crossing of that lake's outlet and a trail intersection at 11.6 miles. The path to the right leads to Taggart Lake Trailhead. Bear left and follow Taggart's east shore toward Bradley Lake to continue on the Valley Trail.

The trail climbs the moraine separating the two lakes and then descends to another intersection above Bradley's north shore. Bear left toward Amphitheater Lake. This is one of the prettiest sections of the Valley Trail. The path parallels Bradley's east shore to a footbridge over its narrow neck. Stunning views of Mt. Wister, Nez Perce and the South Teton are enjoyed from the bridge.

The path ascends Bradley's moraine then traverses wooded terrain to an intersection with the Amphitheater Lake Trail at 14.1 miles, the high point of the hike at 7,400 feet. Bear right at this intersection. The trail steadily descends over 700 feet to Lupine Meadows Trailhead.

Northern Jackson Hole

Introduction

John D. Rockefeller Memorial Parkway—the narrow strip of land between Grand Teton and Yellowstone National Parks—Teton Wilderness, Buffalo Valley and adjacent Washakie Wilderness define the northern reaches of Jackson Hole and beyond. This vast area contains some of the most stunning backcountry in the entire region. The beauty and comparative remoteness of these hikes place them near the top of the list for anyone seeking wildness and solitude.

Flagg Canyon and Huckleberry Hot Spring hikes are within the scenic parkway. The parkway is administered by Grand Teton National Park. Huckleberry Lookout, Gravel Ridge, Enos Lake, South Fork Falls, Holmes Cave, Breccia Peak and Brooks Lake Mountain fall within vast Teton Wilderness, administered by the Buffalo Ranger District of Bridger-Teton National Forest. Toppings Lakes and Rosie's Ridge outings also fall under the Buffalo Ranger District purview.

Wind River Lake, Jade Lake, Upper Brooks and Kisinger Lake Loop trails lie within the DuNoir Special Management Area administered by Shoshone National Forest.

Teton Wilderness

Close to 900 square miles in size, Teton Wilderness abuts Washakie Wilderness to the east and Yellowstone National Park to the north. Its southern end borders the Gros Ventre Wilderness. Grand Teton National Park rims its western extent. Three times bigger than the park itself, this immense expanse of meadows, forests, peaks and plateaus makes up the second largest wilderness area in the lower 48 states, yet its backcountry use is only a third of its famous neighbor. If you are seeking a wilderness experience, point your hiking boots toward this region.

The volcanic mountains and plateaus of the southern Absaroka Range characterize the eastern end of the wilderness. The highest point in Teton Wilderness is 12,165-ft. Younts Peak (the highest peak in the Absaroka Range overall is 13,153-ft. Francis Peak in the Washakie Wilderness). Breccia rock, a mixture of pebbles and stones loosely held together by lava, forms beautiful striated cliff bands that abruptly rise above flowered fields. When the snow melts in the spring, intermittent waterfalls spill over the lips of the high volcanic plateaus in this pristine wilderness.

In contrast, more subtle valleys, meadows and deep box canyons define the western half of Teton Wilderness—prime roaming ground for grizzly bears that inhabit the region. The terrain is cut by numerous streams and covered with thick forests that yield few recognizable landmarks. Unlike the eastern half, the trails receive scant use and can be easily confused with game trails. Old blazes cut into the trees by army troops almost

100 ago are helpful in keeping yourself oriented, particularly across large meadows where trails have already been reclaimed by lack of consistent use. Don't be surprised if the clearly marked trail on your USGS map cannot be found on the ground.

Roughly 500 miles of trails bisect Teton Wilderness, most following streams. Horsepacking outfitters are the main users, accounting for over three-fourths of the backcountry traffic. Horses often attract flies, adding to the summer hordes of mosquitoes. Their impact is minimized if you wear long-sleeve, lightweight shirts and long pants instead of shorts.

One of the prettiest seasons in Teton Wilderness is early fall, but it is best avoided by hikers. From mid-September on, hunting season in one of the most famous big game areas in the country is underway. This is when the trails receive their heaviest use by outfitters and are busiest. A far bigger concern than encountering other parties, however, is the danger of your movement being mistaken for that of an animal. If you do chose to venture into the wilderness during hunting season, be sure to wear bright-colored clothing and make a fair amount of noise.

July is a wonderful month in the wilderness. Statistically it is the driest and the mountain wildflowers are at their best. The snow has left most of the trails but a pretty frosting remains on the higher peaks. Even though visitation in Jackson Hole is at its apex, you'll rarely see another party on the trail.

Teton Wilderness Regulations

The following acts are prohibited in Teton Wilderness:

- Possessing or using a motor vehicle, motorboat, motorized equipment, hang glider or bicycle.

- Landing an aircraft or dropping or picking up any material, supplies or person by means of aircraft, including a helicopter, except in cases of life-threatening injuries.

- Traveling in groups exceeding 20 people

- Grazing stock with a half-mile of Enos, Bridger, Crater, Rainbow, Bertha, Golden, Mackinaw and Ferry Lakes, or other areas where posted.

- A combined number of pack and saddle stock greater than 35 animals.

- Camping within 200 feet of a designated trail.

- Occupying one campsite or area for more than 14 consecutive days without a permit. Each new campsite or area of occupancy must be at least five miles from any previous campsite or occupied area.

- Failing to pack out unburnable refuse and depositing it in designated garbage disposal sites.

- ► Cutting or limbing of live trees.

- ► Using soap, detergent or bleach in springs, lakes or streams or dumping waste water within 50 feet of such waters.

- ► Tethering pack and saddle stock, digging toilet pits within 100 feet of springs, lakes or streams and not covering toilet pits to ground level before breaking camp.

- ► Using signs, tape or flagging or other artificial markers.

- ► Taking unusable animals (cripples or unbroken) into the wilderness.

- ► Leaving a fire unattended without completely extinguishing it.

- ► Operating or using any audio devices such as portable radios, musical instruments or other noise-producing devices in such a manner and at such times to disturb other persons.

- ► Discharging firearms in the vicinity of camps and over lakes or other bodies or water.

- ► Placing or maintaining a cache or leaving gear in the Wilderness.

For further information on the trails contained in this section, other routes and rules and regulations of the wilderness contact:

Bridger-Teton National Forest
Buffalo Ranger District
Box 278
Moran, Wyoming 83013
307-543-2386
www.fs.fed.us/r4/btnf/offices/buffalo

Shoshone National Forest & the DuNoir Special Management Area

In 1891, Congress authorized the President to set aside forest reserves; Yellowstone Timberland Reserve, now the heart of Shoshone National Forest, was the first to be established.

The General Land Office of the Dept. of the Interior administered the reserves until 1905, when President Teddy Roosevelt transferred the land to the newly created U.S. Forest Service. The new agency faced the massive task of inventorying thousands of acres that had been hastily designated forest reserves by Presidential Proclamation. It took two years to organize the reserves into a national forest system Most of Yellowstone Timberland Reserve was included in Shoshone National Forest in 1907, named for the Shoshone tribe that inhabited the area. The forest is honored as the first of what would grow to be over 150 national forests today.

Covering more than 3,800 square miles, Shoshone National Forest is the seventh largest forest in the contiguous US, and the ninth largest overall. Its 2.4 million acres extend from the eastern border of Yellowstone National Park north to Montana and south to Lander, Wyoming, encompassing portions of the Beartooth, Absaroka and Wind River Ranges. The varied terrain includes dense forest, meadows, sagebrush flats, spectacular river canyons and jagged mountains draped in snow most of the year. Gannett Peak—the highest point in Wyoming at 13,804 feet—lies within the forest.

Over half of Shoshone's acreage is designated wilderness. The trails included in this publication fall within the 28,967-acre DuNoir Special Management Area, an integral part of the large Washakie-Teton Wilderness Complex. The DuNoir provides critical habitat for elk, antelope, moose, bighorn sheep, wolverine, lynx and bears. Ten known male grizzlies and eight known females grizzlies reside in the management area. The DuNoir is also used by the Washakie wolf pack and is believed to serve as a corridor for the Big Piney and Pinedale packs.

The Upper Wind River empties into the DuNoir Valley, a scenic vale blanketed by old growth spruce, Douglas fir and whitebark pine. Banded cliffs of volcanic rock ring the valley. Kisinger Lakes lie at its heart beneath the magnificent spires of Pinnacle Buttes.

The Wind River District of Shoshone National Forest administers the DuNoir Special Management Area. It has jurisdiction over the following trails included in this publication:

► Wind River Lake to Brooks Lake

► Jade Lakes

► Upper Brooks and Rainbow Lakes

► Bonneville Pass and Kisinger Lakes Loop

Off-road vehicular traffic is prohibited and motorized trail vehicles are prohibited on all but the Wind River Lake to Brooks Lake outing. All other general USFS use regulations apply. The Wind River Ranger District is headquartered in Dubois. For further information, write or call:

Wind River Ranger District
1403 W. Ramshorn
P.O. Box 186
Dubois, Wyoming 82513
307-455-2466
www.fs.fed.us/r2/shoshone/contact/districts

46 Flagg Canyon

Distance: 5 miles RT
Elevation change: Approx. 120 ft.
Maximum elevation: Approx. 6,800 ft.
Maps: Flagg Canyon. Book map pg. 139
Season: Late May/early June through October
Use restrictions:

> Mountain bikes and pets prohibited. A Wyoming State Fishing license is required to fish; all stated license regulations must be followed. Backcountry camping prohibited within 100 feet of flowing streams, rivers and other bodies of water and 250 yards from roads and developed areas. A permit is not required for backcountry camping in the Rockefeller Parkway.

Just south of Yellowstone National Park, the Snake River flows through Flagg Canyon. The relatively little-known but spectacular chasm was formed when rhyolite, a form of volcanic rock, flowed south from a large eruption in Yellowstone 600,000 years ago. Over the slow course of geologic time, the Snake carved a canyon through the lava flow. Scenic Flagg Canyon Trail follows the lip of the chasm, threading through mostly flat meadows and forested terrain on the east side of the Snake. Quiet hikers often spy moose, elk, squirrels, waterfowl and otters. The trail draws only light to moderate use, even in the peak summer months.

Driving Directions

From the Town of Jackson, drive north approximately 30 miles on U.S. Hwy. 89/191 to Moran Junction. Turn left onto U.S. Hwy 89/287. After passing through the park entrance station at .2 mile, drive north 24.5 additional miles to the turn-off to Grassy Lake Reclamation Road and Flagg Ranch. Set your odometer here, but don't turn in: stay on the main highway. It is 1.6 miles farther to the South Gate Boat Launch and Picnic Area access road on the right side of the highway. The sign for the turn-off is hidden in the trees so it's easy to miss. If you drive by it, continue another .5 mile to the pullout area by the South Entrance to Yellowstone National Park and turn around.

Trail Description

The well-defined path parallels the Snake River. Shade from lodgepole pine supports a luxurious understory of Utah honeysuckle, Oregon grape, phlox, lupine, grouse whortleberry and wild strawberry on the rim The foliage draws a host of birds that find the habitat to their liking.

The trail soon gently bears west closer to the road, but still parallels the canyon rim. Here, the Snake River is glimpsed only by taking one of numerous short side trails closer to the rim. As you continue to walk south, you'll see it more clearly.

A 1.3 miles, you'll reach a signed junction. The trail to the right leads to Polecat Loop Trail and eventually the Flagg Ranch parking area. Continue straight. The trail soon bends right, slightly away from the west bank of this placid section of the Snake, and enters a level stretch of open lodgepole forest and grassy meadowland. Look for elk and moose on the forest bench below.

Top and left: The Snake River flows through scenic Flagg Canyon, located just south of Yellowstone National Park.

Ahead, on the opposite side of the river, the burnt slopes of Huckleberry Mountain are seen. The charred trees mark the perimeter of the Huck Fire, a huge wildland fire that started on August 20, 1988, when winds exceeding 60 mph blew a tree across a powerline. The wind-fanned fire sped through Teton Wilderness and into Yellowstone National Park. It easily jumped the highway and threatened nearby Flagg Ranch. Interagency fire crews set backfires in advance of the facility to successfully protect it, but the extremely dry conditions and high winds made it impossible to extinguish the conflagration. By the time winter snows finally suppressed the fire, its perimeter enclosed a mosaic of 90,000 acres of burned and unburned trees. Burn scars from old tree rings reveal that fires of this intensity and magnitude only occur every 200-400 years.

At 1.8 miles, you'll notice a tributary stream on the opposite side of the river tumbling down the canyon wall in a series of cascades and small waterfalls.

The path descends a knoll and skirts a small willow-fringed pond to your right before reaching a bridge over the park road a 2.5 miles. Across the roadway, a parking lot and picnic area mark a popular river access point. Retrace your steps to return to your vehicle.

47 Huckleberry Hot Springs

Distance: .7 mile to first spring
Elevation change: Negligible
Maximum elevation: Approx. 6,850 ft.
Maps: Book map, opposite page
Season: Late May/early June through October
Use restrictions: Mountain bikes and pets prohibited.

In the mid-1970s, residents and visitors to Jackson Hole could swim in three commercial pools filled with water from nearby hot springs: Astoria, Granite and Huckleberry. Astoria Hot Springs was sold to a developer in the 1990s and has been bulldozed out of existence. The developed pool and campground at Huckleberry Hot Springs were removed in 1980 when administration of the parkway between Grand Teton and Yellowstone was transferred from the U.S. Forest Service to the National Park Service. Only the pool at Granite Hot Springs, constructed by the CCC boys in the 1930s, remains.

Skiers and hikers still actively use Huckleberry Hot Springs. The springs are found along a branch of Polecat Creek north of Flagg Ranch. The naturally heated mineral water attains temperatures of 130 degrees, cooling as it is exposed to air and flows into colder Polecat Creek.

Users have constructed a number of pools by building small rock dams. These 100 to 105 degree caches provide places to soak and enjoy the rolling meadowland near Yellowstone National Park's south entrance.

While not prohibited, the National Park Service subtly discourages people from visiting the springs. A bridge over Polecat Creek accessing the springs was removed. The features do not appear on park maps or trail information handouts distributed at the park information station at Flagg Ranch. And a number of years ago, the park service widely-publicized the possible presence of a harmful bacterium, naegleria fowleria, in the mineral water. Naegleria fowleria, read the NPS warning, "causes a sudden fatal form of meningitis." True—but to date there has not been a recorded case of anyone contracting meningitis at Huckleberry Hot Springs.

Some people wear swimming attire in the pools. Some don't. Don't be surprised if you see folks au natural.

Note: The springs are in recognized grizzly bear habitat and are best avoided mid-to late April through mid-May, when the bears emerge from their winter sleep. They are ready to replenish their fat stores and are quite active.

Driving Directions

Drive north from the Town of Jackson approximately 30 miles on U.S. Hwy. 89/191 to Moran Junction. Turn left onto U.S. Hwy. 89/287 and drive 24.7 miles

Huckleberry Hot Springs/Flagg Canyon Trails

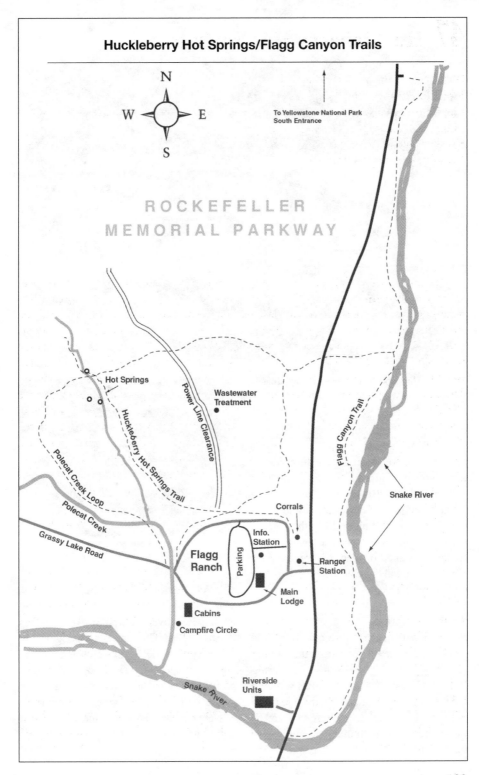

N
W E
S

To Yellowstone National Park
South Entrance

ROCKEFELLER
MEMORIAL PARKWAY

Hot Springs

Wastewater
Treatment

Power Line Clearance

Huckleberry Hot Springs Trail

Flagg Canyon Trail

Snake River

Polecat Creek Loop

Polecat Creek

Grassy Lake Road

Corrals

Info.
Station

Parking

Flagg
Ranch

Ranger
Station

Main
Lodge

Cabins

Campfire Circle

Snake River

Riverside
Units

The trail to Huckleberry Hot Springs follows a placid section of Polecat Creek. Right: Muskrat burrow along the creek's banks.

to Grassy Lake Road on the left side of the highway. Turn in and take the first right into Flagg Ranch. Park in the large lot near the information station and horse corral. The most direct trail to the springs begins on the trail near the corral. This route, not signed or identified on the park handout map, also avoids a wide crossing of Polecat Creek.

Trail Description

The path travels through lodgepole forest on a level course. At roughly .4 mile, it bears closer to meandering Polecat Creek, that here follows a placid course through meadow. Swans and other waterfowl are often seen along this stretch of the creek and both muskrat and beaver burrow along its bank.

As you near a large group of springs, you'll reach an improvised plank and stick bridge over the first of two branches of the creek. This creek crossing is not as deep or wide as the crossing on the signed Polecat Creek Loop Trail (see map). Beyond the crossing, you'll see steam rising from a series of hot springs of varying heat intensity and depth. Test the water temperature carefully before entering.

48 Huckleberry Mountain Lookout

Distance: 11.4 miles RT
Elevation gain: 2,880 ft.
Maximum elevation: 9,615 ft.
Maps: Huckleberry Mountain
Season: July through September
Use restrictions: Wilderness regulations apply.
   Closed to mountain biking and motorized vehicles.

As a former U.S. Army administration site, historic fire lookout station and location of hideout cabins for the notorious elk tusk hunters at the turn of the century, the area around Huckleberry Mountain is rich in local lore. Superb views of the northern end of the Teton Range and southern end of Yellowstone National Park are enjoyed from the summit.

Much of the terrain leading to the lookout was burned in the 1988 Huck Fire, started August 20 when high winds blew a tree onto a powerline near the trailhead. The conflagration consumed over 90,000 acres before firefighters were able to contain its perimeters.

The blaze was one of 249 fires in the greater Yellowstone area the hot, dry summer and fall of 1988. When the last blaze was finally controlled on November 18, the tally of money spent and acreage burned was as startling as the blackened landscape. Over 25,000 fire fighters had worked to minimize damage to property and humans, at a cost of over $120 million dollars. Close to 1.4 million acres had been partially or totally burned. Two hundred and ninety large animals had perished; no count was taken of birds or smaller mammals.

For many, charred forest is not a pleasant sight. Yet, there is now widespread recognition among ecologists that fire has always been a part of the natural cycle. Nutrients released into the soil fertilize the ground, and fallen snags reduce snowmelt and rain run-off. This richer, sun-exposed terrain supports a greater diversity of trees and plants and improves wildlife habitat for a large number of wildlife species. Twenty-five to 30 years after an area has been burned, a forest attains its greatest plant and wildlife diversity.

This is clearly seen on the hike to the lookout. Lodgepole seedlings are thriving. The ground is covered with thick grasses, magenta fireweed, dogbane and snowbrush; all thrive in areas that have been burned. Elk and deer browse the slopes. Bluebirds, kestrels, woodpeckers and small owls that nest in snag cavities have taken up residence. The trail to Huckleberry Lookout is not the same as it was—but it offers a different kind of beauty and an uncommon opportunity to view natural cycles at work.

Hikers are advised that the open path can be quite hot and dusty, and most of Sheffield Creek's small tributaries are dry by August. Bring plenty of water.

Driving Directions

Drive north on U.S. Hwy. 89/191 to Moran Junction. Turn left onto U.S. Hwy. 89/287 and drive approximately 24 miles to a dirt road signed Sheffield Creek off the right-hand side of the highway. The road is located just before the bridge crossing the Snake River near Flagg Ranch. If you are coming from Yellowstone, the turn-off is approximately three miles beyond the park's south entrance and is on the left side of the highway. The short dirt road ends at the trailhead. Although called Sheffield Creek Trail on the topo map, the trail sign and common usage identify the trail as Huckleberry Ridge.

Trail Description

The trail traverses a burnt area and passes a sign marking the Teton Wilderness boundary before beginning a steady climb up Huckleberry Ridge. It ascends over 1,600 feet at a moderately steep grade before dipping across a branch of Sheffield Creek at 2.0 miles. The downhill respite is short, as the trail soon resumes its upward course through charred forest and open slopes.

It descends briefly to hop a small creek, then resumes climbing to the crest of 9,200-ft. Huckleberry Ridge, reached at 4.8 miles. Over seven miles in length, this grassy, open ridge extends from Arizona Creek north toward Yellowstone, offering fine views of the Teton Range and the southern end of Yellowstone's high plateaus and canyons. Its high point is 9,615-ft. Huckleberry Mountain.

Once on the ridge the grade abates. The trail travels southeast about half a mile to a small trail sign that reads, "Fire Tower," and the lookout is finally visible above. Unfortunately, the trail beyond the sign is not in the best of shape. The path is littered with deadfall and has consequently become little used. Most hikers chose to leave the trail near the sign and walk up the steep slope toward the saddle between the lookout and Huckleberry's summit. En route, you'll intersect a distinct trail to the lookout. It steeply switchbacks up rocky terrain to the saddle, then bears right (S) to the historic structure.

Huckleberry Ridge was originally called "Soldier's Hill," as it was used as a lookout point by U.S. Army troops. (The army administered the park until the formation of the National Park Service in 1916.) In 1938, CCC crews built a 15x17 foot, two-story fire lookout on the ridge with locally obtained logs. Mules packed in cement, hardware, shingles, glass and other materials for the structure. The bottom floor was used for storage. The upper story was used to survey the surrounding landscape. Two hundred panes of glass wrap around all four sides of the upper level, accessed outside by a log staircase.

Huckleberry was one of six lookouts the Civilian Conservation Corp built on the northern half of the forest in the 1930s. The others were strategically located at Deer Creek, Munger Mountain, Baldy Mountain, Signal Mountain and Blacktail Butte. Changing fire policies, reporting done by public and private aircraft, and more efficient detection methods eventually made the lookout towers obsolete. Huckleberry was last used as an active lookout the summer of 1957.

When the Forest Service began to dismantle the lookouts, protection was sought for the two-story structure. In 1980, Bridger-Teton Recreation Staff Officer Bob Perkins wrote in a nomination form for historic site designation that the Huckleberry Lookout "is a significant example of rustic design employed by the United States Forest Service and built by the Civilian Conservation Corps during the first half of this century."

Top: Huckleberry Fire Lookout. The structure is on the National Register of Historic Places. Middle: the Tetons and Jackson Lake from the lookout. Bottom: The Huck Fire of 1998 created lush regrowth.

The U.S. Dept. of Interior granted historic designation, and the building was placed on the National Register of Historic Places. It is the only lookout still standing on the northern portion of the forest. Five lookouts—in various states of disrepair—still stand on the southern half of the forest.

At the turn of the century—well before the lookout tower was built—Huckleberry Ridge was the site of hideout cabins for notorious elk tuskers William Binkley, Charles Isabel and Charles Purdy.

The BPOE (Elk's Club) formerly used the animal's canine teeth, or tusks, as its insignia. With each tusk fetching a lucrative $100, this use unintentionally fostered illegal poaching.

Tuskers Binkley, Isabel and Purdy slaughtered thousands of elk before game wardens were finally able to apprehend and prosecute two of the trio in 1907. Binkley and Purdy were each sentenced to three-month terms at the army guardhouse at Mammoth in Yellowstone National Park. Isabel was never apprehended.

143

49 Gravel Ridge
50 Enos Lake

Gravel Ridge
> Distance: 5.2 miles one-way
> Elevation gain: Approx. 1,900 ft.
> Maximum elevation: 8,859 ft.
> Maps: Rosie's Ridge, Gravel Mountain
> Season: Mid-June through October
> Use restrictions: All wilderness regulations apply.
> > Closed to mountain biking and motorized vehicles

Enos Lake
> Distance: 11 miles one-way
> Elevation gain: Approx. 2,000 ft.
> Elevation loss: Approx. 1,250 ft.
> Maximum elevation: 8,859 ft.
> Maps: Rosie's Ridge, Gravel Mountain
> Season: Mid-June through October
> Use restrictions: All wilderness regulations apply.
> > Closed to mountain biking and motorized vehicles

Enos Lake—the largest lake in vast Teton Wilderness—is a popular destination for outfitters who can easily cover the 11-mile distance. Despite soft mud shores and an influx of Utah chubs, it offers reasonably good fishing, as do Pacific Creek and other streams in the vicinity.

For those seeking a shorter outing, the jaunt to the top of 8,859-ft. Gravel Ridge is rewarded with panoramic views of Teton Wilderness and the after effects of a rare high-altitude tornado. According to the Forest Service, the massive July 21, 1987, twister—believed to be the highest elevation tornado ever recorded—leveled trees along a path 20 miles long and up to two-miles wide. Two hundred mile an hour winds toppled and tossed over 14,000 acres of lodgepole and fir around like matchsticks. The storm resulted in some area trails being permanently closed. It took Forest Service and volunteer work crew four years to finish clearing and re-routing the sections of trail that were re-opened.

The toppled trees fueled a conflagration the summer of 2000 that resulted in most of Teton Wilderness being closed to public access that August. Hikers travel through portions of this burn on the way to Enos.

Driving Directions
Drive north of Jackson approximately 30 miles on U.S. Hwy. 89/191 to Moran Junction. Pass the turn-off to Grand Teton National Park and head east toward Dubois

Top: The historic Enos Lake Patrol Cabin, circa 1965. Middle: Teton Wilderness near Gravel Ridge. Bottom: After effects of a high-altitude tornado.

on U.S. Hwy. 26/287. Three-and-a-half miles beyond the junction, turn left onto the signed Buffalo Valley Road. Drive approximately nine miles to the signed Box Creek Trailhead access road on your left. It is .7 mile to the parking area at the end of the rough road. (Note: The trailhead has been relocated since the 1965 Rosie's Ridge topo map was drawn. The map shows the trailhead starting roughly a mile to the west. Although you can still begin there, mileage and description of his hike begin at the new trailhead.) Hikers going to Gravel Ridge and Enos Lake share the first 3.6 miles of trail.

Trail Description

The trail immediately begins climbing sage-covered hills. Quaking aspen, fir and pine trees provide intermittent shade.

145

You'll soon pass a trail to your left; this leads to the old trailhead.

A weathered wood sign marking the Teton Wilderness Boundary is reached at 1.0 mile. Beyond it, the trail climbs at an easy grade along dirt two-track, testimony to its use by outfitters. The grade eases as the path crosses open meadow colored with sunny balsamroot and fragrant lupine early summer. The opening provides nice vistas of the Buffalo River Valley and the forested highlands surrounding Mt. Leidy to the south.

The trail gently climbs and drops through a marshy area before reaching a meadow bordered by dead snags at 2.4 miles. Birders and those who appreciate wildlife may want to spend quiet time here. Snags in Jackson Hole are home to a rather amazing 19 birds of prey, nine kinds of woodpeckers, 22 kinds of songbirds, 15 kinds of small mammals and six species of squirrels and chipmunks. Nuthatches, woodpeckers, bluebirds, kestrels and owls all nest in snag cavities.

After crossing a creek .4 mile farther, the path ascends to a long, rolling meadow awash with color mid-summer. Scarlet gilia, Indian paintbrush, bracted lousewort, yampah, groundsel, buckwheat and arnica are among the many blossoms that adorn this clearing.

A junction marked by a wood sign that reads, "trail" is reached at 3.6 miles. This is where hikers going to Gravel Ridge and Enos Lake part company.

To Gravel Ridge

Continue straight at the junction. The path hops a creek and moderately ascends the lower slopes of Gravel Ridge. At 4.6 miles, the trail begins to drop. Leave the trail here and ascend north up the open slopes for .6 mile to reach the summit of 8,859-ft. Gravel Ridge. On a clear day, you'll enjoy both Teton and Absaroka vistas, the remains of the blowdown and the sparkling waters of Enos Lake to the distant northeast.

To Enos Lake

Bear right at the trail sign. The trail turns sharply south and hugs the base of Gravel Ridge for .4 mile. It then bears north and steeply climbs 260 feet up the ridge, opening views of Gravel Mountain to the west and Box Creek Canyon and the Absarokas to the east.

The path gradually drops off the ridge and enters a long meadow at 5 miles. It hops a tributary of Box Creek .4 mile farther and proceeds northeast over mostly flat terrain to a sketchy intersection with Lava Creek Trail at 7.0 miles. A small wood sign near the base of a tree identifies the faint crossroads to your left (W).

Continue straight, dropping steeply then more gradually as your traverse two narrow meadows and a small canyon to reach the intersection with Divide Creek Trail at 8.5 miles. This intersection is well signed. Stay to the left here.

The trail to Enos climbs 200 feet out of the canyon and enters the meadows south of the lake, where the trail forks again. Take the right fork, a level walk through flowered fields. The trail crosses the outflow of the lake near the patrol cabin at 9.6 miles. It climbs up a ridge above the west side of the lake then drops to its north shore and the best camping spots near the lake.

The body of water and creek are named in honor of John Enos, Chief Washakie's Shoshone cousin. Enos worked as a guide for both Bonneville and Fremont in the early 1800s. In 1915, at the age of 102, he was presented at the San Francisco Exposition.

He died four years later at the age of 106. Enos often camped at the lake that bears his name.

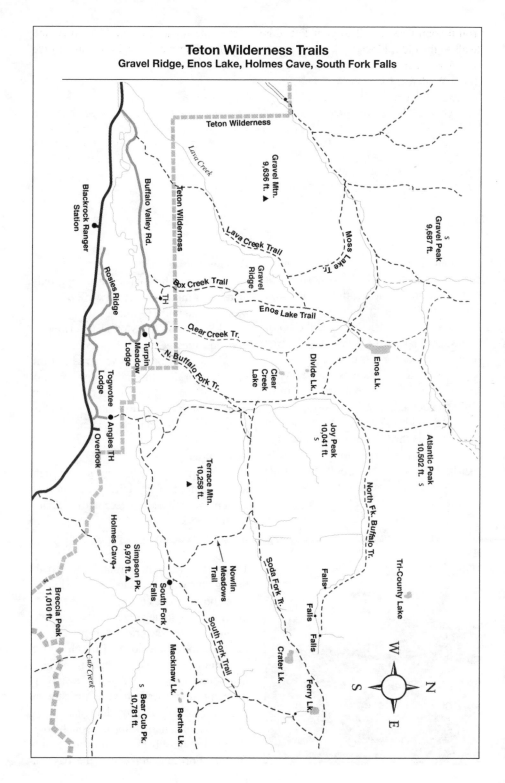

Teton Wilderness Trails
Gravel Ridge, Enos Lake, Holmes Cave, South Fork Falls

Teton Wilderness

Lava Creek

Gravel Mtn.
9,636 ft. ▲

Moss Lake Tr.

Gravel Peak
9,687 ft. s

Blackrock Ranger Station

Buffalo Valley Rd.

Teton Wilderness

Lava Creek Trail

Gravel Ridge

Rosies Ridge

Box Creek Trail

TH

Enos Lake Trail

Enos Lk.

Clear Creek Tr.

Turpin Meadow Lodge

N. Buffalo Fork Tr.

Clear Creek Lake

Divide Lk.

Togwotee Lodge

Angles TH

Overlook

Joy Peak
10,041 ft. s

Atlantic Peak
10,502 ft. s

Terrace Mtn.
10,258 ft. ▲

Nowlin Meadows Trail

North Fk. Buffalo Tr.

Holmes Cave

Simpson Pk.
9,970 ft. ▲

South Fork Falls

Soda Fork Tr.

Falls

Tri-County Lake

Breccia Peak
s 11,010 ft.

Cub Creek

Mackinaw Lk.

South Fork Trail

Bear Cub Pk.
s 10,781 ft.

Bertha Lk.

Crater Lk.

Falls

Falls

Ferry Lk.

W

N

S

E

51 South Fork Falls

Distance: 11.3 miles one-way
Elevation gain: Approx. 1,460 ft..
Elevation loss: Approx, 2,380 ft.
Maximum elevation: 8,520 ft.
Maps: Angle, Togwotee
Season: July through September
Use restrictions: Wilderness regulations apply.

South Fork Falls is possibly the most spectacular waterfall in Bridger-Teton National Forest. The South Buffalo Fork, squeezed into a slot half its size by a large rock pillar, rushes toward the lip of a sheer-walled, narrow chasm and dives over 80 feet to its moss covered bottom.

The impressive falls is reached via a long trek through the southern reaches of Teton Wilderness, limiting most traffic to outfitters and backpackers. Ambitious, fit hikers can do the hike in a very long day.

Anglers often hike to the bridge to fish both banks of the South Fork Buffalo River. A Wyoming fishing license is required.

The hike to the falls may be started from Turpin Meadows or the Angles Entrance to Teton Wilderness, the option described here.

Driving Directions

Drive north from Jackson approximately 30 miles on U.S. Hwy. 89/191 to Moran Junction. Continue straight (E) on U.S. Hwy. 26/287 toward Dubois. Sixteen miles beyond the junction you'll see Togwotee Lodge on your right. Turn into the parking lot and follow the dirt road on the left (W) end of the lodge. Stay right when the road forks and drive to the developed trailhead parking area.

Trail Description

The trail heads north through lodgepole forest for .4 mile before starting a steep, switchbacking descent to the South Buffalo Fork. It steadily drops 1,520 feet in 2.5 miles to a bridge spanning the river. (A signed short-cut trail is passed at the 1.6 mile mark. This up-and-down path through the woods cuts the distance by 2.5 miles but requires an icy ford of the river, often difficult to negotiate safely until late summer.) Cross the bridge and ascend 200 feet to a lodgepole-covered bench above the South Buffalo Fork. The trail divides just before it crosses a small side stream. Take the upper trail. It hops the stream and climbs 180 feet, providing nice views of the scenic, narrowing canyon below, before dropping back down to the South Buffalo Fork and traversing the base of

steep, rocky cliffs to your left.

After crossing a small flat, the trail ascends to a small saddle at 5.3 miles that provides nice views west of the terrain you just negotiated. You descend to the river once again, soon passing the Angles cutoff trail junction at 5.5 miles to reach a set of pretty, small cascades and waterfalls that offer a nice place to take a break.

The trail soon climbs above the river again and enters dense conifer forest. The lush forest floor is sprinkled with berry bushes; keep a sharp ear out for bears frequently seen here early August when the fruit ripens.

At 7.5 miles you'll enter long Lower Pendergraft Meadows; from here to the end of the trail, water is scarce. Make sure you are carrying plenty with you. To your left (N), 10,258-ft. Terrace Mountain rises in steps, giving the mountain its name. The limestone cliffs of Angle Mountain to your right (S) hide Holmes Cave, described in hike no 52.

The path re-enters lodgepole and fir forest. Roughly a half-mile farther you pass a junction to Cub Creek Trail on your right at 9.9 miles. Continue straight and steeply climb 200 feet via switchbacks. At the top of the climb a faint but signed trail to your left leads to Nowlin Meadows and the Soda Fork Trail at 10.5 miles. Stay on the main trail. Watch for an unsigned trail to your right a half-mile farther. This is the spur trail that leads to the South Buffalo Fork Gorge and South Fork Falls, 11.3 miles from the trailhead. At the lip of the gorge, turn left and walk up canyon for the best view of the falls.

South Fork Falls plunges to the bottom of South Buffalo Fork Gorge, seen below. Both are scenic highlights of Teton Wilderness. Opposite page: The bridge over South Fork of the Buffalo River. Anglers often hike to the bridge to fish both shores of the South Fork.

52 Holmes Cave

Distance: 8.8 miles RT
Elevation gain: 1,500 ft.
Elevation loss: 680 ft.
Maximum elevation: 10,040 ft.
Maps: Angle Mountain, Togwotee Pass
Season: Mid-July through September
Use restrictions: Teton Wilderness regulations apply.

The hike to Holmes Cave leads you into the heart of the fabulous pinnacle country near Togwotee Pass. The vast expanse of rolling meadow colored with red foliage and patches of late-blooming lupine brings hikers back every September—unless they are lured there in the summer months to catch the height of the wildflower bloom. And, yes, there is an interesting cave at the end of the walk. Holmes is one of the largest caverns in northwest Wyoming. The multi-chambered cavern is known to extend over 4,000 feet and is still being explored.

Driving Directions

Drive north from Jackson approximately 30 miles on U.S. 89/191 to Moran Junction. Set your odometer here and continue straight (E) on U.S. 26/287 toward Dubois. Twenty miles beyond the junction, immediately past a highway speed limit sign, is an unmarked dirt turn-off on the left. Turn here and drive .1 mile to an obvious parking area on your right. Walk up the badly rutted road, soon passing a small cabin. Left of and beyond it is a wood sign that reads "Holmes Cave." This is the start of the hike.

Trail Description

The clear trail—not plotted on the topo map—climbs through scattered forest. It gains approximately 400 feet before dropping to cross an unnamed tributary of Blackrock Creek. The trail then climbs above the creek, recrossing it again at 1.6 miles before paralleling it on a sustained, steep climb up its drainage that gains almost 500 feet in the next half-mile.

At 2.6 miles, you'll pass a wilderness boundary sign. The trail continues its ascent for another .2 mile, reaching the hike's high point of 10,040 feet at an obvious ridge crest. From the crest it descends to a large cairn and disappears. Walk to the far right—almost due east—and head toward the subalpine fir below you. You'll pass three more cairns as you drop 440 feet to the meadow. If you keep right, you'll soon see the trail again.

Hop a stream at 3.6 miles and begin a short but moderately steep climb up a wooded draw. The trail switchbacks once before leveling and skirting the right side of an unnamed lake at 4 miles and a small pond just beyond it. Shortly past the pond, the trail divides. Take the left fork to reach Holmes Cave.

The path descends 200 feet into a large depression. Water from the entire area drains into this sinkhole—the entrance to Holmes Cave. Head toward an obvious, 20-foot high, rock-covered hillside ahead

Top: The pinnacled terrain en route to Holmes Cave.
Left: The entrance to the cave. Technical equipment is required to safely explore the cave.

of you. The cave entrance is at its foot.

Holmes Cave extends approximately 4,000 feet underground. Edwin Holmes, John Holland, and Neil Matheson discovered it in September of 1898. The labyrinth was explored seven years later, September 6-9, 1905, by T.R. Wilson of Afton, Wyoming, and two others. They named its two large rooms Holland and Wilson. Holland, the largest chamber, is 754 feet long and 452 feet wide. (A third chamber, Neda, has since been discovered.)

The obscure cave was re-explored 18 years later in July of 1933. One of the participants, Esther Allen, described the chilly spelunking expedition in an unpublished history of Bridger-Teton National Forest:

"We had to crawl through a small stream that came out of the small entrance to enter a tunnel inside. Through the arrow-shaped hall entry, we passed over ground to the 31-foot waterfall which descended into the Holland Chamber...."

An expedition two months later determined that the breccia formation was an extinct volcano. The cave has since been entered numerous times. Adventurous spelunkers hope to yet discover new tunnels and chambers.

Looking right (NE) from the cave entrance one can discern a faint trail heading toward a saddle. From the saddle, the trail descends 200 feet to a small stream. From here, it is possible to walk up 9,910-ft. Simpson Peak.

53 Breccia Peak

54 Brooks Lake Mountain

Breccia Peak

    Distance: Approx. 3 miles one-way

    Elevation gain: Approx. 1,800 ft.

    Maximum elevation: 11,010 ft.

    Maps: Togwotee Pass (Not plotted)

    Season: July through September

    Use restrictions: Wilderness regulations apply.

        Closed to mountain biking and motorized vehicles

Brooks Lake Mountain

    Distance: Approx. 2.2 miles one-way

    Elevation gain: Approx. 1,700 ft..

    Maximum elevation: Approx. 11,000 ft.

    Maps: Togwotee Pass (Not plotted).

    Season: July through September

    Use restrictions: Wilderness regulations apply.

        Closed to mountain biking and motorized vehicles

Breccia Peak and Brooks Lake Mountain define the southern reaches of the Absaroka Range and the boundary of Teton and Washakie Wilderness. Both summits are the apex of massive cliffs born when a volcanic near Mt. Washburn in Yellowstone National Park erupted 50 million years ago. Lava and debris spread south and east. The volcanic conglomerate was cemented by flows cooling at different rates and mineral deposition, a geologic process that eventually forms breccia (pronounced bret-cha). This easily eroded rock strata creates pinnacles and cliffs of great beauty that are wonderful to view, but awful for technical climbing: nothing can be trusted not to crumble or peel off. Walking up the slopes of Breccia Peak and Brooks Lake Mountain is the best way to explore these beauties.

The hikes up both are relatively short but vigorous ventures that offer unsurpassed loveliness, luxuriant wildflowers and superb views of the pinnacled landscape that defines the southernmost stretch of the Absaroka Mountains. The peaks share the same trailhead. Energetic hikers seeking an extended outing can do both in one longer day.

The high, open meadows and slopes encountered on this pair of hikes are frequented by grizzlies digging for roots and grubs. Numerous claw marks on trees and shredded bark are vivid reminders that hikers should travel in groups and adhere to bear country precautions.

Driving Directions

Drive north from Jackson approximately 30 miles on U.S. 89/191 to Moran Junction. Continue straight on U.S. 26/287 toward Dubois for 24 more miles and

The view looking northwest from the summit of 11,010-ft. Breccia Peak.

begin looking for a large pullout/parking area off the right side of the highway—the last pullout before reaching the summit of long Togwotee Pass. As of this writing, highway construction has temporarily obscured the start of the trail on the opposite (N) side of the highway. By driving to the signed summit of Togwotee Pass, then backtracking to the pullout, you'll see a segment of trail heading up slope, which will help you get your bearing.

The trail divides almost immediately. Bear left. At the second split, reached a short distance farther, continue straight to reach Breccia Peak. Take the right fork to hike to Brooks Lake Mountain.

Breccia Peak

The trail moderately climbs then flattens as it traverses subalpine fir forest. It parallels an unnamed tributary of Blackrock Creek to your left for about five minutes before splashing through the shallow waterway. Beyond, the rocky tread climbs at a moderate then steeper grade. After crossing a stream twice in

quick succession, views of spectacular Breccia Peak ahead of you open up.

The path ascends to an open meadow, where it flattens and bends right before again assuming an upward course. It zigzags left then right near a streambed and splits. Keep left.

The clear path soon peters out. Keep walking on a straight course across the open meadow toward Breccia Peak ahead. As the meadow narrows, you'll regain the trail. It bears right and enters a second, long meadow framed by the Breccia Cliffs. Mid- to late July, this high expanse is graced by a riot of Indian paintbrush, generous patches of elephant's head, monkey flowers and bluebells. The trail is faint in spots, but generally travels up the right (E) side of the meadow.

Near the meadow's end, leave the path and begin angling left (NW) toward an obvious shoulder of Breccia Peak that dips to the horizon ahead. It is a steep hike up this ridge through grasses interspersed with rock and talus to a high plateau. Once the plateau is reached, you climb at a more moderate grade to the summit, where you'll see a metal U.S. Survey marker.

The panorama is spectacular. The Breccia Cliffs dominate the foreground to the immediate north, while the Tetons frame the distance skyline. Small Lost Lake lies below you to the west.

Look for the summit register and sign yourself in. While you grab a bite to eat, entertain yourself by reading the remarks left by those who have gone before you. Senior Exum guide Ron Matous hiked up the peak with his 13-year-old daughter, Anna, on July 7, 2001. He had two broken arms at the time. A participant on a NOLS Outdoor Educator's Course mused that, "Martha Stewart is the devil incarnate." Dr. "Big Stride" Bill Greenway penned my favorite on July 16, 1998: "Look long and carry the wild places home."

Brooks Lake Mountain

From the junction, the unofficial but clear path climbs very steeply through pleasant fir and pine forest before leveling and descending a short distance. It then resumes climbing, bearing right (SE) as it ascends at an easy to moderate grade to a junction. Stay left here. The trail soon begins paralleling a creek and becomes quite steep.

The grade moderates as the trail crosses open slopes below the rocky crest of the cliff band. Here, the path crosses the creek, turns left and enters forested terrain. It steadily ascends to high meadows and an open bowl that offer great views of the Teton Range.

The grade increases near the head of the bowl and the trail disappears, but the route is obvious. Keep ascending the open slopes until you reach a small saddle between Peak 10,908 to your left (N) and Brooks Lake Mountain to your immediate right, identified by a pole on top of the summit.

If you don't want to ascend the final, steep 100 feet to the summit, the view of the surrounding terrain from the saddle is more than satisfying.

Hikers ascend the open slopes below the summit of Brooks Lake Mountain.

154

55 Wind River Lake to Lower Brooks Lake

Distance:
 Wind River Lake to Lower Brooks Lake: 4.6 miles one-way
 Wind River Lake Loop: 16.6 miles
Elevation change:
 Wind River Lake to Lower Brooks Lake: Approx. loss of 500 ft.
 Wind River Lake Loop: Approx. 1,200 ft.
Maximum elevation: 9,540 ft. at Wind River Lake
Maps: Lava Mountain, Kisinger Lakes
Season: Mid-July through September
Use restrictions:
 Off-road vehicle travel prohibited. Old road is open to motorized vehicles but traffic is infrequent. Be alert, however, to the possibility of encountering vehicles. Avoid travel when conditions are wet.

Wind River Lake to Lower Brooks Lake can be done as an out-and-back hike through scenic terrain or as a loop mountain bike ride. The outing travels through the famed pinnacle country near Togwotee Pass on the old Lander to Yellowstone Highway. The loop option exits onto the present highway to return to the Wind River Lake picnic area. Wind River Lake is a sparkling tarn nestled at the toe of rugged 10,537-ft. Sublette Peak.

Snow typically renders this higher elevation outing impassable until early to mid-July. Mountain bikers are further advised that the old roadway travels through clay and shale soils that turn into plastic gumbo during or following wet weather. Red goo will glom itself onto wheel rims in layers thick enough to halt tire rotation. This is not theory speaking: it is personal experience.

But if the snow has melted and the sun is shining, this ride/hike is a superb scenic and historic delight. Mountain bikers not wishing to ride the highway should shuttle a vehicle to the wide turnout at the entrance to Brooks Lake Recreation Area, shortening the outing almost seven miles and eliminating the 1,200-foot climb back to Wind River Lake.

Driving Directions

Drive north from Jackson approximately 30 miles on U.S. 89/191 to Moran Junction. Pass the turn-off to Grand Teton National Park and head east toward Dubois on U.S. Hwy. 26/287. Signed Togwotee Pass is reached 24.8 miles beyond the junction. Wind River Picnic Area, located off the left side of the highway, is .7 mile farther. The turn-off is a bit abrupt; start looking for it after you crest the pass.

Those who wish to do a car shuttle should drive an additional 6.8 miles past Wind River Lake to the turn-off to Brooks Lake Recreation Area on the left side of the highway. Park off-road in the pullout and return to Wind River Lake picnic area. The picnic area has tables and a vault toilet, but water is not available.

Trail Description

The road you will be hiking/riding gently descends to historic Brooks Lake Lodge and Lower Brooks Lake before traveling south to its terminus at U.S. Hwy. 287 in 9.8 miles. It was constructed under the auspices of the U.S. War Department in 1898 as part of a military road to connect Fort Washakie near Lander with Fort Yellowstone as well as provide road access between the Northern Pacific and Union Pacific railheads. Capt. Sanford of the U.S. Corp of Engineers reasoned in an 1899 report that the road would provide cavalry stationed in Fort Washakie direct access into Jackson Hole, where conflicts between state game wardens and Indians residing on the Fort Hall and Wind River Indian Reservations, "were to be feared." He also made the politically shrewd observation that since most of newly formed Yellowstone National Park was in Wyoming, Wyoming residents should have direct access to it.

The rough military swath was little more than a wagon road not crossed by automobiles until 1916. At the urging of Lander and Casper residents eager to develop Yellowstone tourism, Wyoming Governor Joseph Carey acquired funds from the National Park Service to improve the route over the pass in 1921. Sections of the road, including the one you are on now, were eventually rerouted to become today's U.S. Hwy. 287.

The road travels east from the picnic area, crossing the first of numerous run-off streams at .2 mile. These create a lush environment that helps support verdant meadows, subalpine fir forest and remarkable wildflower displays.

Gently curving in places, the road climbs short grades but generally descends, passing run-off streams at .8, 1.2 and 2.0 miles before reaching open Barbers Point at 3.1 miles. The point provides superb views of 9,704-ft. Pilot Knob across the meadows to the south. The rugged, stratified volcanic cliffs above Lower Brooks Lake rise to the north. These stand in quiet testimony to the violent volcanic explosions that rocked the Absaroka Range some 50 million years ago.

Beyond the point, the road drops at a consistent grade to the entrance to Brooks Lake Lodge at 4.4 miles. The impressive log structure was one of a string of guest lodges built by Eugene Amoretti between Lander and Yellowstone in the early 1900s. When improved automotive technology enabled travelers to comfortably cover more ground, business at the log hostelry declined. Its owners revived the operation by converting the lodge into the Diamond G Dude Ranch.

The ranch went through a series of owners and a name change through the 40s and 50s before it was closed for a period of time. In 1983, a Minnesota doctor purchased the property and succeeded in having it placed on the National Register of Historic Places, a designation that enabled him to receive federal restoration funds to repair the lodge.

Under the direction of the Carlsberg family, extensive renovations were completed in the late 1980s, and the lodge was rededicated and opened to the public. The present owners operate Brooks Lake as a high-end guest ranch.

Brooks Lake and the campground are reached less than a quarter-mile beyond the lodge. The campground has running water during the summer months, for those needing to refill water bottles, and vault toilets are available.

Top: Wind River Lake picnic area is the start of the hike/bike along the former Lander to Yellowstone Highway. The scenic lake is framed by impressive breccia cliffs. Left: The old highway is a popular destination in the winter as well.

U.S. Hwy. 287. Expect vehicle traffic on this section. If you are doing the loop outing, bear right onto the highway and climb 1,200 feet on paved roadway to reach Wind River Lake picnic area in 6.8 miles.

The lodge, creek and lakes are named in honor of Bryant Brooks, governor of Wyoming from 1905 to 1911. Brooks discovered the lake that bears his name while on a hunting trip in 1889. His notes of the event captured his impression:

"Among the pines glistened a lake… what a sight! Tracks of elk and bear. Where I sat on my horse stretched a broad, peaceful valley. I stood closer that day to nature's heart than ever before."

The road briefly climbs as it leaves the campground. It then descends on a high standard, gravel road 5.2 miles to

157

56 Jade Lakes

Distance:
  Upper and Lower Jade Lakes: 5 miles RT
  Jade Lakes Loop: 5.5 miles
Elevation change
  Upper and Lower Jade Lakes: 630 ft. gain
  Jade Lakes Loop: 740 ft. elevation change
Maximum elevation: 9,700 ft.
Maps: Togwotee Pass. Book map pg. 161
Season: Late June through September
Use restrictions: Motorized trail vehicles prohibited.

Dropping down Togwotee Pass toward Dubois motorists are treated to one of the most stunning roadside panoramas in the West—a two-mile stretch of stratified volcanic cliffs and pinnacles that soar over a thousand feet into the sky. The deep green waters of Upper and Lower Jade Lakes in the Absarokas reflect these multi-colored banded formations and surrounding countryside beautifully. This is one of the most rewarding half-day hikes in the region. Backpackers enjoy numerous good campsites near Upper Jade and fisherman try their luck landing the cutthroat trout that inhabit both lakes.

Driving Directions

The trail to the lakes begins near Brooks Lake Campground. Drive 30 miles northeast of Jackson on U.S. Hwy. 89/191 to Moran Junction. There, pass the turn-off to Grand Teton National Park and head east toward Dubois on U.S. Hwy 26/287. Roughly 32 miles beyond Moran Junction you'll see a signed road to Brooks Lake Recreation Area off the left side of the highway. Turn in and follow the high-standard forest service road 5.2 miles to Brooks Lake Campground. Park

in the boat-ramp parking area left of the campground and walk to the signed trailhead.

Trail Description

To control erosion and limit impacts on the wet meadow near the start of the trails to Jade, Upper Brooks and Rainbow Lakes, the Forest Service and area volunteers have constructed a series of bridges and wood plank sidewalks through the meadow and re-routed the initial climb to Jade Lakes away from a badly eroded hillside. Please use the trail described here.

The new Yellowstone Trail traverses a large meadow over four bridges and a plank sidewalk to a signed trail intersection at .5 mile. The trail to Jade Lake gently ascends and enters a predominantly Douglas fir forest, soon reaching a buckrail fence. Beyond it, the forest opens for a brief stretch and the grade increases a bit. The trail re-enters the trees, bears left and levels on a ridge above Brooks Lake, offering great views of it and the Pinnacle Buttes.

At 1.0 mile, you'll reach a restoration trail sign. Stay on the new trail to the left. You'll soon reach a second split; keep left

Upper Jade Lakes in Washakie Wilderness is a rewarding half-day hiking destination.

again. The trail crosses an open stretch that unveils the Breccia Cliffs ahead. The trail bends right (N) and splits. Keep right here. You'll soon parallel a willow-lined tributary of Brooks Lake Creek to your left. The trail crests a rise and passes a tiny pond to your right. It then heads up a draw that opens views of the striated cliffs ahead. At the top of the draw, the trail broadens into a two track and gently descends to Upper Jade Lake at 2 miles.

The volcanic cliffs above the lake are best reflected in the mirror-like stillness of dawn and dusk, times you are also most likely to see wildlife coming to the lakeshore to drink. Good camping sites are found near the lake's outlet on the north shore and on its southwest shore. Remember that it is illegal to camp within 100 feet of the shore.

Lower Jade Lake lies .4 mile to the northeast. While it lacks the stunning reflections of cliffs and pinnacles found in Upper Jade's still waters, the peaceful lake offers both good fishing and seclusion. The trail to that lake circles the east shore of Upper Jade, then descends through spruce and fir forest to Lower Jade's west shore.

Those wishing to travel a different route back to the trailhead should hike to Lower Jade Lake's narrow neck near the lake's northwest corner, where the trail splits. Bear right at this junction. You'll soon reach a second junction; a branch is over the fork to the right. Keep left here. The path climbs a short rise before curling right (E) through forest and descending at a moderate than steeper grade. You'll pass a spring to your left by a stand of willows before reaching Lower Jade Lake's outlet stream. Look for a log spanning the stream 20 yards ahead. Cross the stream and bear right (S) on the path. The level trail soon reaches a side channel of Brooks Lake Creek that is easily spanned by rock hopping. Just beyond is an intersection with the trail to Upper Brooks and Rainbow Lakes.

Turn right (S) to return to the trailhead in 2 more miles.

57 Upper Brooks and Rainbow Lakes

Distance:
    Upper Brooks: 7 miles RT
    Rainbow Lake: 8.2 miles RT
Elevation gain:
    Upper Brooks: Approx. 250 ft.
    Rainbow Lake: Approx. 250 ft.
Maximum elevation: 9,230 ft.
Maps: Togwotee Pass. Book map pg. 163
Season: Late June through September
Use restrictions: Motorized trail vehicles prohibited.

No grunt climbs up Teton-size hills. Great fishing. Beautiful scenery. All can be found at Upper Brooks and Rainbow Lakes, less than 90 minutes from downtown Jackson. Nestled beneath striking volcanic pinnacles, these pretty lakes provide the near perfect summer getaway. The "near" is a reflection of two items that need to be mentioned. The first is that cattle graze the lower meadows crossed on this hike. Most agree the scenery more than compensates for their presence.

The second item is a good deal smaller than peaceful bovines, but a far bigger distraction. Abundant water makes this area an excellent breeding ground for mosquitoes. Those who neglect to bring repellent on this hike—or wear a long sleeve shirt and pants—will wish they had.

Driving Directions

The trail to the lakes begins near Brooks Lake Campground. Drive 30 miles northeast of Jackson on U.S. Hwy. 89/191 to Moran Junction. There, pass the turn-off to Grand Teton National Park and head east toward Dubois on U.S. Hwy 26/287. Roughly 32 miles beyond Moran Junction you'll see a signed road to Brooks Lake Recreation Area off the left side of the highway. Turn in and follow the high-standard forest service road 5.2 miles to Brooks Lake Campground. Park in the boat-ramp parking area left of the campground and walk the short distance to the signed "Yellowstone Trail" near the lakeshore.

Trail Description

The first section of this trail is shared with people hiking to Upper and Lower Jade Lakes (see hike no. 56). It traverses a large meadow to a signed trail intersection at .5 mile. The path to Upper Brooks Lake continues north around the west side of Brooks Lake. As you approach the northern end of Lower Brooks Lake you ascend a short, steep hillside, virtually the only noticeable grade on the whole trip. Thick conifers block the view to the left, but straight ahead and to your right (N and E) the colorful volcanic cliffs above Bonneville Creek and jagged outcroppings of Pinnacle Buttes slice the sky.

Jade Lakes, Upper Brooks Lake and Rainbow Lake Trails

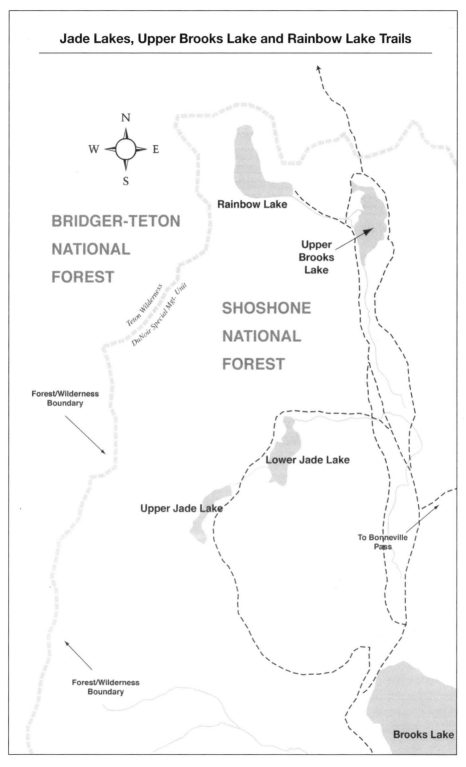

N
W E
S

Rainbow Lake

BRIDGER-TETON
NATIONAL
FOREST

Upper
Brooks
Lake

Teton Wilderness
DuNoir Special Mgt. Unit

SHOSHONE
NATIONAL
FOREST

Forest/Wilderness
Boundary

Lower Jade Lake

Upper Jade Lake

To Bonneville
Pass

Forest/Wilderness
Boundary

Brooks Lake

The trail stays atop a level grassy ridge between two shallow drainages, gradually descending to an informal use trail to your left to Lower Jade Lake not shown on the 1965 Togwotee Pass topo map. Keep to the right and cross wide Brooks Lake Creek before entering the trees. Shortly, you'll pass the Bonneville Pass Trail on your right, incorrectly shown on the Shoshone Forest Service maps as being nearer Brooks Lake. Stay left on the main trail. Yet another junction is reached a short distance farther. Both forks of the trail rejoin before reaching Upper Brooks. The left branch is preferred to avoid the slightly undulating course of the right fork and muddy terrain created by seeps. The flat, grassy terrain is sprinkled with a wildflower garden, amply watered by Brooks Lake Creek tributaries.

At 2.9 miles, you'll get your first view of Upper Brooks Lake. The trail crosses the creek and bears right to skirt the east side of the lake. To gain access to the best campsites, follow the trail to the north side of the lake.

Although not on the topo map, a less developed trail loops around the northern end of the lake and follows the creek's west tributary to Rainbow Lake at 4.1 miles. Visited almost solely by fishermen, this lake offers seclusion.

Those desiring a longer outing can continue on the trail past Upper Brooks Lake to Bear Cub Pass, three-quarters of a mile beyond the northern end of the lake. Little more than a wooded hilltop, the pass marks the boundary between Shoshone National Forest and Teton Wilderness. From the pass the trail drops two miles to beautiful Cub Creek drainage.

The hike to Upper Brooks and Rainbow Lakes begins by skirting the west shore of Brooks Lake.

58 Bonneville Pass
59 Kisinger Lakes Loop

Bonneville Pass
> Distance: 5.2 miles RT
> Elevation gain: Approx. 740 ft.
> Maximum elevation: 9,980 ft.
> Maps: Dundee Meadows
> Season: July through September
> Use restrictions: Motorized trail vehicles prohibited

Kisinger Lake Loop
> Distance: 12.8 miles
> Elevation loss/gain: Approx. 2,680 ft. gain, 2,900 ft. loss
> Maximum elevation: 10,120 ft.
> Maps: Dundee Meadows, Kisinger Lakes
> Season: July through September
> Use restrictions: Motorized trail vehicles prohibited

Exceptional views of the unique DuNoir area, an impressive cirque and flowered meadows await hikers en route to Bonneville Pass. Those continuing beyond the pass take pleasure in a series of comely, clear lakes that reflect jagged breccia pinnacles, stretches of dense forest and wonderful solitude. This is country in which to revel—located on the fringe of perhaps the wildest country remaining in the lower 48 states—and is well worth the drive from the town of Jackson.

But don't explore this terrain alone: the trail traverses grizzly bear habitat. One summer day, our party of veteran backcountry users was vividly reminded of this when it chanced upon the largest grizzly tracks anyone had seen. One member remarked hopefully that at least the bear was going the other way, before quietly relinquishing the lead and slipping to the back of the group. It is safest to travel in a group of four or more.

Driving Directions
Drive 30 miles northeast of Jackson on U.S. Hwy. 89/191 to Moran Junction. There, pass the turnoff to Grand Teton National Park and head east toward Dubois on U.S. Hwy 26/287. Roughly 32 miles beyond Moran Junction you'll see a signed road to Brooks Lake Recreation Area off the left side of the highway. Turn in and follow the high-standard Forest Service road to the signed intersection with the Bonneville Pass/Kisinger Lake trailhead access road (USFS Road #516) to your right at 4.1 miles. Turn here and carefully drive the sometimes potholed artery road 1.7 miles to the signed trailhead. There is

163

Top: Beyond Bonneville Pass, the trail follows Dundee Creek as it steeply drops to Dundee Meadows. Bottom: Hikers enter the old-growth forest for which the DuNoir is named.

an information kiosk at the trailhead. No water is available.

Note: The Kisinger Lakes outing is a near loop completed by walking on the trailhead access road. If you prefer to not walk on the road on the way back, have members of your group drive two vehicles. Park one in the trail parking area located off the right side of the road just before the turn-off to USFS Road #516 to Bonneville Pass. (You'll see trail information signs at the Pinnacle Trail trailhead once you turn in.) This option cuts off 1.8 miles of road walking at the end of the hike.

Trail Description

The first section of the trail to Bonneville Pass and the Kisinger Lakes Loop begins by hopping a tributary of broad, shallow Bonneville Creek and walking on a closed logging road that soon narrows to trail width. The path parallels the creek to your right as it gently ascends terrain pleasingly forested with spruce and fir. Small clearings in the canopy offer enough sunlight for lupine, yarrow, geraniums, fireweed and other wildflowers to thrive. At roughly .5 mile, the grade increases to moderate and the trail steadily ascends. It leaves the forest at one mile and enters steep, open meadows. To your right, spectacular Jules Bowl is unveiled. This memorable cirque has a relatively flat headwall rimming its mid-section. The craggy spires of Pinnacle Buttes rise to the right and left. It's terrain worth a closer look if an off-trail adventure beckons. Jules Bowl and the surrounding Pinnacle Buttes area was the site of controversy in the 1960s, when the U.S. Forest Service issued large timber contracts to U.S. Plywood and closed recreational access to the area. Results of the large-scale timbering are still evident over four decades later near the end of the Pinnacle Trail.

Beyond the bowl, the grade of the trail become steeper. It hops a rivulet and bears right (ENE). In the next 10 minutes, you'll hop over two more rivulets before reaching the south end of a gently sloping meadow at 2.1 miles. The well-defined path, occasionally marked by cairns, hugs the right side of the half-mile long expanse. A small lake rests just below 9,960 ft. Bonneville Pass, a grassy saddle 2.6 miles beyond the trailhead that offers fine views of the surrounding pinnacle country. Ramshorn Peak and Coffin Butte define the distance horizon to the east, while the vertiginous cliff walls that define the Continental Divide lie to the west and north.

A wood sign near the pass identifies the boundary of the DuNoir Special Management Area beyond and reminds travelers that, *"the trail is the thing, not the end of the trail. Travel too fast and you'll miss all that you are traveling for."*

The tarn/pass area makes a fine destination for those seeking a shorter outing. Beyond the pass, the trail hops Dundee Creek and steeply descends east via a series of short switchbacks to Dundee Meadows. The 800-plus foot descent is through the remnants of spectacular old growth forest that gives the management area its name. "DuNoir" (roughly, of black, in French) referred to the expanse of dense forest that formerly covered much of the area. In 1914, the Wyoming Tie and Timber Company established its headquarters at the DuNoir tie hack camp west of Dubois. Between 1914 and 1946, the company supplied 400,000 ties annually to the Chicago and Northwestern railroads as well as timber for mine props—all cut from this area.

The now level trail hugs the right side of the meadow, often within the edge of trees fringing it. Near the end of the larger cliff-framed meadow the trail bends right (E). You'll soon hop a stream and travel through a short, forested section before entering another, smaller meadow and passing an old wood sign for Bonneville Pass. Beyond, the trail bends right (S) and climbs about 100 feet through subalpine fir forest before gently descending approximately 240 feet to a signed trail junction that is a bit confusing. The path that angles left leads to Clendenin and Murray Lakes. The one you are on continues straight. Head for Kisinger Lakes Trail to your right. You'll splash through West DuNoir Creek and skirt the west side of a meadow watered by the same. The trail is indistinct here. Head for the poles and stay on the right side of the expanse and you shouldn't lose your way. The path hops tiny Spruce Creek and a tributary of West DuNoir Creek before gently ascending to drier terrain and becoming more distinct.

It eventually bends more directly south and travels through a small open park, paralleling a tributary of West DuNoir to your left. The path gently drops to a crossing of Grizzly Creek. Beyond, it climbs at a moderate grade before leveling in pretty Basin Creek Meadows at 6.6 miles, where fine views of the dramatic Pinnacle Buttes to your right (W) unfold. Fed by two springs that form the creek, the meadows are a nice camping option.

The first lake of Kisinger Lakes lies just .4 mile farther. Day hikers looking for a great place to eat lunch or take a break should ascend through whitebark pine forest another quarter mile to the second larger and more scenic lake, backdropped by the craggy spires of Pinnacle Buttes.

Beyond the second lake, the trail crosses an outlet stream between the lakes, skirts the west shore of a third lake, and steeply ascends to a small saddle at 9,720 feet. It then climbs at an easier grade through an attractive whitebark

The Pinnacle Buttes create a spectacular background for the second of four Kisinger Lakes.

pine forest, its floor graced by grouse whortleberry. The path contours around the southeast shoulder of Pinnacle Buttes. You'll climb in and out of the small drainage created by the upper reaches of Wolf Creek before entering a high, alpine meadow and ascending to a broad 10,000-foot saddle. Here, a new trail sign marks the intersection with the Pinnacles Trail angling right ((NW) off the saddle. This is the path you want to complete the loop.

The trail drops below the saddle, then steeply re-ascends to the high point of the hike at 10,120 feet, 9.9 miles beyond the trailhead. This steep, rubbly spur of the butte is prone to sliding, and extensive trail work has been done through the slide paths.

The path tightly jogs right then left and begins its steady descent through forest. You'll hop over several small run-off streams spilling down the sides of the butte before reaching an area of forest that was obviously clear-cut. Occasional slash piles and stumps from 40 plus years ago still mark the activity. The terrain levels as you approach the parking area for Pinnacle Butte Trail. If you didn't shuttle a car, walk through the lot and bear right onto the road. In .1 mile, you'll reach the signed access road to Bonneville Pass. From here, it is 1.7 miles to your vehicle.

Bonneville Pass is a nod to Capt. Benjamin Louis Eulalie de Bonneville, a fur trader and adventurer who opportunistically worked for the army as well. In 1832, Bonneville led an historic expedition of 110 men and 20 wagons through South Pass to the Green River, and is credited with the first ascent of Gannett Peak—the highest summit in Wyoming—in September of 1833.

Washington Irving used Bonneville's detailed journals and maps when he wrote the classic *Adventures of Captain Bonneville*.

166

60 Rosie's Ridge

Distance:
3.6 miles to turn-around
4.5 miles to radio tower
Elevation gain: Approx. 170 ft.
Maximum elevation: 7,862 ft.
Maps: Rosie's Ridge
Season: Mid-May through October
Use restrictions: Closed to motorized vehicles Nov. 1 - June 15.

A two-track road travels the length of Rosie's Ridge in Buffalo Valley, offering rewarding views of the north end of Jackson Hole and the Teton Range. Although it can be hiked, it is best suited for mountain biking and skiing from November 1 to June 15, when the road is closed to motorized vehicles.

Driving Directions

Drive 30 miles northeast of Jackson on U.S. Hwy. 89/191 to Moran Junction. Set your odometer at the junction and continue east on U.S. Hwy. 26/287 toward Dubois for 12.7 miles to the signed Turpin Meadows/Four Mile Meadow Road on your left. Turn in and drive .3 mile to access the start of Rosie's Ridge Road (F.S. # 30060) on your left. Park off road.

Trail Description

The graveled two-track is an access road that leads to a radio tower perched at the end of the ridge. It gradually ascends and passes a food/meat storage pole at .2 mile. You'll reach a gate in another .2 mile. A metal bar here bars onward motorized vehicle traffic from November 1 through June 15. The road skirts an attractive meadow to your left at 1 mile. At the 2-mile mark, views of the Grand Teton open up. Recreationists take advantage of many nice camping spots in the vicinity.

The track begins ascending at 2.5 miles, cresting a small rise at 2.8 miles that unveils views of the Tetons. Even better views of the Tetons and the Absaroka Range to your right are enjoyed at 3.3 miles. The nicest viewpoint is at 3.6 miles, just before the road drops around a sharp curve a tenth of a mile farther. This viewpoint is a good place to turnaround.

Beyond the curve, the drop roads sharply for .2 mile and then ascends to the end of the road at 4.5 miles. Here, a gate over the road bars onward travel to the radio tower. It is possible to parallel the fence around the facility and walk uphill about 10 minutes to the end of the hill and views of the range.

The ridge is named in honor of Rudolph "Rosie" Rosencrans, an Austrian native who began working for Teton National Forest in 1904. Rosie reportedly came to America because he had seen Buffalo Bill touring in Europe and was very impressed by him. It was one of Rosie's greatest honors as a ranger to

Top: Panoramic views of the northern end of Jackson Hole and the Teton Range are enjoyed by visitors to Rosie's Ridge. Right: Rudolph "Rosie" Rosencrans at the age of 78. Photo taken in 1954 by Elizabeth McCabe.

escort Buffalo Bill through the forest in 1914. When Buffalo Bill asked Rosie what he could give him, Rosie asked for a lock of his hair—which Buffalo Bill promptly cut off with a hunting knife. It was a prized keepsake for the remainder of Rosie's life.

Rosie mapped much of the surrounding area and constructed the Blackrock Ranger Station, now on the National Register of Historic Places. He retired relatively early because of failing eyesight, but was to live many more years before dying on September 22, 1970, just three months shy of his ninety-fifth birthday.

61 Toppings Lake and Ridge

Distance: 4.4 miles RT
Elevation change: Approx. 1,200 ft.
Maximum elevation: 9,034 ft. at the ridge
Maps: Davis Hill, Mt. Leidy. Book map pg. 170
Season: Late June through October
Use restrictions: Closed to motorized vehicles Nov.1 - June 15.

If you only have a morning or an afternoon to hike—or if you are looking for good fishing—place Toppings Lakes near the top of your short list. Fred Toppings, for whom the lakes are named, stocked the two tarns with grayling. Fred and Eva started the Moosehead Ranch in the late 1920s. They gradually expanded their operation, hosting game hunters in the autumn and dudes in the summer. The latter were treated to a horseback ride to the lakes.

At its height in the 1960s, Topping's Moosehead Ranch had over 40 cabins, a school and its own post office, registered under the name of Elk. Both the school and post office were closed by 1969. Fred died in 1970, Eva in 1988. The ranch is still in operation under new owners.

Driving Directions

The unmarked trail to this pair of mountain jewels is reached by driving 24.5 miles north of Jackson on U.S. 89/191 to a signed Teton National Forest access road on the right, almost directly opposite from the Cunningham Cabin turn-off on the left (W) side of the highway.

Turn right onto the access road. Pass an information kiosk at .7 mile. A short distance farther, the road forks, with Road #30310 turning sharply left and Road #30333 continuing straight. Take the left fork. It immediately switchbacks up a steep hill that crests at 1.1 miles. Bear right at 2.3 miles where a logging road veers left, and drive up the cobbled grade. At 2.9 miles, you'll pass Dry Lake, frequently covered with striking pink algae bloom before seasonally disappearing as summer progresses.

Stay right at 3.2 miles where the road forks. The unimproved dirt road gets progressively rougher, but is passable for sedans if you travel slowly and carefully. At 4.7 miles, park in the graveled area to your right.

Trail Description

Walk .1 mile up the road to a gate (usually barred). You'll see a wood trail marker but no sign of a trail. The trail begins approximately two minutes up the road on the right-hand side. Look carefully. If you are still on the road as it swings noticeably to the left, you've missed it.

The trail abruptly climbs through lodgepole forest, switchbacking slightly west but heading predominantly southeast through cool forest. Good eyes will spot a wonderful assortment of edible berries, typically ripe and ready to pick early to mid-August. Thick foliage hides a stream to your left that is heard but not visible. This is the outflow of a pond above you.

At 1.1 mile, you'll see the first indication that you are in the right place: A

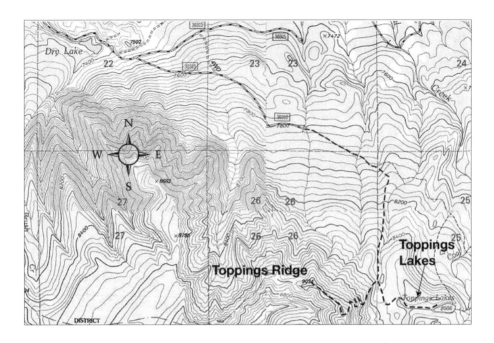

The ridge west of Toppings Lakes offers memorable views of the Teton Range.

small, wood forest service sign that reads "Toppings Lakes." The sign is placed just before a trail junction. The right fork steeply climbs .5 mile to a ridge above the lakes. Turning left once on the ridge and walking 10 minutes to a high point gains vistas of Mt. Leidy rising above Toppings Lakes. Walking right yields panoramic view of the Teton Range and Jackson Lake. Those who are lakebound may wish to add this rewarding side trip.

Bear left at the junction to proceed directly to the lakes. The path drops to the pond whose outlet you have been paralleling then gently descends open, flowered terrain to the first lake. It skirts that small lake's left (N) shore to its outflow to reach the second, prettier lake 1.7 miles beyond the trailhead. Look closely at the trees ringing this tarn: claw marks high on the trunks offer mute evidence that you are in bear country. Both lakes, but

the lower lake in particular, are partially covered with pond lilies. Wise fishermen know this means the lakes are generally too deep for hip waders.

The Gros Ventres

Introduction

The Gros Ventre Range, a rugged, weathered group of sedimentary peaks that trend northwest to southeast, defines the east side of Jackson Hole. A dozen summits surpass the 10,000 foot mark; an additional eight top 11,000 feet. Sheep Mountain and Pyramid Peak dominate the northwest end; Doubletop Peak, the highest in the range at 11,682 feet, rises near the eastern end.

First included in Teton Forest Reserve in 1897 and later in Teton National Forest in 1908, the bulk of the 300,000-acre range was placed under wilderness protection when Congress passed the 1984 Wyoming Wilderness Act. Wilderness designation protects the resource from both timbering and mining activity. The latter played a noteworthy part in the range's natural history. Coal was discovered near the upper end of Slide Lake in 1890. Two years later local businessmen formed the Jackson Hole Coal Company and began digging a 60-foot tunnel to access the 15-foot long vein. The mayor of Jackson burned the first lumps from the venture in 1924, but transportation problems prevented it from being more widely extracted. In more recent years oil and gas exploration and pressure from timbering companies, many of which have since closed or moved away, made passage of the wilderness bill a political dogfight.

Luckily, conservationists prevailed. The largely intact range is home to a large number of elk, deer, moose, bighorn sheep, black bears and grizzlies. Over 200 miles of trails rise from the sage-covered valley floor through flower-filled meadows, aspen and lodgepole. Engelmann spruce and alpine fir shade the trails as they near the crest. There are relatively few lakes but numerous streams and waterfalls, including spectacular three-tired Shoal Falls described in this section. Most of the trails are snow-free by late June.

Geologically, the Gros Ventre is a fascinating region. The sedimentary rocks were once the bottom of a long vanished inland sea. Roughly 50 million years ago a major uplift formed the peaks we know today, exposing a panoply of different sediments in the limestone, sandstone and shale that compose the range. The Red and Lavender Hills are a striking example of this striated, colorful rock.

The forces that uplifted the peaks are still active. Eight decades ago a sizeable tremor dislodged over 50 million cubic yards of earth and rock from the face of Sheep Mountain, sending it crashing to the bottom of the Gros Ventre River Canyon and 400 feet up the other side in less than three minutes. It has been estimated that if the Panama Canal had been excavated at the same rate of speed, the 51-mile trench would have been completed in less than an hour. The area, known as the Gros Ventre Slide, can be hiked and is also included in this section.

The Gros Ventres were first visited by Native Americans following game herds near what is now Pinedale, through the Upper Green River drainage and across the range into Jackson Hole. French trappers gave the migrants and the range its name in the early 1800s. One account holds that the Indians rubbed their hands over their stomachs to designate their tribal sign of three stripes around their waist. This was misinterpreted by the French as being the sign for the "big bellied" Indians, or "Gros Ventre." A second account believes that when the trappers saw the open canyons of the range, they exclaimed, "Gros Ventre!" or great opening.

Several trails included in this section are accessed from the National Elk Refuge but lie within the Jackson District of Bridger-Teton National Forest. These include Goodwin Lake, Sheep Creek Canyon and Curtis Canyon. In addition, one trail in this section is located in the National Elk Refuge: The Elk Refuge Nature Trail. Regulations specific to that hike are listed in the hike write-up. With these exceptions, unless otherwise signed, it is prohibited to leave the road in the National Elk Refuge.

Gros Ventre Wilderness Regulations

In addition to general forest regulations listed in this book's introduction, the following special regulations apply to the Gros Ventre Wilderness:

► Group size is limited to 15 persons and 25 pack and saddle stock.

► The maximum length of stay at any campsite is 16 days.

► Camping within 200 feet of any lake is prohibited.

► Tethering or picketing of stock within 200 feet of any lake, stream or trail is prohibited.

► Do not tie pack or saddle stock to any tree in a way that would cause injury or damage to the tree, vegetation or soil.

► Motorized and mechanized equipment is prohibited, including bicycles, chainsaws and hang gliders.

The Jackson District of Bridger-Teton National Forest administers the Gros Ventre Wilderness. For further information, please call or write:

Bridger-Teton National Forest
Jackson District
Box 1689
Jackson, Wyoming 83001
307-739-5400
www.fs.fed.us/r4/btnf/offices/jackson

62 Coyote Rock

Distance: 2 miles one-way
Elevation gain: Approx. 960 ft.
Maximum elevation: 7,670 ft.
Maps: Shadow Mountain
Season: Late June through September
Use restrictions: Wilderness regulations apply.

Coyote Rock is a large volcanic boulder hurled from a cataclysmic eruption in Yellowstone over two million years ago and subsequently carried by a glacier to its resting spot. Its name is derived from a mythical story written years ago by students participating in a course at nearby Teton Science School. The school often hikes its charges to the boulder to teach field geology.

The distinctive Huckleberry Ridge tuff boulder offers a nice turn-around destination for a wonderful ridge walk that offers near continuous Teton views and spectacular wildflowers.

Driving Directions

Travel approximately seven miles north of Jackson on U.S. Hwy 89/191 to the signed Gros Ventre Junction. Turn right and drive 7.2 miles to Kelly. It is an additional 1.2 miles to Gros Ventre Road on your right. Turn in and drive 2.2 miles to a Grand Teton National Park boundary sign. If you look up the hillside to your left, you will see a dirt two-track. This is the start of the hike. Drive .1 mile beyond the sign and park in the Forest Service pullout; there is a large information kiosk in the lot. Walk the short distance back up the road. The track angles off the north side of the road between the parking area and the park boundary sign.

Trail Description

The very steep, cobbled track initially heads west, then quickly bears right and travels north up open sage grassland slopes. As you climb, you immediately get a taste of the superb views that define this ridge walk. To your right (E), the Gros Ventre Slide dominates. Behind you is a scenic slice of the Gros Ventre River. The western horizon, of course, belongs to the Teton Range. Sulphur buckwheat, lupine yellow paintbrush, stickseed forget-me-not, balsamroot and salsify provide a colorful foreground in all directions.

The track parallels a pole and wire fence. As you continue ascending, it climbs at an easier grade until you reach a knoll with a fence line running over its apex. Here, you'll intersect a clear trail, Bear left onto it. The trail affords wonderful views right (E) into Turpin Creek drainage, and a panoramic sweep south to west of the town of Kelly, Snake River Range, Blacktail Butte and the Tetons from the Pass to Mount Moran. Sego lilies, blue flax, penstemon and groundsel thrive on the windward side of the ridge, and large amounts of elk scat indicate the terrain is often traversed by this ungulate.

Beyond the knoll, the trail gently climbs open slopes before dipping and re-ascending to Point 7578 on the Shadow Mountain topo map. It then gently des-

Top: The hike to Coyote Rock, pictured to the left, is characterized by near continuous Teton views and memorable wildflower displays.

cends again on the undulating ridge. Coyote rock appears ahead in the distance. Here, almost the entire length of the Tetons, framed by gorgeous wildflowers in season, comes into view.

You'll soon reach a junction. The trail to the left drops down to meadows and eventually Teton Science Schools' Kelly Campus. Continue straight.

The path gently descends then levels. Below you, to your right, you'll see an old cabin and beaver-created ponds in pretty Turpin Creek drainage.

The path descends before the final climb up, briefly obscuring Coyote Rock on the undulating ridge before it again pops into view.

Coyote Rock—composed of Huckleberry Ridge tuff—and the tongue of land upon which it rests, is the turn-around point of this hike. It's presence is a visual affirmation of the power of volcanic eruptions that rocked Yellowstone 2.2 million years ago. The gigantic eruptions spewed ash and debris over 800 miles into present day Nebraska, a phenomenon known as pyroclastic flow.

Molten rhyolite works its way to the surface of the Earth through faults. As the magma works its way to the surface, the pressure of overlying rock diminishes. This allows gas trapped in the magma to rapidly expand, propelling hot rocks and volcanic debris upward at supersonic speeds.

175

63 The Wedding Tree

Distance: .5 miles RT
Elevation gain: Negligible
Maximum elevation: Approx. 6,800 ft.
Maps: None needed
Season: May through October
Use restrictions: No camping. Forest regulations apply.

The stroll to the Wedding Tree is technically not a hike: it is a short walk that provides superb views of the Teton Range, framed by handsome Douglas fir and Engelmann spruce. One tree, in particular, offers such a spectacular foreground for that "perfect Teton shot" that it has become a popular spot for locals tying the knot. Conveniently, the access path to the site is located off a parking pullout area.

The destination is a great place for a picnic (remember to clean up after yourself!) or to enjoy a lazy afternoon soaking up the sun and reading a good book. It is also near the start/terminus for the Atherton Ridge hike (see no. 67) and should not be missed as a worthwhile extension to the day. Thus, it is included in this book.

More of a walk than a hike, the excursion to the Wedding Tree is a great place to picnic, relax and enjoy the amazing view.

Driving Directions

Drive approximately seven miles north of Jackson on U.S. Hwy 89/191 to the signed Gros Ventre Junction. Turn right (E) and drive 7.2 miles to the town of Kelly. Roughly a mile beyond town you'll see a paved road on the right that leads to Lower Slide Lake. Turn here and drive 3.6 miles to the wide pullout/parking area located at the elbow created by the road curving left. You'll see the obvious trail trending west off the right end of the parking area.

Trail Description

The level but at times rocky path heads almost due west toward the Tetons. In about a quarter-mile, the path ends at the aforementioned tree and lookout area. Beyond, the hillside drops away steeply. One of the nicest times to visit the Wedding Tree is early spring, when a riot of knee-high balsamroot are in bloom, painting the earth the color of sunshine. This plant's impressively long taproot allows it to thrive in dry climates. Elk and deer graze on the young shoots, and bighorn sheep munch on its leaves and flowerheads. Native American peoples also made extensive use of this hearty plant for medicine and food, steaming or roasting the leaves, roots, flower stems and seeds.

64 Gros Ventre Slide

Distance:
>Interpretive hike: .4 mile loop
>Slide: 1.6 miles one-way

Elevation gain:
>Interpretive hike: Approx. 60 ft.
>Slide: 720 ft.

Maximum elevation:
>Interpretive hike: Approx. 7,200 ft.
>Slide: 7,640 ft.

Maps: Shadow Mountain, Blue Miner Lake
Season: May through October
Use restrictions: No camping. Forest regulations apply.

On May 18, 1927, the small town of Kelly was destroyed by a tremendous flood that demolished its buildings and claimed six lives. The settlement was washed away by a wall of water so massive that the town of Wilson, miles away on the other side of the valley, was submerged under six feet of water before the flood subsided.

The event was the second act of a dramatic geologic play begun two years earlier. The afternoon of June 23, 1925, 50 million cubic yards of dirt, shale and Tensleep sandstone—heavily saturated by rain and loosened by earth tremors—slid off the face of Sheep Mountain. Gaining momentum quickly, the debris swept down the mountain at an estimated 50 miles per hour into the Gros Ventre River Canyon 2,000 feet below, then climbed 400 feet up the opposite side—all in under three minutes. The slide formed an earthen dam 225 feet high across the river, completely blocking it's flow and creating a five-mile long body of water that today is known as Lower Slide Lake.

State surveyors and engineers who subsequently visited the site believed the dam would hold permanently. They were wrong. Exceptionally heavy winter snow and rain in May of 1927 caused the lake to overflow the earthen dam and wash it away, creating the sudden and disastrous flood that decimated Kelly 3.5 miles downstream. Within hours the level of Lower Slide Lake dropped over 50 feet.

The event is clearly explained and the results viewed on a .4 mile interpretive trial constructed by the forest service and the YWCA.

Sadly, the deaths that occurred were preventable. Forest Service Ranger Charles Dibble and a man named Jack Ellis were removing driftwood and debris away from the Kelly bridge when they saw a hayrack floating down the river. (The hayrack had been floating in the newly-created Lower Slide Lake.)

Dibble and Ellis jumped into Dibble's Model T and drove toward the dam to check its condition. Upstream from Kelly, they saw a wall of water roaring down the canyon. They raced to a nearby house and had the resident telephone in an alarm. When they arrived back in Kelly, people had 15 minutes to flee to safety. Most did, but Milt Kneedy reportedly didn't believe the water was coming. He refused to leave and would not allow his foster son, Joe, or his wife, to go. All three perished. Clint Stevens was trying to save his livestock when he was hit by the wall of water and drown. Similarly, May Lovejoy and her sister, Maude Smith, had loaded their wagon with valuables. They left so late that their horse became frightened by the oncoming water and raced toward it. The water swallowed the wagon in its path. May's body was never found; Maude's was recovered when the flood subsided.

Driving Directions

Travel seven miles north of Jackson on U.S. Hwy 89/191 to the signed Gros Ventre Junction. Turn right and drive 7.2 miles to the town of Kelly. It is an additional 1.2 miles to Gros Ventre Road on your right. Turn in and drive 4.6 miles

The Gros Ventre Slide, seen from the USFS loop.

to the Gros Ventre Slide Interpretive Trail pullout on the right.

Trail Description

The Forest Service interpretive trail begins near the restroom. Signs every 30 or so yards identify points of interest, including trees, bushes and geology. As the loop trail nears Slide Lake, benches provide a nice spot to enjoy the view.

After reading the display and walking the interpretive loop, skilled hikers may wish to visit the slide itself. This is most easily accomplished by following the main drainage up the slide's face, a difficult cross-country route that involves walking through heavy brush and loose talus.

To reach the face of the slide, drive 150-200 yards past the interpretive pullout to a dirt road on your right that leads down to the lake. The narrow road crosses the bridge below Slide Lake in a half mile. Turn right onto a jeep trail shortly after crossing the bridge and park. Hike along the jeep trail, staying right of the creek. Bear left toward the drainage as the jeep trail begins to turn right. Climb above the brush on the loose rock, avoiding the steeper slide wall as you work your way up the boulder fields.

Three-quarters of a mile up the slide you'll reach a group of conifers that provide a good stopping point to view this incredible geologic phenomenon. The trees themselves have a story to tell. Several near the toe of the slide grow at peculiar angles. They were swept down the slide with their roots intact in the soil, stopping at the position they grow today.

The drainage can be ascended to the top of the fracture, a challenging boulder route that should not be attempted by the inexperienced. Hikers are advised that the terrain and rock on the slide path is unstable and rough. Proceed with appropriate caution.

65 Atherton Ridge

Distance: 4.5 miles one-way
Elevation gain/loss: Approx. 1,420 ft.
Maximum elevation: Approx. 8,400 ft.
Maps: Shadow Mountain. Book map pg. 181
Season: Late May through October
Use restrictions: Motorized use prohibited.

Sweeping views of the Teton Range, Red Hills and Gros Ventre Slide make this walk a favored outing. Its mid-range elevation makes it accessible comparatively early in the season. While not exceedingly long, several steep, sustained pitches leave you feeling that you've gotten exercise for the day. Good off-road parking is available at both ends. Because walking east to west provides the best sustained views of the Tetons, this direction is described below.

Driving Directions

Drive approximately seven miles north of Jackson on U.S. Hwy. 89/191 to the signed Gros Ventre Junction. Turn right (E) and drive 7.2 miles to the town of Kelly. Roughly a mile beyond town you'll see a paved road on the right that leads to Lower Slide Lake. Turn here and drive 5.9 miles to Atherton Campground on the right side of the road. Park near the campground or the boat ramp. The unsigned but clear trail begins opposite the campground off the left side of the Gros Ventre Road. The descent from the plateau comes out near the parking area for the Wedding Tree. (See hike no. 65). If you are in a group and are shuttling a vehicle, leave one of the vehicles here.

Trail Description

The jeep trail immediately ascends open, south-facing grassy slopes dotted with aspen and spruce and colored with cornflower, desert parsley, evening prim-rose, wild strawberry, agoseris and vetch. The trail jogs right (E) then left (NW), soon reaching an area dotted with small ponds that dry up as the season progresses. It soon veers east and steeply climbs a dry, south-facing slope smattered with limber pine to reach the south end of a north/south trending spur, where you'll gain your first views of the stunning Red Hills.

Once on the ridgeline you'll pick up a distinct trail. Bear left (N) and continue ascending to Point 7925 on the Shadow Mountain topo. Here, views of the south end of the Tetons unfold.

The path curls left (N) and gently descends a short distance, skirting a forest of limber pine and subalpine fir to your right, before resuming a brief but steep climb up the undulating ridgeline. You will dip and climb twice more before reaching the top of the ridge and a well-used trail. Turn left (W) here. The path cuts through open terrain that opens spectacular views of the Gros Ventre Slide to your left (SW). Violets and lupine sprinkle the ground beneath your feet. The path soon intersects a two-track used by mountain bikers. The old 4WD track is part of a network of roads/trails between Turpin, Atherton and Horsetail Creeks. Armed with a topo map, GPS or compass, there are many

179

Top: The Atherton Ridge hike showcases the Teton Range and the Gros Ventre Slide. Right: Evening primrose, sego lilies, and other wildflowers that flourish on dry, sunny slopes are seen on the ascent.

route/trail options to explore on this broad plateau. To complete the ridge walk, bear left.

The path curls more directly south and begins descending at a moderate, steady grade through open pine forest and grass and sage-covered slopes. It skirts a stand of Douglas fir before gently ascending a short distance to a knoll, where views of the geologically-fascinating Gros Ventre Slide at the 11 o'clock position and the Tetons dead ahead are unveiled.

Panoramic vistas of the latter improve as the trail nears the grassy end of the plateau. Copious scat attests to the fact that grouse, elk and deer frequently visit the area. The path begins dropping off the plateau, bending toward the Gros Ventre Slide, now in front of you. It then gently climbs to a junction. Stay left here and again when the trail divides a second time. The path gently climbs to the top

of a hillock and panoramic vistas. You'll soon reach two sections of buckrail fence. Beyond them, the trail drops very steeply and the town of Kelly pops into view.

After crossing a short, level section of grassy terrain covered with balsamroot and larkspur, the trail drops very steeply to a third split. Again, keep left. It eventually travels under a powerline and drops to the road near the pullout for the Wedding Tree.

If you have shuttled a vehicle, this is the end of your hike. If not, either try to catch a ride from the pullout, or carefully walk against traffic to return to your vehicle in another 2.4 miles.

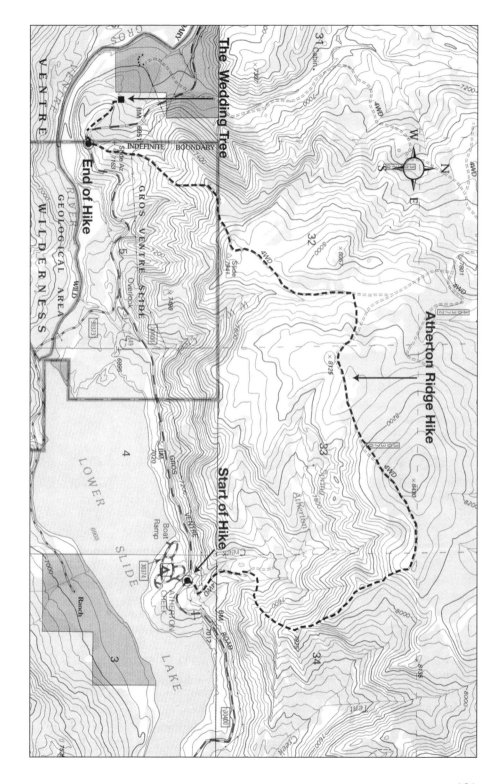

The Wedding Tree

End of Hike

Atherton Ridge Hike

Start of Hike

INDEFINITE BOUNDARY

GROS VENTRE SLIDE

GROS VENTRE RIVER GEOLOGICAL AREA

WILDERNESS

LOWER SLIDE LAKE

ATHERTON CREEK

66 Red and Lavender Hills

Distance: 4.2 miles RT
Elevation gain/loss: 1,460 ft.
Maximum elevation: 8,560 ft.
Maps: Grizzly Lake, Mt. Leidy
Season: Late May through October
Use restrictions: Wildlife winter closure from Dec. 15 to April 30.
Closed to motorized use.

A walk to the Red and Lavender Hills in the Gros Ventre Range northeast of Jackson offers a wonderful panorama of the Tetons and the surrounding area. From atop a ridge, the range skyrockets above a striking foreground of colorful cliffs and slopes that give the surrounding terrain its name.

Driving Directions

Drive approximately seven miles north of Jackson on U.S. Hwy 89/191 to the signed Gros Ventre Junction. Turn right (E) and drive 7.2 miles to the town of Kelly. Roughly a mile beyond town you'll see a paved road on the right that leads to Lower Slide Lake. Turn here and drive 10 miles to the trail sign on the left side of the road. Park in the wide pull-off area on the right (S) side of the road.

Trail Description

The trail gently ascends through terrain sprinkled with blue-eyed grass, groundsel, sulfur paintbrush, cinquefoil, yarrow and wild iris. The big sage just left of the trail is among the largest in the valley, with hardy clumps exceeding five feet in height.

The path soon enters a narrowing draw lined with aspen and willow and begins climbing in a northeast direction at an increasingly steep grade. The red shale and sandstone soil are reminiscent of the desert Southwest, providing a startling contrast to the surrounding forested mountains and jagged peaks.

The grade moderates and the narrow draw widens as you approach a saddle on a 8,160-foot ridge at 1.6 miles. The impressive, gray-blue striated Lavender Hills lie directly north, while rugged 11,000-foot peaks of the Gros Ventre range rise south. This viewpoint is a wonderful place to take a break, soak in the panorama, and have a sip of water. Be sure to bring plenty with you, as none is available on the hike. The unshaded ridges can radiate intense heat on a hot day.

At the saddle, you'll reach a T-junction. The trail to the right gently ascends through grassy terrain to the east end of the ridge, marked as Point 8166 on the topographic map. To continue to the highest viewpoint and fine views of the surrounding terrain, bear left at the junction. The trail climbs quite steeply to the top of a second ridge graced with limber pine. This viewpoint is 400 feet higher and a half-mile farther. It yields

Top: The striated, purplish-gray Lavender Hills are showcased on the hike through neighboring Red Hills. Left: Bighorn sheep frequent the steep slopes.

one of the prettiest vistas in the area, with both the Teton Range and the Red Hills before you. The higher vantage point also opens up views of the Sleeping Indian and sapphire-blue Grizzly Lake.

Sunset is a particularly appealing time to be here. The sun sets the Red Hills on fire before slipping behind the Tetons and rimming the peaks in gold. The Red Hills are part of the Chugwater Formation, 180-

million-year-old layers of gypsum, red shales, sandstone and siltstones that were once on the bottom of an ancient sea. The easily eroded formation also comprises the dramatic badlands terrain near Dubois. The purplish gray clay of the Cloverly Formation gives the adjacent Lavender Hills its distinctive coloration and name. This 120-130 million year old formation covers parts of northern Wyoming and southwest Montana. Like the Chugwater Formation, the Cloverly Formation tends to be unstable and slides easily. Landslides are common throughout the Gros Ventre and are particularly visible along the course of the Gros Ventre Road.

Scan the hills carefully for the bighorn sheep that frequent the area, protected from predators by the steepness of the cliffs. Retrace your steps to your vehicle.

67 Grizzly Lake

68 Blue Miner Lake/Sheep Mtn.

Grizzly Lake

Distance: 3.7 miles one-way
Elevation gain: Approx. 810 ft.
Elevation loss: Approx. 640 ft.
Maximum elevation: Approx. 7,600 ft.
Maps: Grizzly Lake, Blue Miner Lake. Book map opposite page
Season: Mid-May through October
Use restrictions: Motorized use prohibited.

Blue Miner Lake/Sheep Mtn.

Distance:
    Blue Miner Lake: 6.5 miles one-way
    Sheep Mountain summit: 9 miles one-way
Elevation gain:
    Blue Miner Lake: Approx. 2,950 ft.
    Sheep Mountain summit: Approx. 4,400 ft.
Maximum elevation:
    Blue Miner Lake: Approx. 9,750 ft.
    Sheep Mountain summit: 11,239 ft.
Maps: Grizzly Lake, Blue Miner Lake.
Season: Mid-July through early September
Use restrictions: Wilderness regulations in effect.

Grizzly Lake lies in the undulating foothills of the Gros Ventre Range. The pleasant hike to the lake travels through open sagebrush country punctuated with wildflowers, aspen groves and scattered conifers, all backdropped by the colorful Red and Lavender Hills.

Grizzly Lake's low elevation offers a snow-free alternative to higher, often impassable trails early season. It's also a good late-season choice, when snow has closed the high country but lower elevations are still dressed in autumn's patchwork of gold and russet vegetation.

The first portion of the trail to the lake is also the start of the longer hike to Sheep Mountain and Blue Miner Lake. Sheep Mountain is known locally as the Sleeping Indian. It doesn't take much imagination to see the shape of a giant Indian lying down, his stomach and body the long, gradual slope of the main peak to the north and his head—with its pointy nose and headdress—the 11,106 foot subsidiary peak to the south. A scramble to the top of the Indian's belly, the true summit, is blessed with grand views of the valley and the distant snow-covered Wind River Range on the northeast horizon.

Blue Miner Lake rests below Sleeping

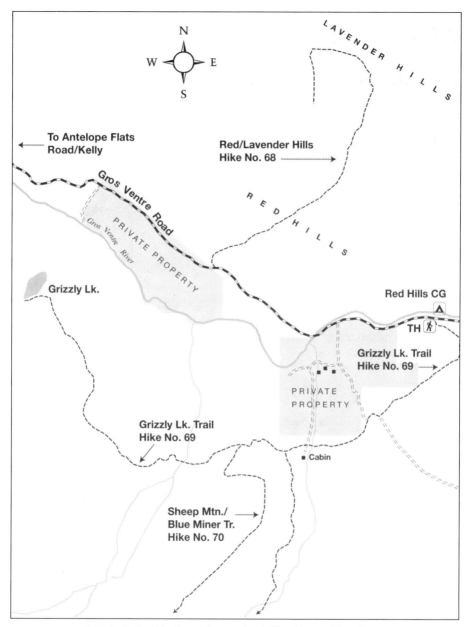

Grizzly Lake, Red and Lavender Hills, Sheep Mtn. Trails

Indian, a sparkling jewel whose beauty is enhanced by its wild, rugged setting. The hike to the lake gains almost 3,000 feet. While it can be done in a long day, the trip is an ideal 2-3 day backpacking trip to allow time to scramble up the Indian and explore the surrounding area.

Driving Directions

Drive north of Jackson on U.S. Hwy.

185

189/191 to Gros Ventre Junction. Turn right at the junction and drive past the town of Kelly at 7.2 miles to the signed Gros Ventre Road at 8.4 miles. Turn right and drive 11.3 miles to the trailhead on the right side of the road, opposite the Red Hills Campground.

Trail Description

The trail parallels the road a short distance before turning southeast and crossing a meadow on an old jeep two-track. In a quarter-mile the signed trail turns right off the track and gradually ascends predominantly open terrain that yields views of the Grand Teton. It then descends to a fence encircling private property and follows it on a mostly level course through open lodgepole forest. You'll pass a faint split left of the trail. Stay on the main path by the fence line until you reach a sign that reads "trail." Bear left here, away from the fence. The trail passes through a section of blue spruce and drops to a bridged crossing of an irrigation ditch. Turn left after the bridge and walk a short distance to a plank crossing of East Miner Creek.

Beyond the creek, the path climbs west at a moderate grade via two switchbacks to the top of small slope, then turns right (N) the descents to a plank crossing of West Miner Creek. You'll reach a small run-off stream, easily jumped over, a short distance farther.

The trail now climbs at a moderately steep grade up open slopes, passing a backcountry cabin set back from the trail to your left at 1.4 miles. The path descends and curls right, then follows an undulating course south as it parallels a small stream right of the trail. It then ascends to a signed junction with the trail to Blue Miner Lake and Sheep Mountain at 1.8 miles.

To reach Grizzly Lake

Bear right at the junction. The trail drops into a wet, willow-lined basin.

The Red Hills are prominently featured on the hike to Grizzly Lake.

Beavers' handiwork can be observed here. A dam flooded a portion of the original trail in the 1970s, forcing it to be rerouted. The path hops two small rivulets then steadily ascends at a moderate grade to the top of a 7,600-foot ridge at 2.4 miles, the high point of this hike. The small rise offers a nice view of the Lavender and Red Hills to the north and the Teton Range to the northwest.

The path descends the hill then follows a level to slightly downhill course through a large meadow before dropping at a moderate grade down an open hillside. It gradually curves right then left and passes an outfitter's area marked by a trough and hitching pole. A short distance ahead, you'll reach a sign that reads "Grizzly Lake." Beyond it, the path drops to the southwest end of the lake.

If you enjoy fishing, Grizzly Lake won't disappoint you. In the early 1980s the Wyoming Game and Fish Department helicopter stocked the lake with both native cutthroat and brook trout. The best camping is found in the scattered trees near Grizzly Lake's southwest shore. The north and east shores of the lake are predominantly open meadowland.

To reach Blue Miner and Sheep Mtn.

Bear left at the signed junction. The trail steadily climbs an open slope. At a blazed arrow it turns left and steeply climbs the crest of a ridge to a point marked "8497" on the Grizzly Lake quad, 3.2 miles beyond the trailhead. The Sleeping Indian dominates the view to the southwest, while the familiar Teton skyline is silhouetted to the northwest.

The trail drops slightly at a saddle before resuming its steep climb, eventually bearing left to the edge of a sheer drop-off. On a clear day, the jagged peaks of the 50-mile distant Wind River Range are seen to the east-southeast.

Beyond the overlook, walk right toward a wildflower-filled clearing and ascend through fir and limber pine to reach an alpine meadow. The trail often fades out along the mile-long path through grass that ensues. Stay toward the middle of the meadow and look for a blazed pine in the left treeline near the meadow's end.

Follow the blazes another half mile to the trees at the edge of the amphitheater above the lake, 6.1 miles beyond the trailhead. The high ridge overlooks the often snow-covered cirque above Blue Miner and a startlingly blue, unnamed lake to the southeast, locally dubbed Betty Davis' Eyes. Continue on the ridge until you reach a cairn marking a route that descends west to Blue Miner Lake 550 feet below you. Campsites can be found on the lake's south and west shores.

From the south shore of Blue Miner, it is a non-technical but steep 1,800-foot scramble to the belly of the Indian. The cirque frequently contains snow until early August. Late season it is usually possible to reach the north ridge of the main summit without crossing significant snowfields.

If you are not dropping to the lake, Sleeping Indian can be climbed by staying on the ridge and walking west. Follow the ridge until it curves south. From here, it is a steep ascent of 1,100 feet and another 2.0 miles to Sheep Mountain's summit.

The Sleeping Indian was tragically the focus of national attention the summer of 1996. Following an August visit to Jackson Hole by President Clinton, an Air Force cargo plane carrying Secret Service personnel and equipment made a night departure from the local airport to return to the capitol.

The pilot ignored or misunderstood flight pattern instructions and crashed into the side of the mountain, killing all nine on board.

69 Alkali Ridge

Distance: 2.4 miles to crest
Elevation gain: Approx. 1,750 ft.
Maximum elevation: 9,348 ft.
Maps: Grizzly Lake
Season: July through September
Use restrictions: Closed to motorized uses and mountain bikes

The ascent to Alkali Ridge is rewarded with sweeping views of Crystal Creek drainage and remote Hidden Basin. Few places in the Gros Ventre Wilderness rival the impressive panorama gained at the ridge crest. Pyramid, Crystal and Antoinette Peaks rise steeply above the narrow creek canyon, framing the wooded chasm from the southwest to the southeast. Views of the Teton Range are enjoyed on the climb to the ridge, wildflowers find the terrain to their liking and elk are often seen in the vicinity. It is unlikely you will spy another soul on this delightful but little-known trail.

Driving Directions

Travel north of town on U.S. Hwy. 89/191 to the signed Gros Ventre Junction. Turn right and drive 7.2 miles to Kelly. Continue an additional 1.2 miles to the Gros Ventre access road on your right. Turn in and drive past Crystal Creek Campground at 11.8 miles to a narrow bridge over Crystal Creek and a signed junction at 12.8 miles. Road #30377 to your right travels to Red Rock Ranch (not open to the public) and Crystal Creek Trailhead. The road to your left leads to Slate Creek. Set your odometer and continue straight. It is 2.4 miles to an unsigned road to Alkali Creek on your

right. Turn in here and drive to a split in the road at .4 mile. The left branch leads to corrals and covered hay storage. Park off road near the split and walk up the right branch of the road. It soon narrows to trail width.

Trail Description

The road climbs at a moderate grade, immediately opening views of the Teton Range to your right (W). You'll soon pass a wilderness sign posted on a tree reminding users that the area is closed to motor vehicles, motorized equipment, hang gliders and bikes. Leave the two-track just beyond the sign and angle right toward a post on a ridge ahead of you. You'll soon gain a clear trail on the ridge near a transect location marker.

The path ascends the ridge at a moderate grade. Early season, the terrain is sprinkled with a garden of wildflowers that includes wild rose, columbine, penstemon, vetch and flax. Tracks and sign indicate elk frequent the area and numerous badger holes are seen—including a rather large, ankle-busting cavity in the middle of the trail.

The trail bears slightly right toward a lone limber pine near a rock outcropping. It stays right of treeline on the open ridge, becoming somewhat faint as it crests a

The hike to Alkali Ridge leads to this view into Crystal Creek drainage.

small rise. As the gradient eases it soon becomes clear again and eventually bears left (E) in a gentle arc, descending slightly before turning south and entering sage-covered terrain. Looking west yields sweeping views of the Tetons.

Bearing east again, the path gently descends through open aspen and spruce forest that provides welcome shade on a hot day. Columbine and bluebells thrive near a small spring.

The trail curls west then south before hopping a small rivulet and climbing at a steeper grade through open forest. A rivulet flows down the draw to your left, its course lined by bluebells. You'll soon reach a meadow colored mid-summer with yellow mule's ears, lavender lupine, fiery red scarlet gilia and mauve sticky geraniums. Beyond, the trail bends left and skirts a deteriorating aspen grove.

Stay left at an unmarked trail junction; the path to the right leads to a herder's camp. The trail climbs at a moderate grade as you re-enter wooded terrain. Upon reaching another open area, it bears left and proceeds at a gentler grade, gradually turning right as it enters open forest. Traveling in and out of spruce forest, the path leads to the toe of a grassy ridge. The moderately steep climb to its crest angles toward a rocky bench dotted with limber pine.

Reaching the ridge crest at 2.4 miles, the trail turns left (SE) and follows its undulating spine, unveiling spectacular views into Crystal Creek drainage and Hidden Basin. Framed by 11,107-ft. Pyramid Peak, 11,407-ft. Antoinette Peak and 10,987-ft. Crystal Peak, the panorama is among the most striking in the Gros Ventre Wilderness. The trail follows the ridge for a mile-and-a-half before petering out. Those skilled in cross-country travel can plot a route to Two Echo Park and the Six Lakes beyond, presenting numerous opportunities for an extended day or backpacking trip.

70 Curtis Canyon

Distance: 3.2 miles RT
Elevation change: Approx. 550 ft.
Maximum elevation: 7,020 ft.
Maps: Gros Ventre Junction
Season: May through November
Use restrictions: Critical winter range. Area closed Dec. 1 – April 30.
Private property at mouth of canyon. No through access.

Away from the bustle of Jackson but still close to town, this lower elevation, short hike is a favorite spring or end-of-the-day summer destination. It begins and ends with views of the Teton Range rising above the large, undeveloped expanse that defines the National Elk Refuge. Stretch your legs by walking this small but scenic canyon after work, then enjoy a picnic dinner at the overlook as you watch the sun set behind the Grand.

Driving Directions

From the Jackson Town Square, drive one mile east on Broadway to the National Elk Refuge. Turn left onto the broad access road. At 3.5 miles, the road turns sharply left at the intersection with the Twin Creek Ranch Road and travels north another 1.1 miles to a second intersection marked by a large National Elk Refuge information sign. Bear right at this junction. The gravel road travels east for 1.4 miles before veering south and climbing via several long switchbacks to the signed Curtis Canyon Viewpoint, a total of 7.1 miles beyond Broadway. Turn into the overlook and park off the side of the road. Cross the road and walk left a short distance to Curtis Canyon Campground. Twenty or so yards down the campground access road, you'll see a single section of cross-barred buck-and-rail fence to your left. The trail begins on the old two-track road behind the fence section.

Trail Description

The grassy two-track—and artifacts you'll see along the trail—date back to the Curtis brothers, early settlers who ranched at the mouth of the canyon and for whom the canyon is named. Their temperaments earned them the nicknames "Slow-up" and "Flare-up."

The level track traverses open terrain spiked with Engelmann Spruce and Douglas fir. Plentiful scat and tracks testify that sheep, moose and elk all frequent the area. You'll soon reach a log anchored in cement abutments baring onward vehicle travel. Here, the track begins descending at an easy grade into the narrowing canyon. Early season, a few hardy bluebells draw enough moisture from snowmelt to poke their nodding heads between the tracks. You'll pass the rusted remains of an old tractor to your right and a small tributary of North Twin Creek to your left. North and South Twin Creeks begin high in the Gros Ventre Range near Jackson Peak. They flow into Nowlin Creek, which in turn flows into Flat Creek. Sandstone and gneiss outcroppings cap the crest of the north canyon wall and large erratics on the canyon floor speak to the chasm's glacial origin.

Top: The wooded character of Curtis Canyon adds to its beauty. Left: An old tractor is one of numerous artifacts of human activity hikers view as they walk through the canyon.

The track hops North Twin and enters pleasant subalpine fir and blue spruce forest. You'll pass a small pond and gravity-fed water pipes on the right. Historically, residents of Twin Creek Ranch at the mouth of the canyon got their water from the spring-fed creek, although few new homes in the subdivision do today. You'll see a pile of rusted, discarded water pipe at the mouth of the canyon.

Continue descending straight where a road to the left heads uphill. (This travels a short distance and ends.) The track

begins dropping at a steeper grade into denser forest. Meandering North Twin passes through a culvert under the track to the left side of the track. Listen for pikas' warning alarm in the numerous small rock slides to your right.

As you near the mouth of the canyon, the trees recede to unveil views of the Teton Range ahead. Here, elk and moose have severely cropped stands of willow lining the creek. These fast-growing deciduous shrubs nonetheless manage to produce new buds each spring, assuring the return of important forage every winter.

The track ends in a flat grassy area interspersed with clumps of aspen at 1.6 miles. Shortly beyond, it joins Twin Creek Ranch Road. This is private property. Please respect property rights and retrace your steps to return to your vehicle.

71 Goodwin Lake and Jackson Peak

Distance:
  Goodwin Lake: 6 miles RT
  Jackson Peak: 10.4 miles RT
Elevation gain:
  Goodwin Lake: Approx. 1,370 ft.
  Jackson Peak: Approx. 2,580 ft.
Maximum elevation:
  Goodwin Lake: 9,500 ft.
  Jackson Peak: 10,741 ft.
Maps: Cache Creek, Turquoise Lake
Season:
  Goodwin Lake: Late June through September
  Jackson Peak: Mid-July through mid-September
Use restrictions: Wilderness regulations apply.
  Mountain biking and motorized vehicles prohibited.

Landmark Jackson Peak is one of the closest hikeable summits to the town of Jackson. From its 10,741-foot apex, sweeping views of the valley and Gros Ventre Wilderness fan out. Pretty Goodwin Lake at its base offers anglers fine trout fishing, making this hike a good choice for a group with different interests.

Driving Directions

The trailhead to Goodwin and Jackson Peak is reached by driving to the end of east Broadway and turning left onto the National Elk Refuge. Follow the switchbacking dirt road as it climbs past the turnoff to Curtis Canyon Campground at 7.5 miles to reach the signed junction with Sheep Creek Road at 9.2 miles. Bear right here and drive another mile to the large trailhead parking area. This last mile can be in bad shape, but is navigable if driven slowly.

Trail Description

Though clear and easy to follow, the trail has been moved south of its plotted location on the topo map. It climbs at a moderate grade via switchbacks through mostly open slopes studded with towering Douglas fir. Wild rose, salsify and sticky geraniums thrive in the shade at their base. Near the crest of the slope, whitebark pine and subalpine fir replace the Douglas fir.

The trail climbs at an easier grade when you reach the crest of the ridge at .9 mile. Views of the Tetons to your right (W) and into Sheep Creek Canyon to your left (E) unfold through breaks in the forest.

The trail steadily ascends the ridge to reach the signed Gros Ventre Wilderness boundary in another .3 mile. Beyond, it leaves the trees and traverses a rocky, shallow draw strewn with large boulders.

On the far side of the draw the trail

Goodwin Lake is a popular fishing and day hike destination for Jackson residents.

re-enters the woods and soon parallels the creek flowing out of Goodwin Lake. It crosses the outlet creek at 2.8 miles, reaching the north end of the lake .2 mile farther.

Paths loop around both sides of Goodwin. The wooded left (E) path leads to good campsites several hundred feet up the trail. The right fork recrosses the creek and follows the west side of the lake. Please respect the signs identifying areas closed for regeneration, and comply with wilderness regulations by camping a minimum of 200 feet away from the lakeshore.

Goodwin Lake is named after a Jackson Hole mountain man who trapped numerous creeks in the area. Goodwin would bring in a pack string of traps and supplies from Idaho before the heavy snows of November made travel difficult. After unloading and setting up a base camp, he'd send the animals home, since he had no means to feed them over the course of a long Jackson Hole winter. He trapped and lived by himself through the winter.

With the arrival of spring, he'd cache his furs and remaining supplies and point his feet toward Idaho, eventually crossing Teton Pass to retrieve his pack string. He'd then return to collect his hard-earned furs.

Jackson Peak

To reach Jackson Peak, stay on the trail around the left side of the lake. It parallels the lake's east shoreline for a quarter-mile, winding through a forest floor studded with large boulders and shaded by mature Engelmann spruce, Douglas fir and limber pine. Early season, swaths of spring beauties form a white carpet.

Near the end of the east shoreline, the trail bends left away from the lake and switchbacks up through the forest to enter

Top: The Sleeping Indian, seen from the summit of Jackson Peak. Right: A hiker surveys the view from Jackson Peak's large summit marker.

an open expanse. It then climbs more gradually toward a small divide. You'll pass a small pond to your left at 3.8 miles that disappears as the season progresses. Near the top of the divide, at 4.3 miles, you'll reach a cairn right of the trail that marks a somewhat fainter trail angling southwest toward the south end of Jackson Peak's summit ridge. This trail—clearly forged after the last edition of this book—is the path you want. Though longer than the former cross-country route it is a good deal easier. The path steadily climbs up to the ridge, the grade increasing as you more steeply ascend small, tight switchbacks leading to the ridgetop at 4.8 miles. From here, it is a moderately easy, though rocky ascent to the summit, marked by a very large cairn that seems to grow every time this author revisits the peak. It is a local tradition to add a rock to the already impressive marker.

Though there are vistas of the length of the Teton Range to the west, the eternally slumbering Sleeping Indian, closer Cache Peak, and waves of the high ridges of the Gros Ventre Range to the east steal the show.

72 Sheep Creek Canyon to the Ski Cabin

Distance: 4.2 miles one-way
Elevation gain: Approx. 1,380 ft.
Maximum elevation: 9, 550 ft.
Maps: Blue Miner Lake, Turquoise Lake.
Season: July through September
Use restrictions: Wilderness regulations apply

The historic ski cabin is located at the head of pretty Sheep Creek Canyon. A very rough access road, numerous creek crossings, uncertain trail in the upper reaches of the canyon and the difficulty of *finding* the cabin means you likely won't see another soul on this worthwhile, but only lightly visited destination.

Driving Directions

The trailhead is reached by driving to the end of east Broadway in the town of Jackson and turning left onto the National Elk Refuge. Follow the switchbacking dirt road as it climbs past the turnoff to Curtis Canyon Campground to reach the signed junction with Sheep Creek Road at 9.2 miles. Bear left here and drive another 2.6 miles to a dirt road on the right. Pull in and drive as far as you want to punish your vehicle. Mileage for this hike is calculated from the intersection of a second entry point on the dirt access road, just over .1 mile from the turn-off. (Consult the updated Blue Miner topo map.) Pull-off road and park.

Trail Description

This description begins with a walk up the rocky road. It travels above Sheep Creek, providing pretty views into the canyon to your right. Left, the flowered hillside is punctuated by large Douglas firs. You'll soon pass a dirt road to your right that leads to an outfitters camp.

Continue straight until the end of the road, marked by a buck-and-rail fence and a sign indicating motorized traffic beyond this point is prohibited.

Follow the narrowing road/trail to a plank crossing over Sheep Creek. A short distance farther, the path again bumps into meandering Sheep Creek. The trail plotted on the Blue Miner Topo indicates the trail crosses the creek and travels up its right side. The existing trail has been moved. Instead of crossing the creek, stay on the path that travels along its left bank as it moderately climbs through shady forest that supports columbine, wild strawberry and bluebells.

After about 20 minutes of walking, you'll reach another creek crossing. Look to your right and you'll see a log over the creek. The summer of 2008, a guide rope had been strung near the log to assist people with balance. The rope may not be there in the future. Guide ropes and bright flagging were put in place that summer to assist volunteers hauling in materials to repair the roof of the ski cabin. The creek here is not deep, but it is lively and wide enough that you'll get your feet wet if you choose to forego the log.

Beyond the crossing, the trail climbs a short hill and enters an open park, then drops and crosses the steam three times in quick order. Logs are in place at the crossings. Shortly after the crossings, an easily stepped over spring bubbles over the path. Watercress grows in abandon here, and it is a nice place to take a break if you are so inclined.

Beyond, the trail moderately climbs, passing a rockslide area to your left. It then travels through forested areas and open parks to reach the signed Gros Ventre Wilderness boundary.

An easy climb through lodgepole forest leads to a large opening with views of the steep sedimentary walls of upper Sheep Creek Canyon. The trail moderately climbs through this open area, then steeply ascends through a forest, traveling parallel to but above Sheep Creek to your right. The tread becomes faint as you enter a meadow. Maintain the same direction, and you should pick it up again in the woods.

The path skirts around spring-created bogs farther on and ascends toward the head of the canyon, generally keeping to the left side, until you enter an open basin defined by rock walls to the east. This is a lovely spot, and a fine turn-around destination for those not comfortable with potential cross-country exploration. To continue toward the ski cabin, angle right and forward as if you were heading toward a 2 o'clock position. You'll travel moderately uphill through forest to a second grassy area. Walk toward a rocky hump, then right through the woods, where you'll likely pick up the "real" trail. It crosses the creek and travels west a short distance before reaching the ski cabin, hidden until almost the last moment. This is definitely an outing where you want to have the Turquoise Lake topo map and know how to read it. Look back frequently so you have a mental picture of the terrain to help guide you on your return. There is nowhere to go but up—but trail travel is certainly easier and a lot more pleasant.

The historic ski cabin will likely be locked as it is open only to winter use. The 16x20 foot structure was built in 1953 by the Jackson Hole Ski Club, which obtained a special use permit from the Forest Service. Probe poles and shovels are stocked inside. A sign on the door cautions users that in January of 1976 and March of 1977, three cross-country skiers were killed in two separate avalanches near the cabin.

Hikers descend the head of Sheep Creek Canyon.

The historic ski cabin, before its 2008 new roof!

73 Cream Puff Peak

Distance: 9.8 miles RT
Elevation gain: Approx. 3,410 ft.
Maximum elevation: 9,685 ft.
Maps: Bull Creek
Season: Late June through mid-October
Use restrictions: Wilderness regulations apply

Cream Puff is a pleasing peak hike. Deer and elk are often seen on the lower stretches of trail. Wildflowers on the open slopes are prolific and varied, including not often seen wild hollyhocks, sugar bowl and sego lilies. And, the view from the 9,685-foot summit is superb. North, the Tetons are viewed from Teton Pass to Mount Moran. The Gros Ventre Range fills the eastern skyline, while the distant Winds are seen to the southeast. Continuing the panoramic circle, the Hoback, Wyoming and Salt River Ranges define the southern sky. West, the peaks of the Snake River Range are displayed. This is a summit on which to linger.

Driving Directions

Drive 13 miles south of Jackson on U.S. Hwy. 189/191 13 miles to Hoback Junction. Bear left toward Pinedale. The highway crosses three bridges over the Hoback River, the last 9.8 miles from the junction. At 10.6 miles you'll reach the somewhat abrupt Bull Creek turnoff on your left. Drive .1 mile up this unsigned dirt road and park in the grassy area to your right. Note: The trailhead has been moved since the topo was plotted. The new path joins the plotted trail at .4 mile.

Trail Description

Walk a short distance up the road, looking ahead to your left toward the edge of the trees. Tucked near treeline is an almost-hidden Forest Service trail marker signed "Cow Creek Trail." The path travels south before bending west and paralleling the highway below, gradually climbing to an intersection at .4 mile. This is the end of the former Cow Creek jeep road shown on the map. Walk straight at the intersection and ascend open slopes. You'll soon pass under a powerline. Its support pole is marked with a "National Forest Wilderness" sign, reminding users that the trail is closed to both motorized equipment and mountain bikes.

Continue to ascend sage-covered hillsides, enjoying views of Beaver Mountain to your left. At .8 mile, the trail briefly switchbacks and begins angling more steadily northwest away from the highway. Cow Creek is heard but unseen below you to your left. The trail drops slightly than resumes its relentless climb up the creek drainage. You'll soon reach the first of many trail divisions up this rutted drainage. Take either side: the paths consistently merge into one trail.

Hop a small rivulet and then the upper reaches of Cow Creek at 1.3 miles, and climb toward scattered groves of aspen. The path enters a welcome, shady stretch .3 mile farther. As it continues to ascend you gain views of the Gros Ventre Range to your right (E) and bare, cone-shaped Peak 10,013 ahead (N). The distinctive

Top and right: The hike to Cream Puff's summit unveils the high peaks and knife-edge ridges of the southern Gros Ventre Range.

monolith behind it to the right is 10,808-ft. Pinnacle Peak.

The trail jumps a small stream at 2.7 miles—2,000 feet above your start—then descends at an easy grade. You'll soon see an outfitters camp below you. Above the camp is a long, grassy ridge. Cream Puff is the peak at its left (SW) end.

The trail drops 200 feet in half a mile and seems to disappear. Look right at the 2 o'clock position and you'll see a clear trail climbing up a hill. Cross a boggy meadow to reach it and resume climbing. Stay left where the trail splits, entering a lodgepole and whitebark pine forest at 3.6 miles. The trail begins climbing very steeply, its path clearly marked by tree blazes. In roughly .3 mile, and a gain of over 200 feet, it forks. The trail to the left leads to Cream Puff's summit. It soon leaves the forest and becomes indistinct.

Angle up the open, grassy slope to the crest of the ridge and bear left to reach the summit. Look back to get a mental picture of the terrain so you can find the trail upon your return. Alternately, stay right at the split. This steep but distinct trail heads west through pine and fir forest, reaching the open slopes of the ridge between Cream Puff and an unnamed peak to the northeast. The trail continues past rock outcroppings as it ascends Peak 9720, a massif whose two summits are separated by a small saddle. Walk to the farthest summit for the best views.

74 Little Granite

Distance: 5.5 miles to Upper Granite Highline Trail
Elevation gain: Approx. 2,670 ft.
Maximum elevation: 9,200 ft.
Maps: Bull Creek
Season: Late June through October
Use restrictions: Wilderness regulations apply. Mountain biking prohibited

The hike up Little Granite Creek leads to its headwaters in a high, timbered basin below the spine of the Gros Ventre Range. A wall of 10,000-11,000 foot peaks rise above a verdant font of grass, shrubs and wildflowers fed by snowmelt cascading down their rock walls.

The first portion of the trail is straightforward and easy to follow. As you progress up the drainage, parts of the overgrown path are lined with waist-high wildflowers, and multiple paths split off the "real" trail. Trails form easily in the clay soils found in Little Granite drainage; wildlife herds and pack strings moving in wet weather both leave their mark on the land. The most confusing portions of the upper trail, however, are on predominantly open slopes where it is easy to orient to a landmark. Your intended destination and route is not difficult to discern. Comparatively few hikers visit this idyllic corner of the Gros Ventre Wilderness.

Driving Directions

Drive 13 miles south of Jackson on U.S. Hwy. 89/191 to Hoback Junction. Bear left toward Pinedale on U.S. Hwy. 189/191. You'll reach the signed Granite Creek Recreation Area Road off the left side of the highway 11.3 miles beyond Hoback Junction. Turn in and drive 1.3 miles to signed Little Granite Creek Road on your left, just before the road crosses a bridge over the creek.

Turn onto the dirt and gravel road. Bear right when the road splits at 1.3 miles and cross a bridge. The road divides again at 1.6 miles. Stay left. You'll shortly reach the broad, grassy parking area near a portable outhouse. This is the trailhead; no other services are available. Before embarking on the hike up Little Granite, walk the fields in front of the parking area. Blue camas bloom in these meadows in June and early July. This beautiful member of the lily family is not widespread in Jackson, and it is a treat to see its striking purplish-blue blossoms.

Trail Description

The clear path heading up the hill in front of you is not the trail up Little Granite. That path lies across unbridged Little Granite Creek. Head toward the wide, knee-deep creek right of the parking area. This placid stream can be swift and potentially hazardous early season. Ford it with care.

Beyond the crossing the trail travels north through willows and a flat meadow, gradually bending closer to Little Granite Creek on your left. The grade steepens as the trail enters a pleasant Engelmann and blue spruce forest. It hops a tributary at .6 mile before passing a sign marking the boundary of Gros Ventre Wilderness. You closely follow the creek the next .4 mile, crossing it again at one mile.

The now wide path climbs through

spruce and lodgepole forest. You'll pass through an old wood range fence as the trail alternately ascends sunny clearings covered with forget-me-nots and shady forest home to columbine and Indian paintbrush.

After a slight descent the trail enters a flowered expanse that opens views of a string of high Gros Ventre Peaks, including 10,304-ft. Cache Peak and 11,180-ft. Gros Ventre Peak. The path drops to ford a narrow but knee-deep branch of Little Granite Creek at 1.6 miles, and then continues crossing the meadow. The easy grade steepens as the path re-enters coniferous forest.

You'll hop the creek shortly before reaching a split in the trail not shown on the topo. Bear left. The trail climbs then levels as it travels through light spruce and fir forest. It skips over a rivulet then gently descends open slopes. Stay right where a fainter trail veers left. (The path to the left is actually the Forest Service trail plotted on the topographic map. The path to the right avoids a deep creek crossing, and thus gets higher use.) The trail bisects a boggy area before re-entering the forest and moderately climbing to an easy, ankle-deep creek crossing.

The path continues its upward course beyond the crossing. The grade becomes quite steep as it ascends a rocky draw, leveling as it nears the top. Expansive views of the grassy slopes ahead are spread before you. The path climbs then drops into a large bowl, framed by the limestone cliffs and bowls of the Gros Ventre Range.

Continue straight at 3.3 miles where the trail to Horse Creek travels left and crosses the creek. Hop a small tributary and keep bearing north to northwest to reach the top of an open slope. Here you may follow the very steep use trail up the right side of the creek, or walk right (E) a short distance and look for a path that angles left up the slopes. Follow this to an intersection with the Horse Creek spur trail, the end of this hike description.

The last section of the hike is quite steep, but the views gained from the extra push are worth the effort.

Those with time will enjoy strolling west along the Highline, where superb views unfold in all directions.

Top: The Little Granite Creek drainage steepens at its head near the intersection with the Granite Highline Trail. Bottom: Blue camas, a rarely seen wildflower, blooms near the Little Granite trailhead.

75 Boulder Basin

Distance: 7.3 miles RT (Includes walk from parking area to trailhead.)
Elevation gain: 1,780 feet
Maximum elevation: 8,486 feet
Maps: Granite Falls
Season: Mid-June through early October
Use restrictions: Motorized use prohibited

The Granite Highline Trail extends over 15 miles northwest to southeast between the head of the North Fork of Horse Creek and Granite Creek, offering an exceptional, extended walk through a segment of the Gros Ventre Wilderness. Boulder Basin is located three miles in from the southeast end of the trail, an appealing destination that provides views of the Wyoming Range and Gros Ventre Wilderness without logging mega miles. A lightning-caused forest fire opened up tremendous views of a high wall of 11,000-foot Gros Ventre peaks to the east, and created lush habitat for moose, elk and deer. Sweeps of aspen and subalpine fir along or below the trail were not burnt, making this a varied, delightful outing that ends in a spectacular basin ringed by soaring limestone peaks.

The Granite Highline Trail makes a long traverse of the Gros Ventre Range. The day hike to Boulder Basin at its southeast end offers a peek at its beauty.

Driving Directions

Drive 13 miles south of Jackson on U.S. Hwy. 89 to Hoback Junction. At Hoback Junction, turn east onto U.S. Hwy. 189/191 toward Pinedale. Drive 11.3 miles to the prominently signed Granite Creek Recreation Area Road off the left side of the highway. Turn in and reset your odometer. The wide, high standard road can become washboarded by midsummer from drivers traveling too fast. Watch your speed! You'll pass signed turn-offs to Little Granite Creek, the Jack Pine Summer Home Area and several private operations before you reach a large Forest Service sign listing various mileages for the Granite Highline Trail off the left (W) side of the road at 7.6 miles. This is the start of the trail; turn right onto the road just past the trailhead and drive to the large parking area, reached after crossing a bridge over Granite Creek. There is an information kiosk with a map of the area but no services. Park in the lot and backtrack .3 mile to the signed trailhead. The small parking spot in the trees opposite the start of the trail is supposed to be for the Granite Highline Trail but people are often camping here.

Trail Description

The path immediately climbs south at a steady, moderate grade through a forest of young aspen. It soon bears west and ascends through mixed forest of aspen, Douglas and subalpine fir. After about 20 minutes of walking, you'll enter a small area charred by fire. There are now several small erosional run-off streams in this section that aren't on the topo map; all can be easily hopped to keep your feet dry.

At 1.3 miles you'll reach the Gros Ventre Wilderness Boundary, designated by a metal sign nailed to a tree right of the trail. A sizeable stretch of forest beyond the sign was burnt in the Boulder Fire, ignited by lightning the summer of 2000. The fire began in Boulder Creek and burned to the north and east below Boulder Basin, charring approximately 4,500 acres. Deer and elk are commonly seen grazing in the lush wildflower parks that now cover the terrain. On the late June day this was hiked, a riot of phlox, waterleaf, wild strawberry, wood violets, valerian, sticky geranium and lupine were among the wildflowers in full bloom.

At 1.6 miles and 1,260 feet higher than the trailhead, the path tops out at a ridge covered in ceanothus. The trail divides at the ridge, with a user-created spur trail heading right to the top of the ridge shoulder. The short jog opens up wonderful views east of the wall of 11,000-foot Gros Ventre peaks, from 11,174-ft. Corner Peak to the left traveling right (SE) to 11,095-ft. Flying Buttress Mountain.

Continue left at the split. The path continues at an easy to moderate grade through a section littered with numerous downed trees that must be stepped over or around. At 2 miles, it gently arcs left and travels through a stretch of young aspen clones and open hillsides sprinkled mid- to late June with hillsides of blooming pink and white spring beauties. The trail eventually re-enters a forest of spruce, fir and aspen just before reaching timberline and following an undulating course through open slopes broken by fingers of aspen stands and isolated subalpine fir. Left, tremendous views of the Wyoming Range compose the southern horizon.

The high point of the hike—a spur ridge that borders the east side of Boulder Basin—is reached just before 2.6 miles. Beyond, the path descends and climbs out of several small drainages before climbing at a noticeably steeper grade around a shoulder of the basin's east ridge at 3.1 miles. It then gently descends to the basin's floor and willow-lined Boulder Creek at 3.65 miles. Named for the creek that flows south from this small cirque into Granite Creek, Boulder Basin is defined by a vertiginous semi-circle of limestone peaks. To the west, a ridge crests at Peaks 10,285 and 10,405 then arcs north and culminates in Peaks 10,654 and 10,623. The ring of peaks tower over 2,000 feet above the basin floor, a pretty meadowed expanse studded with boulders that have tumbled from the peaks above. It is a satisfying destination for a moderate-length out-and-back hike.

The Granite Highline Trail continues in a general northwest trajectory to its terminus near the intersection of Cache Creek Trail with a trail that travels down the North Fork of Horse Creek. Consult the topo map for extended hiking options. Hikers should be aware that the central section of the Granite Highline is crisscrossed by game trails easily forged in the clay soil, and is intersected with trails that lead more directly to Little Granite and Horse Creek. Bring a map and compass or GPS to help navigate a confusing stretch of trail. Area trails receive heavy usage in autumn from outfitters. Check with the district office for permit dates, and wear orange if traveling during hunting season.

76 Shoal Falls Overlook
77 MacLeod Lake

Shoal Falls Overlook:
Distance: 10 miles RT
Elevation gain: 2,250 ft.
Maximum elevation: 8,540 ft.
Maps: Granite Falls, Doubletop Peak.
Season: June through October
Use restrictions: Motorized use prohibited

MacLeod Lake:
Distance: 4.2 miles one-way
Elevation gain: Approx. 3,560 ft.
Maximum elevation: 10,230 ft.
Maps: Granite Falls, Doubletop Peak. Book map pg. 206
Season: July through September
Use restrictions: Wilderness regulations apply. Motorized use prohibited

One of the valley's first resident physicians was Dr. Don MacLeod, who moved to Jackson Hole in the 1930s. The overworked doctor spent much of his rare time off roaming his beloved Gros Ventre Range. When he retired valley residents successfully lobbied to have a lake east of Granite Hot Springs named MacLeod Lake as a tribute to his service. A very steep unofficial trail, not shown on the topo maps, leads to this idyllic spot nestled underneath 11,175-ft. Corner Peak.

Doc called the area surrounding Shoal Falls "the most beautiful in the entire range." Many who visit it would agree. The emerald green meadows at the base of the falls backdrop a snow-capped line of peaks that form the spine of the Gros Ventre Range. Beginning northeast and moving southwest, the 11,000-foot lineup includes 11,404-ft. Palmer Peak, 11,535-ft. Triangle Peak, 11,682-ft. Doubletop Peak

(the highest summit in the Gros Ventre Range) and 11,180-ft. Hodges Peak. Superb wildflowers and opportunities to see elk, moose, deer and beaver seduce even the most jaded "been there, done that" hikers.

This pair of hikes share the same trailhead, and a very small segment of trail before taking off in different directions.

Driving Directions
Drive 13 miles south of Jackson on U.S. Hwy. 89 to Hoback Junction. At Hoback Junction, turn east onto U.S. Hwy. 189/191 toward Pinedale. Drive 11.3 miles to the prominently signed Granite Creek Recreation Area Road off the left side of the highway. Turn in and reset your odometer. Drive 7.7 miles to the marked Swift Creek Trailhead on the right side of the road. The narrow, sometimes rutted dirt road to the trailhead crosses a bridge

over Granite Creek then bears left. Park in the lot. Walk around the road closure gate and up the old road to the start of the trail. It gradually ascends a sage-covered meadow to a signed junction. Bear right to go to Shoal Falls Overlook, left toward Swift Creek to reach MacLeod Lake.

Shoal Falls Overlook Trail

A quarter-mile down the trail, bear left at another signed junction and climb up a steep hillside. Ahead is The Open Door, a mountain whose south-facing vertical slab appropriately resembles a door left ajar.

Stay left where an unsigned trail drops to Granite Ranch. The path climbs northeast through forest of first aspen then spruce and fir. Excellent views of 10,368-ft. Ramshorn Peak behind you are unveiled as you ascend.

The trail turns right and climbs to the low end of a ridge at two miles. A gradual climb up the ridge leads you first to a drainage fringed with willows, then an open meadow at 2.5 miles. The mid-summer displays of wildflowers in this and other clearings are unparalleled. The deep rose-colored Indian Paintbrush found here is especially gorgeous.

At the head of the meadow the trail descends into a small grassy bowl then climbs to the top of a second flowered meadow. Its undulating course continues as it descends a steep hillside to a crossing of West Shoal Creek at 3.4 miles. Beyond the crossing the path stays right of an intermittent stream. It gradually climbs the sage-covered drainage for over a mile before reaching a hilltop that provides a view of the glaciated face of Palmer peak at 4.5 miles.

The trail drops and climbs out of a grassy bowl, reaching Shoal Falls Overlook at five miles. Many people are well satisfied with what they have already seen and turn around at this juncture.

Continuing toward the falls, the trail drops northeast over a number of small plateaus to reach Shoal Creek at 5.6 miles. Upstream a short distance are three beaver ponds worth a closer look. To approach the base of the spectacular, three-tiered waterfall, turn left at the signed trail junction on the east side of the valley. Continuing straight at this juncture leads to a trail that accesses scenic Shoal Lake. One can return to the trailhead from that lake by hiking out the Swift Creek Trail, a superb loop that rates among the best extended outings in the Gros Ventres.

MacLeod Lake

The unsigned, unplotted path to MacLeod Lake departs from the Swift Creek Trail. At the one-mile mark, you'll reach a plank bridge over lively Swift Creek. Beyond the bridged crossing, the creek draw narrows and becomes more heavily forested. After several small dips and climbs, the gradient moderates. The trail traverses a wooded section to reach a gravelly washout area, where a tributary joins the main stream of Swift Creek. Logs help you navigate the double crossing. If you look back, you'll see a sign on a tree that reads "trail." Shortly afterwards, the path splits. Take the unsigned trail to the right. This is the path that leads to MacLeod Lake, still over 2,500 feet above you. It travels at an easy grade across open terrain bound to the north by 11,113-ft. Antoinette Peak. After a short stretch of woods, it crosses a second meadow before re-entering forest. The path slightly descends at a boggy area at 2.5 miles, then re-ascends as it bears right through forested terrain.

At just under 3 miles, the trail curves left (N) and very steeply climbs up a rocky, loose draw to a small dip in a ridge. It then descends, crosses MacLeod's outflow stream and turns left to re-ascend the

Top: MacLeod Lake is nestled below Corner Peak in the Gros Ventre Wilderness. It bears the name of one of Jackson Hole's first doctors. Left: Palmer Peak rises above Shoal Falls, viewed from the overlook. The trail descends to the meadows below for a closer look at the falls.

drainage via tight, rocky switchbacks, eventually crossing of a small outflow stream from an unnamed pond above you. At 3.7 miles the path carves right (E) through talus and ascends to a rocky basin, bears left and gently drops, then resumes its upward course. You'll see the outflow stream of MacLeod Lake, still unseen, below you at 4.0 miles. The trail drops to the richly wildflower-lined outlet, which it follows to the lake.

MacLeod Lake covers the floor of a small cirque dominated by Corner Peak. Shoal Lake lies east of that summit's long south ridge.

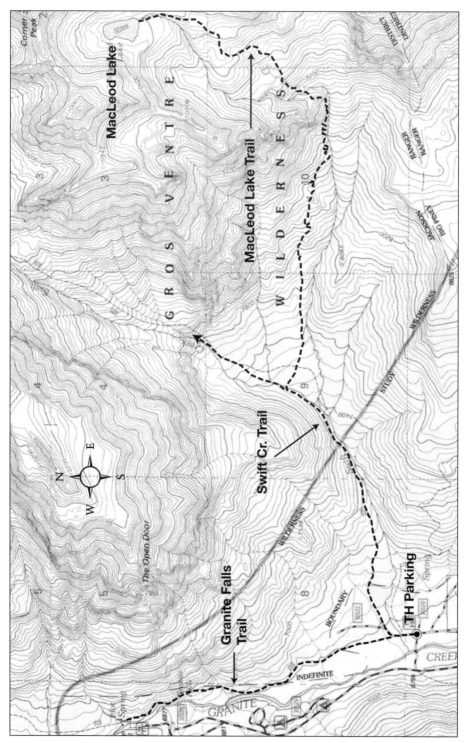

MacLeod Lake, Granite Creek Falls and Hot Springs Trails

78 Granite Creek Falls and Hot Springs

Distance: 2.3 miles one-way
Elevation gain: Approx.. 200 ft.
Maximum elevation: Approx. 7,000 ft.
Maps: Granite Falls
Season: May through October
Use restrictions: Wilderness Regulations apply

Granite Creek Falls, a thundering cascade that spills down the sloping floor of Granite Creek, is a short hike with big rewards. The falls, abundant wildflowers, striking forest and natural and developed hot springs pack a lot of pizzazz into a two-mile outing. Its low elevation makes it a favorite choice for cool spring and autumn days.

Driving Directions

Drive 13 miles south of Jackson on U.S. Hwy. 89/191 to Hoback Junction. Bear left here, driving toward Pinedale on U.S. Hwy. 189/191. At 11.3 miles beyond the junction you'll reach the signed Granite Creek Recreation Area Road off the left side of the highway. Turn in and drive 7.7 miles to the signed Swift Creek Trailhead on the right side of the road. If you pass the turn-off to Granite Creek Campground, you've missed the trailhead and will have to backtrack about a mile.

The narrow, sometimes rutted dirt road to the trailhead crosses a bridge over Granite Creek then turns left. Park at the north end of the lot and look for the trailhead sign to Granite Falls.

Top: View of the high country surrounding Granite Creek from the trailhead. Bottom: Campers and people arriving by road reach Granite Hot Springs by crossing this bridge over the creek.

A hiker checks out thundering Granite Creek Falls, swollen with early season snowmelt.

Trail Description

The path begins on a section of closed gravel road to Swift Creek. After crossing a bridge over that creek, it traverses open, grassy terrain that provides views of the highest peaks of the Gros Ventre Wilderness, including the aptly named Open Door ahead to the northeast and striking 11,113- ft. Antoinette Peak farther distant.

The trail veers close to the east bank of bubbly Granite Creek at roughly one mile. Beyond, it follows a gently undulating course through predominantly Engelmann spruce forest to Granite Creek Falls, reached in another mile. Serviceberry, honeysuckle, penstemon, Oregon grape, arrowleaf balsamroot, wood violets and sticky geraniums are but a few of many plants that thrive in the lush understory.

As you near the falls, several steep user paths to the left lead directly to its base. In the autumn, when the creek volume has diminished, hikers enjoy the natural hot springs found there. In the spring and early summer—when the creek roars with snowmelt from the 11,000-foot circle of peaks above you—it is foolhardy to enter the creek. Instead, continue on the path another .3 mile to Granite Hot Springs, a commercial operation that charges a modest fee.

The concrete pool, built in 1933 by the Civilian Conservation Corp, is fed by natural hot springs. It is typically open from Memorial Day through Labor Day, and again in the winter for snowmobilers and sled dog operations, when its average temperature of 112 degrees Fahrenheit truly appeals. The hot springs concession has changing rooms and restrooms, but no lockers for valuables. Swimsuits and towels are available for rent. A small concession sells bottled water and limited snacks. Free picnic tables are available to the public, but there are no grills.

The concrete pool is drained and scrubbed every evening.

79 Turquoise Lake

Distance: 11.2 miles
Elevation gain: 2,640 ft.
Maximum elevation: 9,490 ft.
Maps: Granite Falls, Crystal Peak, Turquoise Lake
Season: July through September
Use restrictions: Wilderness regulations apply. Mountain bikes prohibited.

Views of sharply glaciated, snow-capped mountains greet hikers en route to Turquoise Lake, a deep blue-green body of water cradled in a pocket at the base of 11,190-ft. Gros Ventre Peak. The trail steadily gains elevation as it climbs through the forests and meadows of lower Granite Creek to the rocky walls of the creek's upper reaches. Hikers can either return the same way or walk to the top of Cache Creek Divide and descend to the Cache Creek Trailhead parking area, completing a 22.7 mile traverse.

Driving Directions

To start or leave a shuttle vehicle at Granite Hot Springs, drive 13 miles south of Jackson on U.S. Hwy. 89/191 to Hoback Junction. Turn left here, driving toward Pinedale on U.S. Hwy. 189/191. Turn left onto the signed Granite Creek Recreation Area road, 11.3 miles beyond Hoback Junction. It is almost 10 miles from the highway to the trailhead parking area at Granite Hot Springs. Be sure to register your vehicle with the attendant at the springs if you plan to leave it in the parking area overnight.

To start or leave a shuttle vehicle at Cache Creek Trailhead, drive east on Broadway to Redmond Street, located across from St. John's Hospital. Turn right on Redmond and drive to Cache Creek Drive. This leads to the trailhead parking area, a total of 2.2 miles beyond the Redmond Street intersection.

Trail Description from Granite Hot Springs

After crossing the Granite Creek footbridge, walk between the hot springs pool and the changing house to reach the start of the Granite Creek Trail to Turquoise Lake. As it gradually ascends through fir forest you cross a tributary and small, open meadows before traversing rocky terrain. This section can be quite dry and dusty as summer progresses.

The trail climbs to the base of a high ridge connecting Pyramid Peak to the north and Antoinette Peak to the southeast. Sheer granite walls breached by meadows and avalanche run-outs at first 2.6 then 2.8 miles dominate the left side of the valley. The trail winds through avalanche debris, talus and sage and passes Bunker Creek drainage at 3.6 miles as it continues its gradual, upward course.

The grade steepens at four miles as you round a slight rise, pass through two groups of conifers and then skirt a rocky basin. Here, 4.4 miles beyond the trailhead, you'll enjoy your first open vista of the surrounding countryside. The sheer face and lower talus fields of 11,107-ft. Pyramid Peak dominates the northern skyline. An impressive but unnamed rocky peak stands to the east/southeast.

As you continue climbing, you'll pass a hunting camp on the other side of Granite Creek at five miles and then begin angling northwest to an unmarked trail junction at 7.6 miles. The trail to the right heads north, eventually intersecting Flat Creek Trail. Keep left and climb steadily to a second trail fork at 10 miles. The right fork leads to Flat Creek Divide, the left to Turquoise Lake.

Shortly beyond the fork one of the most pleasing views of the trip opens up before you. Rocky Gros Ventre Peak, frequently capped with snow through the end of July, reaches over 11,000 feet into the southern skyline. Two unnamed 10,500-foot peaks flank it to the northwest and southeast, forming an impressive upsweep of towering rock.

The trail drops to a tributary of Granite Creek before resuming its gradual climb. At 11.1 miles, you descend the last .1 mile to the turquoise waters that give the lake its name. There are numerous campsites in the vicinity of the lake, many frequently used by horse parties. Choose your site judiciously and be sure to treat your water.

Continuing to Cache Creek Trailhead

Beyond Turquoise Lake, the trail steadily climbs, dropping slightly each

The high country near Cache Creek Divide.

time it crosses one of three tributary branches of Granite Creek, to reach a trail junction 1.1 miles above the lake. Bearing right here would return you to Granite Creek Trailhead. Bear left to continue to Cache Creek.

The trail steadily ascends another .3 mile to reach 10,140-ft. Cache Creek Divide, the high point of the traverse. It then descends almost 700 feet to an intersection with Flat Creek Trail at 13 miles. Keep left here. A quarter-mile farther, you'll reach a second intersection. The trail to the right leads toward Jackson Peak and Goodwin Lake, an alternative traverse of the high country that reaches the Goodwin Lake parking area in another 7.3 miles. This traverse is a bit shorter, but overall gains 800 more feet along its serpentine, undulating course. To continue to Cache Creek, bear left at this intersection.

The trail gently then more steeply descends via a series of looping switchbacks, dropping 1,400 feet to reach an intersection with the Granite Highline Trail at 16.5 miles. Continue straight (W). In .6 mile, you'll leave the Gros Ventre Wilderness near the intersection with a trail heading south up the North Fork of Horse Creek. Keep right here.

The trail winds through forest as it descends the Cache Creek drainage. You'll pass an intersection with the trail leading to Game Creek Divide at 18.8 miles and the Hagen trail at 21 miles. Keep right at both junctions. The Cache Creek Trailhead parking area is 2 miles farther.

Returning via Cache Creek is an attractive option for an extended, multi-day trip but lacks the one advantage gained by retracing your footsteps: a long soak in the hot springs pool. To enjoy the pool at the end of their trip, some people shuttle a vehicle in advance and begin this hike at Cache Creek.

210

80 West Dell Creek Falls

Distance: 8.5 miles one-way
Elevation gain: 1,850 ft.
Maximum elevation: Approx. 8,350 ft. across from the falls
Maps: Doubletop Peak
Season: June through October
Use restrictions: Wilderness regulations apply. Mountain bikes prohibited.

A waterfall and proximity to the highest peaks in the Gros Ventres make the hike to West Dell Creek Falls a favorite choice amongst nearby Bondurant residents. The hike is particularly appealing in autumn, when shimmering gold aspen leaves offer stark contrast to cobalt colored sky and white-capped peaks. By early October, most of the cattle that graze the high meadows have moved to lower ground, surrendering their buffet table to hikers and hunters. Wear safety orange is you are hiking during hunting season.

Driving Directions

Drive 13 miles south of Jackson on U.S. Hwy. 89/191 to Hoback Junction. Turn left here, driving toward Pinedale on U.S. Hwy. 189/191. Roughly 18 miles beyond the junction, almost directly opposite the Elkhorn Store, you'll see Dell Creek Road, a wide, graveled Forest Service artery on the left side of the highway. Turn in and drive past Little Jenny Ranch Headquarters at 3.6 miles to an unmarked dirt road on the left several hundred yards farther. Turn in and drive through a gate, remembering to close it behind you. Straight ahead is the Riling Draw kiosk, near a split in the road. Straight ahead, Riling Draw leads to an

elk feedground operated by Wyoming Game and Fish. To your right is the rough, rutted jeep road up Parody Draw, presently closed as the result of a boundary survey. Park off-road near the kiosk. Mileage for the hike begins at this point.

West Dell Creek Falls is actually a lively cascade that skips down a rock face.

The hike to West Dell Creek Falls is framed by some of the highest peaks in the Gros Ventre Range.

Trail Description

The rough jeep road travels northeast, gradually climbing to a shallow creek crossing of Parody Draw at .8 mile; Rock Creek is crossed .7 mile farther. A short distance beyond, the road splits at a poorly defined junction. Bear right (E) here. The faint, closed road follows a fence marked by a yellow Forest Service boundary sign to a crossing of House Creek. Rock hopping will usually keep your feet dry.

Past the creek crossing the path skirts private property then drops down to West Dell Creek. Here, a long 10,000-11,000 foot ridge rises above pretty aspen groves. Its northern end is capped by 11,682-ft. Doubletop Peak, the highest mountain in the Gros Ventre Range. Those not wishing to hike all the way to the falls will not be disappointed with a hike to the meadows at the base of this impressive massif.

The trail cuts through a clearing studded with house-sized boulders and enters sparse woods. It crosses shallow West Dell Creek several times before entering a long meadow at 5.2 miles. Mid-summer, this is a gorgeous, flowered expanse.

A mile-and-a half farther, the trail recrosses the creek and climbs at a moderate then steeper grade through wooded terrain before again entering open country. Here, numerous cattle trails make you wonder if you are in the right place. Which path you are on is not critical as long as you head generally north above the creek. You'll see the falls spilling down a rock face to your right at 8.5 miles.

Teton Pass

Introduction

The history of Jackson Hole is largely a history of traffic over Teton Pass. For Native Americans it was the natural corridor between the valley and eastern Idaho to access hunting and plant gathering terrain. For trappers, the pass was the direct trading route to Pierre's Hole in Idaho. For the first permanent settlers the 8,431-foot divide was the sole year-round link to the outside world. Mail, groceries, clothing, hardware supplies and other equipment coming into the valley depended on this route to the nearest railhead in St. Anthony, Idaho, staying open.

Native American artifacts found around Teton Pass and Trail Creek date back over 9,000 years. The first known white men to cross the natural divide were members of the 1811 Astoria party. Led by Wilson Price Hunt, the group of 60 explorers and trappers under the employ of the Pacific Fur Company crossed the pass into Idaho while searching for an overland route to the Pacific. The famous mountain man rendezvous of 1832 brought literally hundreds of men and thousands of animals over the same route. But when the fur trade died out, so did traffic over the pass.

In 1860, famed mountain man Jim Bridger led William Raynold's exploratory party over the divide. As a member of the U.S. Topographical Engineers, Raynold's was charged with locating a railroad route to the West. The pass was deemed unsuitable. It was not until the 1880s—when Mormon families and other settlers from Idaho regularly crossed the divide to homestead—that the need for an improved road was eventually recognized. The existing steep track, forged by adventurous travelers, took up to two weeks to negotiate by wagon.

In 1900 Uinta County, then the governmental seat for Jackson Hole, appropriated $500 for a route to be surveyed and hired Otho E. Williams to complete the task. Lacking proper equipment, Williams used a walnut table leaf as a surveying tool. The resulting passage had grades as high as 19%, and was so steep that drivers routinely dragged trees behind them to keep their heavy wagons from running over their horse teams.

A half-dozen years after the road was built the Oregon Short Line Railroad completed a line between St. Anthony and Victor, Idaho, and daily stages began running mail and passengers between Victor and Wilson. In the summer the stage was a wagon and later a truck; in the winter months it consisted of a horse team and sleigh. To accommodate increased traffic, the roadway was widened in 1928.

For many years, automobile traffic was limited to the brief summer season, as the pass was not regularly plowed. After keeping it open for two winters the State Highway Department announced in January of 1940 that clearing Teton Pass of snow was too costly, and simply stopped. Residents took matters into their own hands by confiscating the equipment and plowing the 5.5-mile road themselves. That modern-day vigilante story made national news. When tempers cooled, the keys were returned and the threatened lawsuit was dropped. Since then the highway department has never again said it would not plow this road.

The "Old Pass Road" was used until 1969, when the existing highway over the

Top: An early motorist chugs up the steep grades of the Old Pass Road. Left: The winter of 1936 brought record snowfalls, illustrating the difficulty of keeping the road open year round.

The peak's notorious east-facing Glory Bowl frequently avalanches in winter, occasionally closing the road for days at a time.

In addition to its winter attraction to backcountry skiers, the pass offers a variety of great summer recreation trails and onward access to the west slope of the Tetons and the Snake River Range. Some of the favorites include the trails to Ski Lake and Phillips Pass in the Tetons and Black Canyon on the northernmost boundary of the Snake River Range.

Respect and Responsibility

New trails have recently been constructed or completed on Teton Pass by Boy Scouts from across the country and a group of local cyclists dubbed Teton Freedom Riders. These include the Arrow, Big Rocks, Snotel, History, Jimmy's Mom, Parallel, Powerline Jumps and

divide was completed. Today, recreationists enjoy using the former pass road.

Teton Pass marks the divide between the Teton Range to the north and the Snake River Range to the south. It is situated below 10,086-ft. Mount Glory.

215

Lithium Trails. The new trails and overall increased recreational use of the area has led the Forest Service to adopt a policy of "respect and responsibility" for all trail users. To make the system work for multiple users, trails now have designated restrictions. In addition, the following guidelines are in effect on the Pass:

Dog Owners

- Scoop the poop. To do this, your dog must be in view at all times.
- Ask before allowing your dog to approach other people or dogs.
- Your dog must be under voice control. This means your dog comes immediately upon command and stays by your side. Carry a leash if you have ANY doubt about control amidst distractions.
- Please bring no more than two dogs per group—leash the extras.

Cyclists

- Cyclists must yield to other trail users. Downhill cyclists yield to uphill cyclists. When encountering horses, pull to the side of the trail and wait until they pass.
- Announce your presence around blind corners and when approaching someone from behind.
- The lower two miles of Old Pass Road is a SLOW zone. Expect to encounter others.

Horse Riders

- Know your horse. Easily spooked or inexperienced horses should not be ridden on multi-use trails.
- Offer courteous passing instructions to others; don't assume others know what to do around horses.
- Reduce trail wear: Don't ride when trails are muddy.

Hikers/Runners

- Announced your presence when approaching from behind.
- Yield to uphill hikers and horse riders. Talking to riders lets horses know you are not a threat.
- If you stop to visit or take a break, move to the side of the trail.

For additional information on Teton Pass excursions or trails accessed from Fall Creek Road, contact the Jackson District Ranger Office by calling or writing:

Jackson Ranger District
Box 1689
Jackson, Wyoming 83001
307-739-5400

DRIVING DIRECTIONS

Old Pass Road, Crater Lake , History and Big Rocks Trails
From Hungry Jack's General Store in downtown Wilson, drive west on Wyoming Hwy. 22 toward Teton Pass for 1.1 miles to signed Trail Creek Road on your left, almost directly across the highway from the Heidelberg Inn. Turn onto Trail Creek Road and drive .9 mile to the large trailhead parking area. There is an information kiosk but no restroom facilities or water at the trailhead. Facing the kiosk, the signed path that leads to the History Trail, Black Canyon, Crater Lake and Big Rocks begins just left of the display. The Old Pass Road is right of the kiosk.

Phillips Ridge, Arrow Trail, Ski Lake, Phillips Pass to the Tram
From Hungry Jack's General Store in downtown Wilson, drive west on Wyoming Hwy. 22 toward Teton Pass for 3.9 miles to signed Phillips Canyon road on the right side of the highway. It is also possible to park in the large overflow gravel lot off the left side of the highway. Exercise caution crossing the roadway, as vehicles often exceed the speed limit descending the Pass. Mileage for the hikes listed above begins at the start of Phillips Canyon Road.

Black Canyon, Glory Bowl to Ski Lake ˙
From Hungry Jack's General Store in downtown Wilson, drive west on Wyoming Hwy. 22 for 5.5 miles to 8,431-ft. Teton Pass, marked by a large parking area, information kiosk and "Last and Best of the Old West" sign on the left side of the roadway.

81 History Trail

Distance: 3 miles one-way
Elevation gain: Approx. 1,910 feet
Maximum elevation: 8,416 ft. at Teton Pass.
Maps: Book Map. Map may also be downloaded at www.friendsofpathways.org
Season: June through October
Use restrictions: Hiking and horse use only

The History Trail on Teton Pass follows the natural divide used by American Indians, mountain men, and the valley's earliest settlers. The latter began driving buckboards and covered wagons over the steep terrain in the late 1880s.

The wagon road was eventually replaced by the Old Pass Road, used until the existing highway over the divide was completed in 1969. When tall grasses and undergrowth began to obscure the wagon road, local historian Doris Platts started annually walking and marking its course. Her years of work to keep the route recognizable was described in a September 30, 1998, article in the *Jackson Hole News*. That fall, Bridger-Teton National Forest Wilderness Ranger Bryan Smith and volunteers Keith and Diane Benefiel accompanied her with GPS units to accurately plot the old road on a topographic map, with hopes of turning it into an historic hiking trail.

The long-standing project finally became reality when the Boy Scouts honor society, Order of the Arrow, donated an estimated $1 million dollars worth of labor the summer of 2008 constructing the History and four other Teton Pass trails.

Today, users enjoy stepping onto the trail and into the past as they travel past the remains of old sawmills, buck-and-rail fence, Reed Hotel Rock, and other artifacts. A brochure describing points on interest along the trail was developed through a partnership between the Natural History Interpretation program of Teton Science Schools and the Forest Service. Its contents are reproduced in the description of this hike.

Driving Directions

Follow directions given on page 219.

Trail Description

The access path left of the kiosk immediately splits, with the path to the right leading to Crater Lake. Proceed straight, traveling on a pleasant, level course through shady subalpine fir and Engelmann spruce forest. Keep right where the path divides, soon crossing a bridge over Trail Creek and entering a pretty meadow. Wildflowers have grown up around the rusted equipment to your right, remnants of a once-thriving sawmill operated by R.C. Lundy, Jr. through the 1930s and 40s. Doris Platts recounts in *The Pass* that the new mill began cutting a 40,000 board foot sale in 1931; two years later, Lundy and two other area mill operators donated lumber used in the construction of the sheds and grandstand at the Wilson rodeo grounds.

The first sawmill operated on the Pass was set up by Bill and Howard Schofield,

218

Top: Old marker near the base of the History Trail. The Schofield brothers operated one of three sawmills on or near Teton Pass. Rusted mill artifacts can be found in numerous locations along the trail. Left: Owners of the Reed Hotel in Jackson painted this boulder to advertise their facility sometime between 1908 and 1917.

who milled trees discarded at the base of the Pass. Early travelers dragged log behind their wagons to control the rate of descend on the steep road. Closer exploration of the abandoned equipment will unveil an old concrete marker etched with the Schofield name.

A .1 mile, you'll reach a signed junction. The trail to Black Canyon continues left. Bear right and walk a short distance to another junction, where the Big Rocks and History Trails part company. Continue right on the History Trail. It travels through both shady forest

and open meadow as it ascends toward the Pass. Water (be sure to treat!) is available from a tributary of Trail Creek near Reed Hotel Rock, and from numerous seeps and springs as the trail nears the top of the Pass.

Above the connecting trail to the Old Pass Road near Crater Lake, the History Trail travels through open terrain bisected by powerline poles. Exercise caution in this section as you approach the intersection with the Powerline Jumps mountain biking trail.

The map and contents of the trail's free interpretive brochure, presented with additional information from this author, is included on the following pages. For simplicity, the brochure's detailed History

This wooded section of the History Trail is part of the original wagon route over the pass.

Trail map does not show the Crater Lake Trail that travels between the History Trail and Old Pass Road.

No. 1: Winter on the Pass

The natural environment made traveling Teton Pass challenging—especially during winter. Yet by 1905 this Historic Wagon Route was used enough to keep the snow road "broke out" all winter, despite storms that could drop as many as fifteen feet of snow. Horse-drawn sleds carried people and supplies over the pass from Victor to Wilson. Horses would get stuck up to their bellies, and word has it that going down was easier than coming up!

No. 2: Buck-and-Rail Fences

The steep terrain on this section of the Historic Wagon Route required ranchers to build buck-and-rail fences. These fences prevented cattle from dropping down to the creek. Cattle passed through here single file with cowboys guiding them. Sixty percent of all cattle raised in Jackson traversed Teton Pass to get to the railroad in Victor. This wagon road witnessed numerous cattle drives until the railhead in Victor closed in the 1970s.

No. 3: The Corduroy Bridge

Take a look around you and notice the wet areas. High mountain springs and wet seeps created deep mud holes on this well-traveled path. Settlers cut down trees and laid logs across mud holes to harden the tread, allowing horses and wagons to get through the mud. These structures are called corduroy bridges.

No. 4: Reed Hotel Rock

Can you find a rock used as a billboard? ...The Reeds, who owned a hotel in Jackson, used this natural feature to advertise their business. Ma Reed ran the hotel from 1908 until 1917 when the Crabtrees took it over and eventually renamed it the Crabtree Hotel. The site presently houses a real estate company.

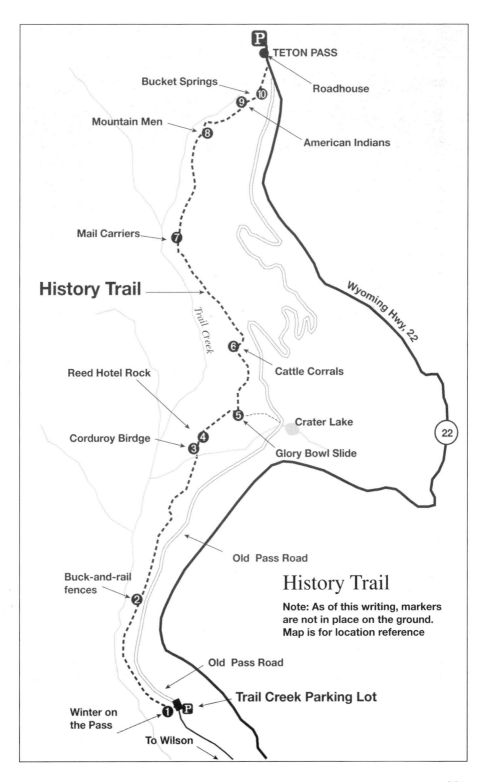

P
TETON PASS

Bucket Springs

Roadhouse

⑩
⑨

Mountain Men

⑧

American Indians

Mail Carriers ⑦

History Trail

Trail Creek

⑥

Cattle Corrals

Reed Hotel Rock

⑤

Crater Lake

Corduroy Birdge ④
③

Glory Bowl Slide

Wyoming Hwy, 22

22

Old Pass Road

History Trail

**Note: As of this writing, markers
are not in place on the ground.
Map is for location reference**

Buck-and-rail
fences
②

Old Pass Road

Trail Creek Parking Lot

Winter on
the Pass
① P

To Wilson

No. 5: Glory Bowl

Avalanches have influenced the nature of Teton Pass and the lives of people who depend on it. Glory Bowl is the bowl-shaped chute just below 10,086-ft. Mount Glory. Snow collects and slides down this bowl throughout the winter. To manage this, the Wyoming Department of Transportation often triggers "controlled" avalanches for greater safety on Teton Pass. Still, from 1911 through the spring of 2009, 10 people have been killed by avalanches on Teton Pass.

No. 6: Cattle Corrals

Cattle were driven from Jackson Hole by the hundreds, corralled at night in this open meadow, and taken over Teton Pass to the railhead in Victor. Can you find their watering holes? Perhaps you notice the difference in the vegetation of this area. These corrals remain as evidence of how cattle influenced Teton Pass. Because of the open grasslands of Jackson Hole cattle ranching was the economic mainstay of the valley by 1913.

No. 7: Mail Carriers

The sheer, rugged nature of this mountain range made communication with the outside world difficult. Before official mail service began in 1892, local residents carried post by foot over the pass. This two-day trip was the only way to send and receive letters and packages. The establishment of the mail service gave residents a timely, dependable means of contacting family and friends. Eight years later, Jackson Hole had five U.S. Post Offices, located in Jackson, Wilson, South Park, Elk and Grovont.

No. 8: Mountain Men

Legendary mountain men like John Colter and David E. Jackson walked this trail in the early 1800s. Teton Pass connected these men to a "hole"—a valley surrounded on all sides by mountains. Jackson's Hole supported a habitat rich in beaver and other fur-bearing animals. The mountain men traveled Teton Pass to "rendezvous" in Pierre's Hole, now modern-day Victor, where they would trade goods and swap stories. With few supplies, mountain men relied heavily on the natural world for survival.

No. 9: American Indians

American Indians depended on the natural world for survival. For nearly 11,000 years prehistoric people used Teton Pass seasonally for its access to plants, animals, and other natural materials. Several outcroppings of obsidian—a glassy, volcanic rock used for making sharp tools—are located near this area. Obsidian from these quarries was traded throughout the United States.

No. 10: Bucket Springs

You have just summited Teton Pass and feel exhausted and thirsty, but where is the water? Water is scarce at high elevations. This small, natural spring supported the weary travelers and their livestock. Bucket Springs, located a quarter-mile from the roadhouse, sustained those who stayed at the roadhouse. This cold-water spring still bubbles today.

No. 11: The Roadhouse

Imagine feeling the relief of finally reaching the top of Teton Pass after an intense struggle with the steep pathway. It often took the early settlers two weeks to get their livestock, families and wagons over the trail. The pass is the break between the Teton Range to the north and the Snake River Range to the south. A roadhouse stood at the summit to refuel tired travelers.

82 Big Rocks Loop

Distance: 2.8 miles
Elevation change: Approx. 660 ft.
Maximum elevation: Approx. 7,100 ft.
Maps: Book map, pg. 225
Season: June through October
Use restrictions: Hiking and horse use only on Big Rocks Trail; multi-use on the Black Canyon section to complete the loop.

Big Rocks Loop is a pleasant trail through lush forest that showcases rich wildflower displays and glacial erratics. The Big Rocks Trail intersects the trail to Black Canyon to complete the moderate loop.

Driving Directions

Follow directions given on page 219.

Trail Description

The access path left of the kiosk immediately splits, with the path to the right leading to Crater Lake. Proceed straight, traveling on a pleasant, level course through shady subalpine fir and Engelmann spruce forest. Keep right where the path divides, soon crossing a bridge over Trail Creek and entering a pretty meadow. Wildflowers have grown up around the rusted equipment to your right, remnants of a once-thriving sawmill operation, described on page 220.

At .1 mile, you'll reach a signed junction. The trail to Black Canyon continues left. Bear right and walk a short distance to another junction, where the Big Rocks and History Trails part company. Bear left onto the Big Rocks Trail.

The trail travels through open terrain a short distance to a log bridge over Trail Creek. Beyond, it enters shady conifer forest. Tall monkshood, baneberry, parrots' beak, pinedrops, birchleaf spirea, Western coneflower, meadowrue, and huckleberry and thimbleberry bushes thrive in the lush understory lining the track. When the huckleberries are ripe, look for not-often-seen pipsissewa, also called Prince's Pine. This small member of the wintergreen family has white to pinkish pendant flowers with five petals and 10 purplish stamens arranged like spokes around a wheel.

The trail climbs at a moderate, steady grade before easing, curving left at the 1-mile mark around a big, coarse-grained granite and pegmatite boulder. A short distance farther, the path turns 90 degrees to the right and soon passes two huge boulders. The rocks that give this trail its name are glacial erratics. They were transported roughly 1,500 feet above the valley floor on the western edge of a large glacier that once covered the floor on what is now Jackson Hole. In their landmark 1968 *Creation of the Teton Landscape,* noted geologists J.D. Love and John C. Reed reported that boulders up to 40 feet in diameter were carried southward from the middle core of the Teton Range as far as Mosquito Creek.

The wooded path climbs via switchbacks before straightening to reach a sign

Top: The boulders that give the Big Rocks Trail its name are erratics dropped by glaciers thousands of years ago. Boulders are large as 40 feet in diameter have been found as far south as Mosquito Creek. Right: Look for pipsissewa along the trail.

at 1.3 miles that warns users a junction with a trail for downhill mountain bikers is just ahead. This is the Lithium Trail, a one-way trail whose use is restricted to mountain bikers. Look carefully before crossing this path to continue on the Big Rocks Trail straight ahead.

Big Rocks enters a small meadow covered with wildflowers, then makes a sharp turn left and enters Engelmann spruce forest. It drops at a steeper grade, then bears right and traverses an open section at 1.8 miles before reaching a junction with the trail ascending Black Canyon. This is a multi-use trail open to all trail users.

Turn left onto the Black Canyon Trail to complete the loop. The wooded trail travels at an easy grade, Black Canyon Creek heard but mostly unseen below and to the right of the trail.

At 2.5 miles, a sign directs you left at the junction. Shortly beyond, the Lithium Trail intersects the Black Canyon Trail to the left.. Continue straight, soon crossing a bridge over Trail Creek and a second plank bridge that completes the loop. Retrace your steps to return to the trailhead.

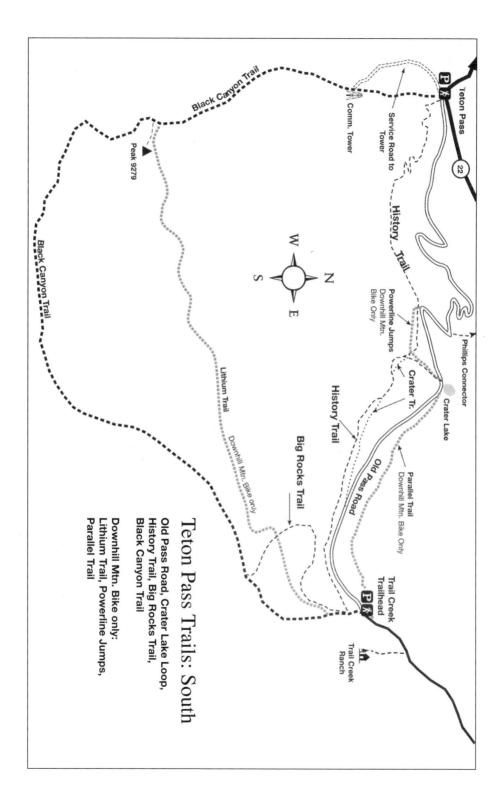

Teton Pass Trails: South

Old Pass Road, Crater Lake Loop,
History Trail, Big Rocks Trail,
Black Canyon Trail

Downhill Mtn. Bike only:
Lithium Trail, Powerline Jumps,
Parallel Trail

Map labels:

Black Canyon Trail

Teton Pass

Comm. Tower

Service Road to Tower

History Trail

22

Peak 9279

Powerline Jumps
Downhill Mtn. Bike Only

Phillips Connector

Crater Tr.

Crater Lake

History Trail

Parallel Trail
Downhill Mtn. Bike Only

Lithium Trail

Downhill Mtn. Bike only

Big Rocks Trail

Old Pass Road

Black Canyon Trail

Trail Creek Trailhead

Trail Creek Ranch

N
W   E
S

83 Crater Lake Loop
84 Old Pass Road

Crater Lake Loop
    Distance: 2.7 miles
    Elevation change: Approx. 670 ft..
    Maximum elevation: Approx. 7,170 ft.
    Maps: Teton Pass. Book map pg. 225
    Season: Mid-May through October
    Use restrictions: Hiking and biking. Horse use prohibited.

Old Pass Road
    Distance: 3.5 miles one-way
    Elevation gain: Approx. 2,000 ft.
    Maximum elevation: 8,431 ft. at Teton Pass
    Maps: Teton Pass. Book map pg. 225
    Season: June through October
    Use restrictions: Hiking and biking. Horse use prohibited.

Crater Lake is a favored destination for dog walkers, joggers and hikers looking for a quick exercise outing. This loop travels via the Old Pass Road to the lake and returns to the trailhead via a forested trail that follows brief sections of the original wagon route over the pass. Wildflowers, Trail Creek and views of Mount Glory, Black Canyon and distant Gros Ventre peaks to the east make this hike particularly appealing.

Continuing up Old Pass Road beyond Crater Lake extends this outing. Users may shuttle a car in advance for a one-way venture, retrace their steps, or return via the History Trail or Black Canyon.

Driving Directions

Follow directions given on page 219.

Trail Description

The old asphalt roadway immediately begins ascending at a moderate grade. Initially lined with towering Douglas and subalpine fir that provide welcome shade on a warm day, the terrain soon opens up. Several minutes into the walk, you'll pass a standing dead tree on each side of the roadway riddled with holes. Look and listen for the woodpeckers and nuthatches that create them, or cavity nesters such as bluebirds, kestrels and flycatchers that use the abandoned holes for nests.

At .7 mile, you'll pass a small spring-fed rivulet to your right that provides ample moisture for some of the many wildflowers and bushes that line the roadway. Because the road is slightly convex to facilitate water run-off, the favorable microclimate has created a parade of wildflowers that at peak bloom look like a planned garden.

A painted yellow "1" on the pavement and a fir tree left of the road appear at the one-mile mark. Crater Lake lies just .2 mile farther. Nestled by a sharp curve at 7,160 feet, the small lake lies at the toe of

Top: Amazing wildflower displays and views of the valley make the Old Pass Road a favorite hike. Left: Tiny Crater Lake is 1.2 miles up Old Pass Road.

Glory Slide in a natural depression created by repeated avalanches. It is a favorite spot for dogs to jump in and cool off. In early days, ranchers driving cattle over the pass to the railhead in Victor often camped here overnight.

To complete the Crater Lake Loop

Walk up the pavement beyond the lake for about 60 yards to a gravel road on your left that is the start of your return route. The roadbed descends at an easy grade through fragrant mixed forest alive with bird song. It soon arcs left, opening a glimpse of the distant Gros Ventre Range, then bends right close to the powerline poles. Ignore the trail to the right: this is the upper History Trail. Instead, take the dirt path to your left after passing the first set of poles. It crosses a short open stretch, circles left and drops into the forest.

As the trail approaches Trail Creek and widens near several large, cut tree trunks, look for a boulder to your left. The faint painted words "Reed Hotel, Jackson" can still be discerned., old advertising for folks heading to Jackson. The original road/wagon route over the pass was close to the creek, following the course of the trail you are walking. The rock was painted between 1908 and 1917, when Ma Reed ran the hotel that bore her name. It was later run by the Crabtree Family and renamed the Crabtree Hotel.

Step over a small channel of the creek; the main creekbed is reached several yards farther. Carefully cross on logs. If the logs are wet, it is safer to just splash through the creek. With the North Fork of Trail Creek and several small run-off steams tumbling into Trail Creek, this section of the trail is often muddy well into the summer season. Stay left where the History Trail merges with the Crater Lake Trail.

The path descends at an easy to moderate grade across open slopes until it intersects Old Pass Road. Rejoin the road here to return to your vehicle, or better, stay on the trail to intersect the road closer to the trailhead parking area.

To continue up Old Pass Road

Stay on the asphalt pavement and continue ascending beyond Crater Lake. In another half-mile, the roadway makes the first of eight hairpin switchbacks as it snakes its way to Teton Pass, 2.3 miles above Crater Lake. Superb views, rocky road cuts, fantastic wildflowers and massive Douglas fir and Engelmann spruce characterize the moderately steep to steep ascending course. Large, easily accessible Engelmann spruce are not widespread in Jackson Hole. Its strong, uniform wood make it a timber sale target for companies interested in selling the quality lumber for mine and timber ties, general use and plywood.

Whenever you see stands of Engelmann, look for grouse, squirrels and chipmunks that gorge on its seeds and porcupines that eat its inner bark.

The Old Road reaches the current highway just below the summit of Teton Pass. If you haven't shuttled a vehicle, retrace your steps to return to your vehicle, or return to the trailhead via the History or Black Canyon Trails. The Old Pass/History loop is 6.5 miles; the Black Canyon Loop, 9.5 miles.

The view along Old Pass Road as it nears the top of Teton Pass.

85 Black Canyon from Teton Pass

Distance:
Mt. Elly Overlook: 3.3 miles RT
Black Canyon: 5.8 miles
Elevation change:
Mt. Elly Overlook: Approx 1,000 ft gain; 200 ft, loss
Black Canyon: Approx 1,100 ft. gain; 3000 ft. loss
Maximum elevation: 9,279 ft. at Mt. Elly Overlook
Maps: Teton Pass. Book map pg 225
Season: July through Mid-October
Use restrictions:
None. Users should be prepared to encounter horse, mountain bike and foot
traffic. Please follow accepted right-of-way courtesies.

The hike from the top of Teton Pass down Black Canyon offers wonderful stretches of towering forest, and panoramic views of 10,086-ft. Mount Glory and the Gros Ventre and Snake River Ranges. It begins by following the high crest of the Snake River Range immediately south of Teton Pass, offering stellar views of that range and the valley floor below. Wildflowers typically peak mid- to late July, when numerous courses from nature-based entities in the valley conduct botany excursions on the ridge.

Driving Directions

From Hungry Jack's General Store in Wilson, Wyoming, drive 5.5 miles up winding Wyoming Highway 22 to 8,431-ft. Teton Pass, marked by a large parking area/scenic turnout to your left (S). You may begin walking up the service road to the radio tower at the west end of the parking area or, as described below, on the hillside trail that heads south.

Trail Description

The clear, steep trail steeply ascends as it crosses a precipitous slope en route to a communications tower at 8,637 feet. Because this section feels a bit exposed, those who suffer from vertigo are advised to hike the service road to the tower and pick up the trail.

Beyond the tower, the path continues its southerly direction just below the ridge crest. At the one-mile mark it traverses the head of large, open Olympic Bowl and enters the trees.

The trail passes through forest and small meadows colored with a profusion of wildflowers that includes scarlet gilia, paintbrush, penstemon, silky phacelia and bluebells. You'll reach a broad clearing overlooking the head of Black Canyon and the Snake River Range extending south. Near the signed intersection with the Lithium Mountain Bike Trail to the left, the trail crosses to a clearing (W) of 9,279-ft. Mt. Elly to begin its descent into Black Canyon. It is worthwhile to hike the .1 mile user path to the top of Mt. Elly, a nice turn-around point for a shorter out-and-back hike, and the high point of the Black Canyon hike.

The view looking north along the ridge that leads to Mt. Elly Overlook.

The trail steeply drops 600 feet in .6 mile to a small saddle before descending more gradually into the grassy, open bowl at the head of Black Canyon. As you switchback down, periodic shade is provided by comely groups of Aspen. Ahead, the eastern skyline is defined by the Gros Ventre Range.

The trail hops a small tributary of Black Canyon Creek, then begins paralleling the same at 2.8 miles. The trail follows the creek to the foot of the Pass as it travels through thick forest that gives the canyon its name. Keep a sharp eye out for delicate calypso orchids, commonly called fairy slippers. This exquisite wildflower prefers cool, damp sites; it typically blooms in the canyon in late June.

The path traverses several small clearings before descending via forested switchbacks. After traversing an open bench, it turns right and enters a meadow watered by a small tributary stream. Here, you'll see rusting remains of old sawmill equipment. At one time, three sawmills operated on or near Teton Pass.

You'll re-enter the forest at the end of the meadow and continue following the creek as you descend, occasionally crossing it. As you near the bottom of the pass, you'll intersect the Big Rocks Trails on the left side of the path. Continue straight on the Black Canyon Trail. It travels through the forest at an easy grade, Black Canyon Creek heard but mostly unseen below and to the right of the trail.

At a signed junction near the base of the Pass, a sign directs you left. Shortly beyond, the Lithium Trail enters the left side of the Black Canyon Trail. Continue straight, soon crossing a bridge over Trail Creek, then a second plank bridge. From here, it is a short distance to the parking area at the foot of Old Pass Road, the end of this hike.

86 Glory Bowl to Ski Lake

Distance: Approx. 5.6 miles
Elevation change: Approx. 1,920 ft. gain; Approx. 2,600 ft. loss
Maximum elevation: 10,086 ft.
Maps: Rendezvous Peak, Teton Pass. Book map pg. 233
Season: July through September
Use restrictions: Mountain bikes and motorized use prohibited.

Mount Glory is a double-summit peak that abruptly rises above Teton Pass. The massif extends north over a mile before arcing east, encircling tiny Ski Lake below. Both 10,086-ft. Mount Glory and Ski Lake are popular backcountry ski destinations; the pair makes an equally appealing summer/fall outing.

The unofficial route/trail combination described here quickly accesses the high terrain of the southern Tetons. Superb wildflowers, rugged bowls and grand views—plus the pleasures of a small but charming subalpine lake—characterize this ever-changing hike.

While it can be done in either direction, the steepness of the route between Teton Pass and the top of Mount Glory makes it advisable to ascend rather than descend this section. This description thus begins at the pass. This hike requires a car shuttle. Alternately, it can be extended by hiking back up to Teton Pass. This option adds 2.5 miles and an additional 1,000 foot ascent.

Driving Directions

From Hungry Jack's General Store in downtown Wilson, drive west on Wyoming Hwy. 22 toward Teton Pass for 3.9 miles to signed Phillips Canyon Road on the right side of the highway. If you are shuttling a vehicle, leave one here or in the overflow parking lot across from Phillips Canyon on the south side of the highway. Drive to the top of 8,431-ft. Teton Pass and park in the large lot south of the roadway. Carefully cross the highway to the unsigned but clear trail that ascends north.

Trail Description

It is immediately evident that the path you are on was not created by Forest Service crews conscious of curbing erosion. There are no switchbacks on this easy to follow but vertiginous trail; if sections were any steeper, this would be a climbing route. You'll soon pass a sign placed high on a tree that warns skiers (and summer hikers) that unexploded warheads used in avalanche control may be found on the mountain. Howitzers have historically discharged artillery shells on the pass to trigger avalanches. The shells are roughly four inches in diameter and over a foot long. If you find one, don't touch or disturb it: They are potentially dangerous. The Teton County Sheriff Office and Wyoming Transportation Department ask that you mark the shell's location and report the find.

If you can put aside feelings of impending heart attack as you climb over 1,600 feet in the next mile, you'll notice the trail is lined first with subalpine fir and Engelmann spruce then limber pine. Yellow paintbrush and fireweed both grow in abundance. In the trees, the trail has a hard-pack dirt base. Higher, it cuts through loose talus where extra caution should be exercised.

At the one-mile mark you'll reach the crest of 10,086-ft. Mount Glory. Superb views to the east encompass the valley floor and the distant Gros Ventre Range, with the ever-slumbering Sleeping Indian a prominent landmark. South, the peaks and ridges of the Snake River Range are unveiled. The Grand Teton and Taylor Mountain are seen to the north and northwest. Immediately west is what you will notice first: A large screen with a box at its base. The screen and assorted sheds and equipment are part of a system installed in the 1980s to aid in avalanche control work. Remote-controlled radio signals release charges into the ground, creating a seismic shock wave designed to trigger avalanches on Glory Bowl and Twin Slides to the south.

To reach Ski Lake, walk north on Mount Glory's summit ridge. You'll dip to a high saddle above the upper slopes of Little Tuckerman's Ravine before gently climbing to Glory's 10,032-foot summit at 1.5 miles. Skiers have named the deep dish below its east slope "Unskiabowl."

Stay high on the ridge as you continue walking north. Mid- to late summer, this is one of the most spectacular alpine walks in the Tetons. A riot of colorful wildflowers cover the grassy terrain, framed by the impressive east slope of Taylor Mountain to your left (W) and the Tetons ahead.

The route dips then ascends a grassy hill. In the winter, this mound is blanketed with as much as 30 feet of snow, earning it the nickname "The Great White Hump." You may continue walking north on the ridge and drop right into Horseshoe Bowl (see hike no. 87) or, as described here, begin angling down the right (E) side of The Great White Hump toward an obvious grassy saddle below, reached at 2.0 miles.

From the saddle the route bends left down steep slopes punctuated with fir trees. It then descends into Horseshoe

Hikers traverse the high ridge north of Mt. Glory's summit to complete the Glory Bowl/Ski Lake Loop. The Grand Teton is seen on the distant horizon.

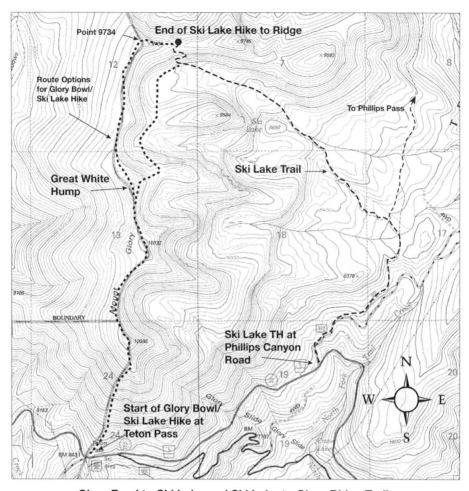

Glory Bowl to Ski Lake and Ski Lake to Glory Ridge Trails

bowl at a more moderate grade to a second saddle.

Drop off this saddle, bending right (E) around a forested hill marked by elevation point 9584 on the Rendezvous Peak topo. As you travel to the north side of this small peak, you'll pick up a trail near treeline. The path travels east through alternately forested and open slopes to reach the eastern shore of Ski Lake at 3.5 miles. The views of both the lake and surrounding terrain on the descent are some of the nicest in the region.

From Ski Lake, it is 2.15 miles to the start of Phillips Canyon Road off Wyoming Highway 22, completing a superb alpine walk. For those who cannot arrange a car shuttle, or want to extend their outing, it is possible to cross the highway to the parking area and pick up the Phillips Connector Trail. This descends to the dogleg of the second switchback above Crater Lake on Old Pass Road. Turn right. You'll gain an additional 1,000 feet on your 1.9-mile walk to the top of the pass and your vehicle.

87 Ski Lake to Mount Glory Ridge

Distance:
    Ski Lake: 4.3 miles RT
    Mount Glory Ridge: 3.6 miles one-way to Point 9734
Elevation gain:
    Ski Lake: Approx. 990 ft.
    Mount Glory Ridge: Approx. 1,980 ft.
Maximum elevation:
    Ski Lake: 8,720 ft. on ridge just above lake
    Mount Glory Ridge: 9734 ft.
Maps: Rendezvous Peak. Book map pg. 233
    Ski Lake: June through October
    Mount Glory Ridge: July through mid-October
Use restrictions: Hike and horse use only.

Ski Lake is an early-season favorite as well as a classic place to enjoy mid-summer wildflowers. The short, well-traveled trail starts half-way up Teton Pass, allowing hikers who have yet to acquire their summer legs and lungs the luxury of climbing under 1,000 feet while still being rewarded with panoramic views. Nestled snugly in a cirque at the southern end of the Teton Range, Ski Lake is virtually hidden until you are upon it.

The trail continues north/northwest around the lake and steeply climbs Horseshoe Bowl to Point 9734 on Mount Glory Ridge, offering superb vistas of the surrounding terrain.

Driving Directions

Follow driving directions on page 219. Mileage for this hike begins at the start of Phillips Canyon Road.

Trail Description

The road climbs at an initially steep than more moderate grade through Doug-

las fir and subalpine forest. The track is lined with balsamroot, sticky geraniums, bluebells, lupine and salsify, a wildflower that thrives in soils that have been disturbed. It is thus often found along fences and roadways. European settlers, who ate the plant's bulbous taproot, imported this distinctive spiky yellow flower. It soon escaped the confines of cultivation, widely planting itself by wind carrying its seeds in dandelion-like puffballs.

At .4 mile you reach a signed intersection to Ski Lake and Phillips Pass. Bear left onto the sage-covered slopes. The trail contours above the old road on a hillside studded with massive Douglas fir and sprinkled with colorful wildflowers during summer bloom. It turns noticeably right just before reaching a small overlook, where one enjoys expansive views south of the Snake River Range.

Beyond the viewpoint the trail drops to the edge of a meadow, circling its left side before reaching a signed junction with the trail to Phillips Pass. Bear left to reach the lake. (This section has been rerouted from what is shown on the 1968 Rendezvous topo. The new trail was relocated to drier ground to mitigate land impacts. Though barricaded with logs, the old path is still visible. Please assist the Forest Service by staying on the new path.)

As you skirt the meadow, look for patches of elephant's head and elk that graze on them. The comical red-violet blooms, curved upward like an elephant's trunk, typically appear in wet, sunny meadows early to mid-summer.

Beyond the junction the trail crosses a drainage and climbs northwest through fir forest before reaching a bridged creek crossing at 1.6 miles. It continues ascending through meadow and open fir and aspen forest. You'll pass an obvious campsite and re-enter the forest before reaching the outflow of Ski Lake Creek. The lake is reached under a quarter-mile farther. Its east and southern shores are bordered by spruce, fir and pine forest. To the north and west, the limestone slopes of unnamed 9,582-foot and 9,584-foot knobs above it encircle Ski Lake's sparkling water. The best views of the lake are obtained by hiking up the trail an additional .1 mile up the ridge that bounds its northeast end.

While the hike itself is short, allow plenty of time to relax and enjoy the lake—and an array of flora so vast and abundant that naturalists choose this hike for interpretive wildflower walks.

Hikers wishing to extend their day should continue on the trail that climbs the ridge encircling the lake. The path ascends to Horseshoe Bowl, then steeply climbs the north wall of the cirque to a small saddle between Point 9734 and Point 9745 on Mount Glory Ridge. From there, it is easiest to access the summit of Point 9734, over 1,000 feet higher and 1.5 miles beyond the start of the ridge

above Ski Lake. The point yields beautiful panoramas in every direction, and while rigorous, is easier than ascending to the summit of 10,086-ft. Mount Glory from Teton Pass (see hike no, 86.)

The series of ridges and bowls at this end of the Teton Range can be confusing to even the most experienced hikers. Don't attempt cross-country routes in this area, especially in poor visibility, unless you are confident of your map and compass reading skills.

Top: Ski Lake, viewed from the toe of the ridge that rises above it. Bottom: Columbine thrive along portions of the trail.

88 Phillips Pass to the Tram

Distance: 12.7 miles
Elevation change: Approx. 4,600 ft. gain; Approx. 1,900 ft. loss
Maximum elevation: 10,450 ft.
Maps: Rendezvous Peak. Book map pg. 239
Season: Mid-July through early September
Use restrictions:
Wilderness and park regulations apply. Mountain bikes, motorized vehicles and pets prohibited.

The high ridge walk from Phillips Pass to the aerial tram in Teton Village is one of the premier excursions of the southern Tetons. The path climbs to the boundary of Jedediah Smith Wilderness then turns more directly north onto Teton Crest Trail, paralleling the eastern side of Moose Creek Canyon. As it scales Moose Creek Divide and drops into Grand Teton National Park, the superb scenery and lush wildflowers make even the most seasoned Teton hikers pause in appreciation.

Many people prefer to start at Teton Village and hike to Phillips Pass to avoid the substantial elevation gain and climbing up the backside of Rendezvous Peak at the end of the hike. Those who have skied, climbed and hiked their knees into submission will appreciate the generally uphill direction described below.

Driving Directions

Follow the driving directions on page 219. Mileage for this hike begins at the start of Phillips Canyon Road. Shuttle a car in advance to Jackson Hole Mountain Resort, reached by driving north on the Moose-Wilson Road (Wyoming Hwy, 390) approximately seven miles.

Trail Description

This hike description begins at the start of Phillips Canyon Road on Teton Pass. That dirt and gravel artery climbs at an initially steep than more moderate grade through Douglas fir and subalpine forest to a signed intersection with trails to Ski Lake and Phillips Pass at .4 mile. Bear left onto the trail and contour above the old road. The path turns noticeably right just before reaching an overlook at one mile. It then drops to the edge of an often-wet meadow, circling its left side to reach a signed junction with the trail to Phillips Pass. Bear right at the junction

The trail soon crosses a plank bridge over an intermittent tributary of Phillips Creek, lushly lined with water-loving monkshood and bluebells early to mid-summer. The gradient eases as the trail traverses subalpine fir forest and open wildflower parks. It curves left, opening fine views of the southern Tetons and the valley floor below, gently descends through mature forest, then bends right at 2 miles and crosses a gully littered with avalanche debris. At 2.8 miles it drops into Phillips Canyon and crosses the Middle Fork of Phillips Canyon Creek, reaching an intersection with Phillips Canyon Trail a short distance farther. Bear left here.

The trail now climbs open slopes, gaining an additional 630 feet on its way to the divide. The appealing open bowl,

236

The dramatic head of Moose Creek Canyon, viewed along the trail between Phillips Pass and the tram.

fed by the upper reaches of the Middle Fork of Phillips Canyon Creek, is covered with wildflowers mid-summer. Lupine, in particular, stage a memorable bloom in mid-July. Later, fireweed puts on a color extravaganza not to be missed.

Keep right at 3.6 miles, where a short spur trail heads left and soon peters out. The path angles right (N), and climbs the final 200 feet to 8,932-ft. Phillips Pass at 4.0 miles. A Jedediah Smith Wilderness sign marks the divide, where expansive views into scenic Moose Creek Basin, framed by Taylor Mountain are enjoyed. Housetop and Fossil Mountains define the northern horizon.

To reach the aerial tram, bear right (N) at the pass. The path gains close to 650 feet in the next three-quarters mile before proceeding at a gentler grade. At 5.2 miles, it steeply drops 200 feet, revealing the talus-covered south slope of 10,927-ft. Rendezvous Peak ahead of you.

Hop a run-off gully and continuing

dropping at a gentler grade. The path levels and seems to disappear a short distance farther. Continue straight and skirt a downed snag and you'll pick it up again. The path traverses pretty, flowered clearings before re-entering coniferous forest. Numerous downed trees span this section of trail—and they look like they had been here for quite a while.

The trail dips to a tributary crossing of Moose Creek and enters a section of towering Engelmann spruce forest. Here it becomes lost in duff covering the forest floor. Aim toward a small hill ahead of you at 11 o'clock and you'll pick it up. Ahead, the limestone benches and verdant, green slopes of upper Moose Creek Basin come into view, watered up the outlet streams of Moose Basin Lakes.

At 7.5 miles you'll reach a signed intersection with Moose Creek Canyon Trail to your left. Continue straight. The trail steeply climbs via four switchbacks to 9,085-ft. Moose Creek Divide and the

Top: the view looking west as hikers climb the back side of Rendezvous Peak to reach the tram. Right: Hikers ascend wooded switchbacks as they climb toward the tram.

boundary with Grand Teton National Park at 8.0 miles, where a sign gives various Teton Crest Trail mileages.

The trail continues trending north at a level to downhill grade, passing a small pond in a quarter-mile as it bisects an open, flowered expanse. At 8.6 miles, you'll reach a signed junction with the Middle-Fork Cut-off Trail. Keep right. The path drops through lush terrain, following small tributaries of the Middle Fork of Granite Creek to a signed intersection at 9.2 miles. The left fork travels down Granite Canyon. Bear right onto the Rendezvous Mountain Trail to reach the tram.

The path drops to a rocky crossing of the upper South Fork of Granite Creek, often dry by late summer. It hops several run-off streams then begins a sustained climb up the backside of the ski area. Conifers provide shade as you steadily climb to a ridge crest.

The trail turns right on the ridge and drops into a rocky bowl that harbors profuse bluebells and columbine fed by snowmelt streams. It then climbs forested switchbacks to the crest of Rendezvous Bowl and a signed junction at 12.3 miles. From here, it is another .4 mile to the tram dock.

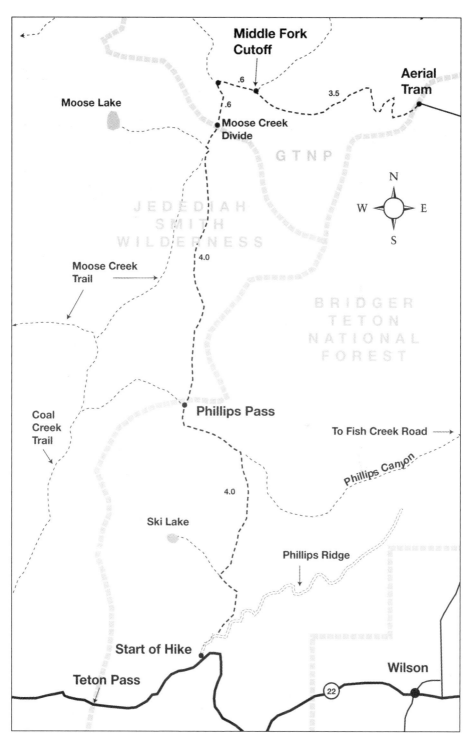

Phillips Pass to Tram Hike

89 Phillips Ridge

Distance:
> Ridge Viewpoint: 2.3 miles
> End of Ridge: 3.4 miles

Elevation change:
> Ridge Viewpoint: Approx. 785 ft. gain, 75 ft. loss
> End of Ridge: Approx. 770 ft. gain, 435 ft. loss

Maximum elevation:
> Ridge Viewpoint: 8,442 ft. at weather station
> End of Ridge: 8425 ft.

Maps: Rendezvous Peak. Book map opposite page
Season: June through October
Use restrictions: None.

Phillips Ridge is a wooded bump of land that extends over two miles in a southwest to northeast direction. Its northern end drops into Phillips Canyon. Its south end subsides into the natural divide that crests at Teton Pass. Phillip's high point provides fine views of the valley floor and Tetons to the north, the Snake River Range to the south.

The ridge is popular with mountain bikers, who follow a dirt two-track road the length of the ridge before dropping down a two-mile trail built the summer of 2008. The "Two Tower Trail" connects a power tower on the ridge to a lower tower on the powerline road. Mountain bikers/hikers eventually exit via a connecting trail onto Fish Creek Road. (This connecting trail and lower road segment is described in hike no. 96).

The Phillips Ridge Road was built to install the high-tension Fish Creek power- line overhead, and vegetation has been cleared below the line. This makes walking to the end of the ridge and beyond unattractive to hikers. The viewpoint, however, is reached before the powerline becomes a major distraction. It offers a fine after-work or half-day alternative for those seeking a short outing close to home.

The trail to Phillips Ridge begins at the start of Phillips Canyon Road on Teton Pass. The first .4 mile of this venture is shared with those heading to Phillips Pass and Ski Lake.

Driving Directions

Follow driving directions for Phillips Ridge given on page 219. Mileage begins at the start of Phillips Canyon Road.

Trail Description

The road climbs at an initially steep then more moderate grade through sub-alpine and Douglas fir forest. The track is lined with balsamroot, sticky geraniums, bluebells, lupine and salsify. You'll soon pass a signed intersection with the Arrow Trail to your right This multi-use trail eventually intersects Phillips Ridge Road, and is an alternative to walking a portion of the dirt track. (See hike no. 90.) This description follows the road until you reach a signed intersection to Ski Lake and Phillips Pass at .4 miles. Bear right here. The rocky two-track climbs at an easy to moderate grade, its course sporadically

240

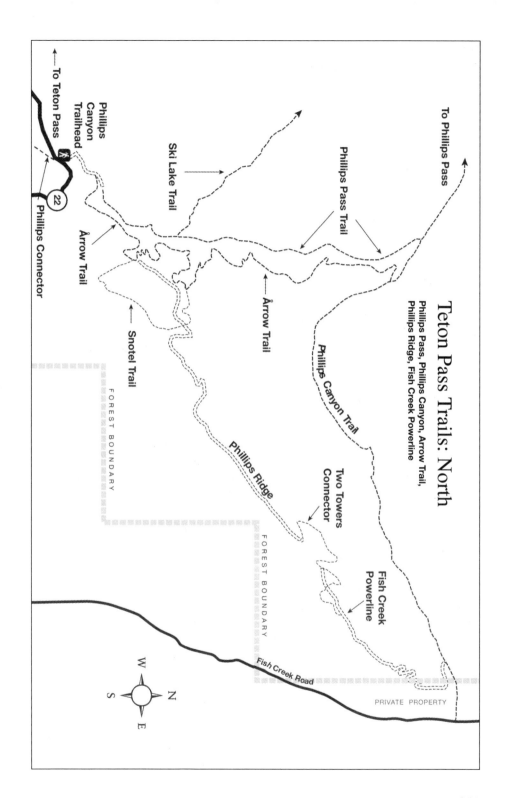

Teton Pass Trails: North

Phillips Pass, Phillips Canyon, Arrow Trail,
Phillips Ridge, Fish Creek Powerline

To Teton Pass

Phillips Canyon Trailhead

22

Phillips Connector

Ski Lake Trail

Arrow Trail

To Phillips Pass

Phillips Pass Trail

Arrow Trail

Snotel Trail

Phillips Canyon Trail

FOREST BOUNDARY

Phillips Ridge

Two Towers Connector

Fish Creek Powerline

FOREST BOUNDARY

Fish Creek Road

PRIVATE PROPERTY

W N
S E

shaded by massive Douglas fir and Engelmann spruce. Continue straight where a dirt two-track, not shown of the topo map, crosses the road. The track curves around an open, grassy hillside before passing a steep jeep track to your left. Stay on the main road, which curves right at an easy grade before bending left and resuming its upward, northeast course.

Top: An old tower used for fire and weather observation is located on Phillips Ridge. Bottom: A panoramic vista of the Snake River and surrounding terrain, viewed from Phillips Ridge.

A number of jeep two-tracks criss-cross this area. Keep on the main road to reach the ridge, traveling on a generally upward course through wooded terrain. At 1.8 miles the road turns noticeably right and the powerline crosses it overhead. Here, expansive views of 10,086-ft. Mount Glory and the Snake River Range to the west and southwest open up. A short distance farther, the road divides, with the right branch leading to the viewpoint, and the left to the end of the ridge.

To reach the viewpoint

Bear right at the split and follow the jeep road for another .3 mile to the wooded crest of the ridge. A use trail extends beyond the jeep track another .2 mile. Nice views of the southern end of Jackson Hole and the braided Snake River are enjoyed along the ridge. You'll pass an old weather tower on the crest, hidden in the trees until you are upon it. Its steel frame is capped by a small wood lookout on top. The tower is locked and no longer in use. It has not been structurally maintained; for your own safety please do not attempt to scale it.

To reach the end of the ridge

Bear left at the road split. Ahead, views of the valley floor open up, dominated by the Sleeping Indian. North, the southern slopes of 10,927-ft. Rendezvous Peak frame the horizon. The rocky two-track curves sharply left then switchbacks right as it drops to the low end of the ridge at an easy to moderate grade. It levels near a pretty grove of aspens before descending on a somewhat gentler course. After ascending a small rise, the aerial tram and the Grand pop into view.

The track gradually climbs again as it approaches the end of the ridge, 300 feet lower than its crest.

90 Arrow Trail

Distance: 5 miles
Elevation change: Approx. 890 ft. gain; Approx. 460 ft. loss
Maximum elevation: Approx. 8,240 ft.
Maps: Book map pg. 241
Season: Mid-July through early September
Use restrictions:
Wilderness and park regulations apply. Mountain bikes, motorized vehicles and pets prohibited.

The Arrow Trail was designed for mountain bikes—and is best suited for that purpose. It is, however, open to hikers and trail runners, and provides a connecting link for a loop hike and other trails. It is thus included in this book.

The serpentine trail travels in-and-out of forest and open meadow as it travels generally north to connect with Phillips Canyon Trail. It is named in honor of the Boy Scouts who constructed the path the summer of 2008. Over 1,000 scouts belonging to the Boy Scouts of America (BSA) honor society, Order of the Arrow, converged in Jackson that July to construct the Arrow Trail and three others: the History, Two Towers and Big Rocks trails. The project was part of ArrowCorp5, a massive BSA service project on five national forests. Over the course of five weeks, scouts donated $5.6 million dollars of work in what has been hailed as the largest volunteer service project ever conducted on US National forests. The Arrow Trail is the flagship project of the endeavor.

Driving Directions

Follow directions given on page 219. Mileage begins at the start of Phillips Canyon Road.

Trail Description

The road climbs at an initially steep then more moderate grade through sub-alpine and Douglas fir forest, its course lined with balsamroot, sticky geraniums, bluebells, lupine and salsify. You'll soon reach a signed intersection with the Arrow Trail that angles off the right side of the road.

The trail gently descends and contours a hillside a short distance before beginning an easy to moderate climb through open forest interspersed with wildflower-covered meadows. At .4 mile, it traverses a longer open stretch, then curves left and crosses a dirt two-track road at .6 mile. The path travels just inside treeline as it parallels a long meadow to your left. It then traverses sage-covered slopes and re-enters the forest.

You'll reach an intersection with the Phillip's Ridge Road at 1.2 miles. Continue straight across the road. The path climbs up a series of open, banked switchbacks obviously designed for mountain biking, then enters a pretty wooded section graced by large Engelmann spruce and Douglas fir. At approximately 2.5 miles, you'll reach an intersection. Across the road, an old dirt two track continues straight. Cross the road and take the path that

243

Top: Cliffbands near the intersection of the Arrow and Phillips Canyon Trails. Right: The start of the Arrow Trail passes between two large fir trees.

angles slightly right. It travels through a split in a large boulder to reach a signed intersection at 2.6 miles. The trail to the right is the Sno-Tel path; the Arrow Trail branches left.

The Arrow Trail crosses a plank bridge at 2.9 miles, then follows a slightly up-and-down course through forest. At 4.3 miles, views of the Sleeping Indian and Jackson Peak to the east open up.

A half-mile farther, you'll cross the Middle Fork of Phillips Canyon Creek. The junction with Phillips Canyon Trail is reached in another quarter-mile.

Retrace your steps to return. Hikers can also descend Phillips Canyon to Fish Creek Road, or turn left and walk up canyon for .3 mile to the intersection with the Phillips Pass Trail. Turning left here will return you to the trailhead in 2.8 miles, completing an 8.1 mile loop.

Arrow Trail hikers are advised to expect a fair amount of mountain bike traffic.

The West Bank

Introduction

Scenic Fall Creek and Fish Creek Roads at the base of Teton Pass provide access to the Snake River Range and the southernmost eastern flank of the Tetons. Phillips Canyon, Munger Mountain, Taylor Mountain and Rock Creek Traverse are among the rewarding excursions close to the Wilson and Teton Village. The Snake River dikes—the official demarcation boundary for "The West Bank"—have also evolved into a recreation corridor for fishermen, mountain bikers, hikers and skiers.

Jackson Hole Mountain Resort in Teton Village rounds out the recreation opportunities west of the Snake River. Covering over 3,000 acres, the resort encompasses 10,450-ft. Rendezvous Peak and 8,426-ft. Après Vous Peak one-and-a-half miles to the northeast. Casper Bowl lies between the two. Although conceived as a winter sports playground, the Village has turned into a popular summer destination as well. The 7.2-mile service road crisscrossing Après Vous and Rendezvous Peaks makes an ideal trail to the summit of Rendezvous. A trail constructed by the National Park Service on the backside of Rendezvous provides a connecting link to the Crest Trail, Granite Canyon and destinations such as Moose Lake on the west slope of the Tetons. The resort has also constructed several fine self-guided interpretive trails, including the .3-mile Summit Loop Hike and the 4.2-mile Rock Springs Bowl Hike.

The top of Rendezvous Mountain is one of the best places in the valley to view the meandering, braided path of the Snake River, dubbed "Mad River" by trappers who found the waterway difficult to float. The 1000-mile plus waterway courses through Jackson Hole on its way to the Columbia River and eventually the Pacific Ocean. From the summit one can see Housetop Mountain, Battleship Mountain, Mount Meek and Fossil Peak, all rising on the crest between the Teton's east and west slopes.

Because of its high elevation, trails that start or lead to the top of the mountain are often closed due to snow until early July, if not later. For current information on mountain conditions, the cost of the aerial tram and operating hours, call Jackson Hole Mountain Resort at 307-733-2292, or visit: www.jacksonhole.com/info/ae.summer.tram.asp.

For additional information on West Bank trails, contact the Jackson District Ranger Office by calling or writing:

> Jackson Ranger District
> Box 1689
> Jackson, Wyoming 83001
> 307-739-5400

91 Snake River Levees

Distance:
    Northeast levee to first gate: 3 miles RT
    Northeast levee to second gate: 4.9 miles RT
    Southwest levee to gate: 4.4 miles RT
Elevation change: Negligible
Maximum elevation: Approx. 6,200 ft.
Maps: None needed.
Season: Year-round
Use restrictions:
    Northeast dike is occasionally closed when the gravel pit farther north is operating.
    Fishermen need a Wyoming license and must comply with all regulations.

The Snake River levees—popularly known as "the dikes"—are to West Bank residents what Cache Creek is to town dwellers: a close-to-home place to recreate. Mountain bikes, dog walkers, runners, skiers and fishermen utilize the hardpack dirt and gravel roads atop the levees year-round. With its continuous views of the Tetons, the northeast dike tends to draw the most use.

Driving Directions

From the intersection of Wyoming Hwy. 390 (the Moose-Wilson Road) and Wyoming Hwy. 22, travel east toward the town of Jackson to the first gravel pullout on the right side of the highway, just before the bridge. This is the parking area for the southwest dike. To access the northeast dike, continue across the bridge over the Snake and turn into the first gravel road on your left, a half mile beyond the Moose-Wilson Road junction. If you are coming from town, turn off Broadway/U.S. Hwy 89/191 onto Wyoming Hwy. 22 and set your odometer. It is 3.5 miles to the gravel access road to the northeast dike, located on the right side of the highway just before a prominent brown and white sign for the Teton Village Resort Area. For the southwest dike, continue across the bridge and turn left onto the first gravel road, a total of 3.8 miles from the Broadway/ Hwy. 22 junction.

Trail Description

The levees are flat, gravel roadways bordered by the Snake River on one side and towering cottonwood trees on the other. The northeast dike draws the most people for its ongoing views of the Teton Range and numerous side ponds and quiet pools. In the last two years, however, the southwest dike has gained in popularity— primarily because it gives access to the "Wilson Beach." Massive amounts of gravel were dredged and redeposited to alter the course of the main channel of the river near a developed boat launch area off the northwest dike. The reconstruction created grassy areas, gravel bars and large, shallow channels on the south side of the bridge. The channels and pools are sufficiently warmed by the sun to make swimming the typically ice-cold waters of the Snake tolerable. Braided river channels shift and change, so it is anyone's guess how long the "beach" will be in existence. While it is, valley residents will continue to enjoy it to the fullest.

Top: Cottonwoods reflected in a side pond along the levee. Right: The Grand, seen from the NE levee.

Prominent ranching families constructed the first Snake River levees in Jackson Hole in the 1940s to protect pasture land. Higher levees on one side of the river created flooding on the other, propelling ranchers on the opposite bank to construct their own. This, in turn, created problems downstream. The ranchers and other influential valley residents marshaled their considerable political clout to secure passage of the 1950 Flood Control Act, federal legislation that mandated the Army Corp of Engineers build a network of Jackson Hole levees. Over 20 miles of levees were reconstructed by the Corp from 1957-1964, at a cost of $2.2 million. It presently costs over $400,000 annually to maintain the levees and restore damage done by lateral pressure of the river.

While levees help protect land from flooding, they are damaging to river ecosystems. Cottonwood trees need periodic flooding to successfully seed new trees. The contained river gouges deeper, swifter channels that affect fisheries and eagles and osprey dependent on fish to survive. The levees block traditional spawning areas and side channels and foster a false sense of security that encourages development in the floodplain on the west bank of the Snake. They have been called one of the biggest ecological challenges in Jackson Hole. It is widely acknowledged among river experts that, given what is known about their impact, the levees would likely not be constructed today.

92 Rock Creek/Poison Creek Traverse

Distance: 4.2 miles one-way
Elevation change: Approx. 720 ft. gain, 750 ft. loss
Maximum elevation: Approx. 7,040 ft.
Maps: Munger Mountain, Jackson. Book map pg. 253
   Use restrictions: Closed to ATVs. Open to motorcycles July 1-September 9. Motorized users may not access trail directly from Rock Creek trailhead, as labeled on the trail map on page 253.
Season: Late May to early November

Easy ascents and descents through pleasant creek drainages make this a premiere mountain bike ride or early season hike. It is equally stunning in autumn, when flourishing aspen groves lining the trail dress themselves in shades of gold. Lush wildflowers that attract a bevy of hummingbirds compete for your attention with winning views of 9,862-ft. Powder Peak, the Tetons, a slice of the Snake River and Munger Mountain. Red-tailed hawks cruise the open meadows looking for dinner, while elk can be spied near the meadows' edge. Alas, there is often a s—t load of bovines milling about, too. A short car shuttle makes this a pleasant half-day outing.

Driving Directions

From Wilson, turn onto Fall Creek Road and drive 12.6 miles to the unsigned Rock Creek pullout on the left side of the road, identified by a talus slope on the south side of the creek drainage. Those wishing to do a car shuttle should leave a vehicle parked at the end of a dirt two-track on the left side of the road, 9.7 miles from its start; the hike exits here. (Traveling north on Fall Creek from Snake River Canyon, it is 5.1 miles to the trailhead; 8 miles to the shuttle point.)

Trail Description

Walk northeast up the old roadbed.

Bubbling Rock Creek is to your right, semi-hidden by healthy willow thickets. The trail traverses just above the toe of open, sage-covered slopes before dipping down to cross a bridge over a tributary stream. It then ascends to the crest of the ridge bounding the east side of Rock Creek. The undulating path travels through forest punctuated by scattered, small openings. Early one summer, a ruffed grouse, red fox, and a grumpy badger kept this author company on the ridge.

The path reaches the border of a large, grassy meadow at 1.3 miles and splits. The right fork heads a short distance toward Munger Mountain before disappearing. Keep left. The trail crosses a small bridge and curls right, heading north on a level grade along the left edge of the meadow. At the end of the meadow, it bends left and climbs up grassy slopes before entering the trees and ascending to an overlook of Powder Peak and the Snake River Range at 2.4 miles.

Beyond the viewpoint, the trail bears right (NW) and climbs an open slope covered with Wyethia (commonly called mule's ears for the shape of its leaves) and reaches a 4-way junction. The trail to your left leads south to the top of Point 7081. Wally's World trail—named for its originator—continues straight. It ascends a ridge and follows its length before descending to Fall Creek Road, exiting

Top: The view looking back toward the Snake River Range near the start of the Rock Creek Traverse. Bottom: Hikers head into the remarkable Aspen groves encountered near the end of the hike. The groves are among the prettiest in the region.

near a Forest Service information kiosk .8 miles south of the end of the Rock Creek Traverse, and presents a nice alternative descent. To complete the traverse, bear right at the junction. The path gently descends to a pleasing meadow liberally strewn with lavender violets. At meadow's end it enters an Engelmann spruce and aspen forest, crosses a boggy area, and descends at an easy then progressively steeper grade down Poison Creek drainage. You'll soon see that small stream to your left, which you follow for the remainder of the hike.

As the descent continues, pleasing vistas of the Tetons and the braided Snake River on the valley floor pop into view. Cross a bridge over the stream and continue descending at an easier grade to a second bridged crossing a half-mile farther. Beyond, the path widens into dirt two-track and enters remarkable aspen groves. What appear to be many trees may, in reality, be clones of only one. In mountains where wind blown seeds may not land in a suitable place to germinate, shoots grow from horizontal roots of the parent tree, an adaptation that ensures its survival.

Proceed northwest at a level grade to a wood post and barbed wire fence at 4.1 miles. Loop the wire off the post to open the gate—making sure you close it behind you—and continue straight cross a grassy area where the trail is somewhat fainter. (A sketchy dirt two-track parallels the fence line. Another track crosses the creek and heads up a hill on the opposite side. These are not the paths you want.) The path becomes clear again when you re-enter the aspens. As you continue gently descending you'll see a powerline to your left, and then glimpse a section of Fall Creek Road. You reach the road at the 4.2-mile mark, the end of this hike.

93 Munger Mountain

Distance:
  Via Lookout Pack Trail: 2.0 miles one-way
  Via Summit Loop Trail: 2.5 miles one-way
Elevation gain: Approx. 2050 ft.
Maximum elevation: 8,383 ft.
Maps: Munger Mountain. Book map pg. 253
Use restrictions: Single-track motorized use permitted on Summit Loop Trail
  July 1- September 9. Critical wildlife habitat. Stay on designated route and keep
  dogs under voice control.
Season: Late May through mid-October

Munger Mountain is a distinctive landmark in the south end of the valley. It's apex was the site of a fire lookout constructed by the Civilian Conservation Corps (CCC) in the 1930s, chosen for clear, unobstructed views of the Teton Range to the north, Snake River Range to the west, the Wyoming Range to the south and the Gros Ventre Range to the east.

The lookout enticed hikers through the late 1950s, when the Forest Service stopped using the structure. New fire policies, reporting done by public and private aircraft and use of radio repeaters had doomed fire towers to extinction. Some hikers and skiers continued to visit the lookout—often staying overnight—until the Forest Service destroyed the structure in 1976.

The pack trail to the lookout was abandoned and gradually fell out of use. It is not difficult to access the summit, however, and it is worth the walk up. A section of the pack trail is presently overgrown and is more of a route. Local boy scouts are considering improving this section as a service project; check with the Forest Service for its current status. Hikers uncomfortable with route finding—or pushing through waist to shoulder high wildflowers—may prefer hiking the Summit Loop Trail, detailed at the end of this write-up. Both trails share the final stretch to the summit, and are thus presented together.

Driving Directions, Pack Trail

At Hoback Junction, turn south toward Alpine on U.S. Hwy. 26/89. Drive 4.2 miles to signed Wilson-Fall Creek Road on your right. Turn in and drive 3.3 miles to a bridge over Fall Creek. Just beyond the bridge, turn right onto a narrow dirt road. (Alternately, you may reach this point by driving south down Fall Creek Road 14.5 miles from its start off Wyoming Hwy. 22 in Wilson).

Cross the cattle guard and find a place to park off-road. Two-tenths of a mile farther, a dirt two-track heads left (N). This is the start of the hike.

Trail Description

The dirt two-track stays left of s small creek as it travels north through open, sage-covered terrain. The track soon narrows to trail width, and you'll see a path cutting steeply up the base of the slope. This is a steep shortcut trail prone to erosion. Please stay on the main trail

Top: Looking northeast from Munger's summit. Right: A broken foundation, scattered planks, metal hardware and a suvey marker identify the former site of the fire tower on Munger Mountain.

as it bends right then left in a semi-circle and contours at an easy grade around the open slope dotted with large Douglas fir. The grade becomes steeper as the path continues north and eventually disappears in overgrown foliage. Continue ascending, staying right of a clump of chokecherry bushes. Bend right around the upper edge of the clump, and head toward a large, lone Douglas fir. From there, hike toward a group of dead aspen upslope to your right. As you draw near them, start angling left uphill at about the 10 o'clock position toward a dip in the ridge ahead of you. You'll intersect a path that leads to the clear Summit Loop Trail on the ridge. If you don't hit it, keep ascending toward the ridge and you'll pick up the Summit Trail on the ridge. Bear right onto that trail and continue ascending.

The upper sections of the Summit ridge Trail are very steep: climbers will understand the term "5.10" dirt. Poles are recommended to help navigate this section. Hikers are reminded that the Summit Trail is open to motorcyles from July 1 to September 9. Riders often must use a fair amount of speed to ascend this grade. If you near a motorcycle, *step off the side of the trail* for both your safety and theirs.

The upper segment of the Summit Loop Trail is open and can be quite warm. Other than a large beaver-enlarged spring-fed pond resting 20 yards below the track, water is not available.

A concrete foundation, a few rusted

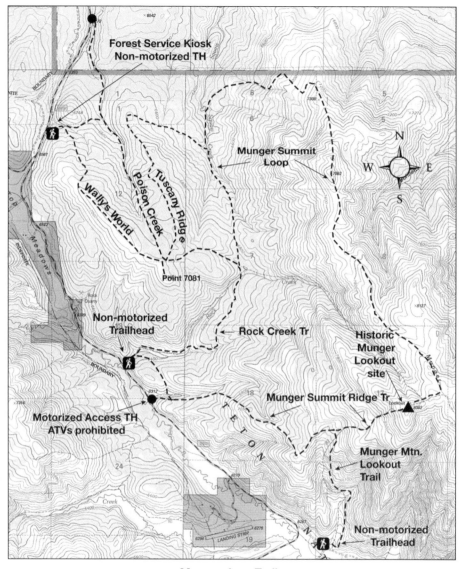

Munger Area Trails

can lids, and a metal survey marker placed by the U.S. Coast and Geodetic Survey in 1946 mark the remains of the lookout.

The trail ascending east from the lookout site is the continuation of the loop trail, an 8.2-mile outing. Munger is named after a prospector who searched for gold at the base of the mountain.

Hikers who wish to hike the Summit Ridge Trail to the lookout site can access the start of that trail .3 mile south of the Rock Creek Trailhead off the east side of Fall Creek Road (approximately 13 miles south of Wilson). The lower portion of the trail is forested. It soon travels through open terrain and intersects the pack trail to the former fire lookout. Though longer, the entire length of the trail is clear.

94 Taylor Mountain

Distance: 1.4 miles one-way
Elevation gain: Approx. 1,090 ft.
Maximum elevation: 8,010 ft.
Maps: Munger Mountain, Teton Pass
Use restrictions: None. Forest Regulations apply.
Season: June through October

Barely cresting 8,000 feet, Taylor Mountain is one of the lowest named summits in the Snake River Range. Open, sage-covered slopes lead to its broad apex, yielding arresting views en route and 360-degree panoramic splendor on top. An array of wildflowers, high peaks clothed in white and the bottle green floor of Jackson Hole make this hike especially inviting early season, when lingering winter snow entombs trails at higher elevations. Elk and deer regularly roam the peak and mountain bluebirds and sage grouse are often spotted. Rarely seen mountain lions haunt both Taylor and Munger Mountain to the east.

Driving Directions

From the town of Wilson turn onto Fall Creek Road and drive 10.8 miles to North Fork Fall Creek Road. Turn right onto it. (It is 6.7 miles and a left-hand turn if you are traveling the Wilson/Fall Creek Road north from Snake River Canyon.) Constructed in 1949, North Fork Fall Creek Road can be a dicey proposition. Sections of the dirt artery are often badly rutted and have to be traveled with care. The road may be impassable for sedans and/or non-four wheel drive vehicles in wet weather.

The road divides at 1.7 miles. A brown wood sign at the intersection indicates the left fork leads to Trails End Ranch in one mile. Bear right to reach the start of this hike, and reset your odometer. Pass dirt two-tracks at .4 and .7 miles before reaching the unmarked Taylor Mountain two-track between .8 -.9 mile. Park as far off the main road as possible so you don't block onward travel for other users.

Trail Description

The two-track immediately climbs at a moderate grade toward a pretty grove of quaking aspens. Balsamroot, sticky geranium and larkspur line the path early season, replaced by lupine, yarrow and Indian paintbrush as summer progresses. Upon reaching the aspens the rutted two-track bends northwest and begins a steep climb through sparse aspen and spruce forest, soon replaced by sage-covered slopes. The steep grade and open terrain continue unabated until you reach the low end of Taylor's southeast ridge, one mile beyond and 720 feet above your parked vehicle.

The steep but pleasant climb to the ridge offers unobstructed views of the crest of the Snake River Range to your left (W) and behind you. Wolf Mountain, the prominent 9,483-foot pyramid seen when you turn around, dominates the southern skyline. The snow-covered peaks of the Gros Ventre Range rise to your right (E). Just off the track a garden of wildflowers that tolerate dry, gravelly soil infuse

The snowy Snake River Range, viewed from the summit of Taylor Mountain early season.

the silvery green, sage-covered slopes with color. Early bloomers include field chickweed, small-flowered woodland star, stone-crop, waterleaf, nuttall violets, cutleaf daisies, sage buttercup, an occasional Indian paintbrush and sweetly fragrant, sunny yellow prairie rocket, an attractive member of the mustard family.

Upon reaching the ridge, you will see engaging vistas of Jackson Hole unfolding to the north. Settlements along the west bank of the Snake River are visible beneath the craggy peaks of the Teton Range. The meandering Snake River cuts a wide, lazy swath through the verdant valley floor. East Gros Ventre, West Gros Ventre and Blacktail Buttes rise above the town of Jackson, preamble to the Gros Ventre Range further east. To the distant northeast, the Sleeping Indian slumbers beneath his blanket of snow.

The two-track turns more directly west on the ridge and drops slightly, skirting a small pond often dry by midsummer. Elk and deer tracks indicate the small body of water is a favored watering hole. Beyond the pond the track resumes

climbing at a moderately steep grade to the next high point then flattens or drops, a pattern repeated twice before reaching the summit.

The ridge rewards hikers with impressive views and air redolent with the scent of many-flowered phlox, longleaf phlox and prairie rocket. Aspen below to your left, interspersed with Douglas fir and limber pine, attract flocks of birds that feed on their seeds and cones. A magnificent, lone Douglas fir on the right skyline signals the final push to the top. This sentinel and the remains of an old metal fence mark the broad, open summit.

The two-track drops off the apex and gently descends toward a group of massive limber pine and Douglas fir, offering a great place to enjoy lunch and savor the view. The ground beneath the group of trees is overlaid with thousands of shooting stars and prairie-smoke.

Fire rings indicate people have camped at this spot, though water is not readily available; by continuing to descend on the two-track, you come to a pond a 100 or so feet below the path.

255

95 Phillips Canyon

Distance: 5 miles one-way to Phillips Pass
Elevation gain: Approx. 2,630 ft.
Maximum elevation: 8,932 ft. at Phillips Pass
Maps: Teton Village, Rendezvous Mountain
Use restrictions:
Multi-use to the intersection with the Arrow Trail, Beyond, use is restricted to hiking and horse use only.
Season: Late June through mid-October

The trail up wooded Phillips Canyon features spectacular mid-summer wildflowers, open bowls, access to the southern reaches of Teton Crest Trail and expansive views of Jedediah Smith Wilderness. Numerous extended day hikes, aided by a car shuttle to Phillips Ridge, Coal Creek or Teton Village, can also be made. These attributes—plus its proximity to Jackson—make this a popular day outing for local residents.

There is limited parking and the trailhead is presently not signed. It has been moved slightly south since the 1968 Teton Village topo was plotted to respect private property rights. Please obey the signage so future trail access is not endangered.

Driving Directions

In the town of Wilson, turn north onto Second Street and drive .2 mile to signed Fish Creek Road to your right. Turn onto it and drive 3.0 miles to an obvious dirt pullout lined with rocks on the right side of the road. Park here. The start of the trail is the wide dirt swath off the left side of the road, across from the parking pullout.

Trail Description

The track climbs a short distance before flattening and bearing right through open forest, staying left of a wood fence that marks private property. (You'll soon see a use trail bearing right toward Phillips Canyon Creek. Stay left.) The path travels west at an almost level grade through shady stretches of Douglas fir, lodgepole, mountain ash and mountain maple. Clematis, thimbleberry, serviceberry, sticky geranium, lupine, wild strawberry and meadowrue thrive in the varied understory.

Keep left at a second junction (the trail to the right soon ends at an old fire ring) to a crossing of the bluebell-lined creek. A two-foot wide log spans the stream, providing a means of keeping your feet dry. Beyond the crossing a use trail comes in from the right. Continue straight. The path proceeds at a level grade through open forest before beginning a gentle ascent to an unmarked junction at .5 mile. The trail to the left leads to the old power line access road. Take the path to the right. It ascends at a moderate to moderately steep grade through Douglas fir and lodgepole forest as it enters the wooded canyon, closely following the Middle Fork of Phillips Canyon Creek.

The path diverges from the topo map where the stream has cut away the

Hikers descend toward Phillips Pass. From the Pass, it is possible to continue to the aerial tram.

bank, climbing north above the creek. It then enters a clearing—opening views of a rocky spur on the north side of Phillips Ridge—before entering aspen groves.

Rock hop a creek tributary at 1.3 miles, the North Fork of Phillips Canyon Creek .4 mile farther. Beyond, the path climbs through open forest at a moderately steep to steep grade, ascending several tight switchbacks before resuming a steady, upward western course through meadow and forest.

Continue straight where the Arrow Trail intersects the left side of the trail at 3.5 miles, and again at 3.8 miles when the Phillips Pass Trail comes in from the left. This path travels south to Wyoming Hwy. 22, passing the junction to Ski Lake, and is a nice alternative hike or ride.

The trail climbs open slopes, gaining an additional 632 feet on its

way to the divide. The appealing open bowl, fed by the upper reaches of Middle Fork Phillips Canyon Creek, is lush with wildflowers mid-summer, consistently offering spectacular displays of color. Lupine, in particular, stages a memorable extravaganza in mid-July.

Stay right at 4.7 miles, where a short spur trail heads left and soon peters out. The path angles right (N), and climbs to the pass, marked by a Jedediah Smith Wilderness sign. The pass yields wide-open views into scenic Moose Basin to the west, framed by Taylor Mountain to the south. Housetop and Fossil Mountains define the northern horizon.

From the pass, it is possible to walk to the aerial tram in Teton Village or drop into Mesquite Creek drainage and hike down Coal Creek. Consult the Rendezvous Peak topo.

96 Fish Creek Powerline

Distance: 5 miles one-way to Phillips Pass
Elevation gain: Approx. 2,630 ft.
Maximum elevation: 7,545 ft.
Maps: Teton Village, Rendezvous
Use restrictions: This is a multi-use trail
Season: Mid-May through October

The road constructed to install the power line dropping off Phillips Ridge to the substation north of Wilson provides a nice hiking or mountain bike ride alternative to well-known and highly trafficked Old Pass Road. The abandoned track is easy to follow and provides superb views of the Aspens, Tetons, the Snake River and Gros Ventre Range.

Driving Directions

In the town of Wilson, turn north onto Second Street and drive .2 mile to signed Fish Creek Road to your right. Turn onto it and drive 3.0 miles to an obvious dirt pullout lined with rocks on the right side of the road. Park here. The start of the trail is the wide dirt swath off the left side of the road, across from the parking area. The bottom of the path traverses private property. Please stay on the trail.

Trail Description

The dirt track climbs a short distance before flattening and bearing right through open forest, staying left of a wood fence that marks private property. (You'll soon see a use trail bearing right toward a tributary of Fish Creek. Stay left.) The path travels west at an almost level grade through shady stretches of Douglas fir, lodgepole, mountain ash and mountain maple. Clematis, thimbleberry, serviceberry, sticky geranium, lupine, wild strawberry and meadowrue thrive in the lush understory.

Keep left at a second junction (the trail to the right soon ends at an old fire ring) to a crossing of the bluebell-lined tributary flowing down Phillips Canyon. A two-foot wide log spans the tributary, providing a means of keeping your feet dry. Beyond the crossing a trail again comes in from the right. Continue straight.

The path proceeds at a level grade through open forest before beginning a gentle ascent. Stay left where the un-marked trail up Phillips Canyon turns right at .6 mile. Shortly beyond you'll reach a concrete bridge spanning the tributary. The single-track trail crosses the bridge and bends left toward a rock face, making a horseshoe turn as it loops east along the old road and climbs at a moderately steep grade. The grassy roadbed turns right (S), then switchbacks left as it continues ascending, opening up views of Rendezvous Mountain and the aerial tram at Teton Village to the north.

The grade lessens as the road turns

Top: View of the Grand Teton from the Fish Creek powerline track. Right: Sticky geraniums are one of many wildflowers that flourish close to the road cut.

right (S). Here the track is shaded by towering fir, and abundant tall grass divides the dirt two-track.

Looking left (E) through the trees, the distinctive Sleeping Indian and the Gros Ventre Range form the far horizon, while the Aspens settlement and braided Snake River are seen on the valley floor below you. The roadbed again turns right (W), then loops north, climbing at a moderate grade through towering Douglas fir. Switchbacking left, you soon cross below the powerline at 1.5 miles, traveling through a big open swath cleared for its placement.

The road continues its switchbacking, ascending course, crossing clearings below the powerline five more times. The grade steepens at the turns, and at times the path narrows to single-track width.

At 2.5 miles, the old access road pass-es close to a steel support tower, marked by Point 7545 on the Teton Village topo, and soon ends. The summer of 2008, the Boy Scouts constructed a trail connecting the lower segment of the road with the road atop Phillips Ridge, extending this outing if desired. Phillips Ridge is accessed via Phillips Canyon Road on Teton Pass. See hike no. 89 for a description.

97 Rendezvous Peak Trail

Distance: 7.2 miles one-way
Elevation gain: Approx. 4,100 ft.
Maximum elevation: 10,450 ft.
Maps: Teton Village, Rendezvous
Use restrictions: Mountain bikes prohibited
Season: July through early September

A 300-mile panorama of seven mountain ranges, the Snake River, and "right there" views of Buck Mountain and the Grand Teton lure' hikers to the top of Jackson Hole Mountain Resort. The resort's dirt service road—built when the tram and chairs were installed—connects the 10,450-ft. apex of Rendezvous Peak to facilities at its base. The meandering 7.2-mile swath rises over 4,100 feet on its way to the top. Most hikers prefer to ride the aerial tram up and walk down, but a large number also opt for the more aerobic choice of ascending the peak. Hikers who walk to the top presently earn a free ride down the aerial tram.

Driving Directions

Drive south out of Jackson on U.S. Hwy. 89/191, turning right onto Wyoming Hwy. 22 at the traffic light by Albertsons. Head west five miles to a bridge over the Snake River. Just over the bridge turn right onto Wyoming Hwy. 390 and drive seven miles to Teton Village, the resort complex at the base of the Jackson Hole Mountain Resort. The turn-off to the Village to the west is well marked.

Trail Description

From the parking lot walk up the gentle slope on the right side of the tram dock. Bear right before you reach the Festival Hall in front of you. You'll see a low angle ski run about 60 yards ahead. Follow the signs to the start of the service road, located on the right side of the run. The road heads north up 8,426-ft. Après Vous Peak before turning southwest and traversing its lower slopes. Signs on the mountain direct you to the tram. You'll pass Casper Bowl, Thunder chairlift and Laramie Bowl before reaching the bottom of Rendezvous Bowl. Steep switchbacks from the bottom of that bowl bring you to the top of the mountain. As you walk up consider this: Every fall, athletes competing in the Rendezvous Peak Run sprint up this stretch. The course record, bottom to top, is just under one hour.

Since the route is the service road the grade is more or less constant—a little steeper in some places and not quite so steep in others. The road winds in and out of the trees but is primarily open. Be sure to bring sufficient water for the hike. There is some run-off on the mountain's face but this dries up as the summer progresses, and in any case, it must be treated for safety. Moose, fox and black bear are occasionally seen by summer visitors to the mountain. Check the ticket window at the base of the mountain for information on recent wildlife sightings.

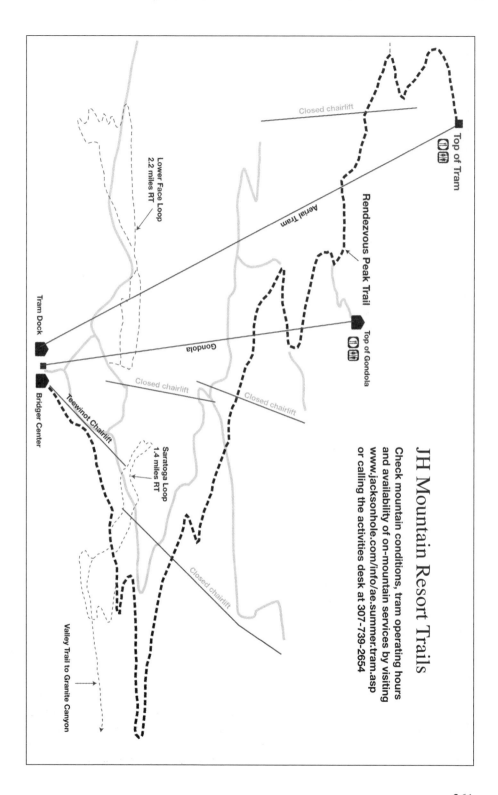

JH Mountain Resort Trails

Check mountain conditions, tram operating hours and availability of on-mountain services by visiting www.jacksonhole.com/info/ae.summer.tram.asp or calling the activities desk at 307-739-2654

Top of Tram

Closed chairlift

Rendezvous Peak Trail

Aerial Tram

Lower Face Loop 2.2 miles RT

Top of Gondola

Gondola

Tram Dock

Closed chairlift

Closed chairlift

Bridger Center

Teewinot Chairlift

Saratoga Loop 1.4 miles RT

Closed chairlift

Valley Trail to Granite Canyon

Cody Peak, viewed along the Jackson Hole Mountain Resort's service road to the top of the ski area.

Once on top, wander to the small rise behind the tram dock to peer into the telescope. On the dock itself signs identify the surrounding mountain ranges and notable peaks. Restrooms and a snack bar are located on the summit.

Bring warm clothing with you so you can linger and soak in the outstanding view. The 10,450-foot summit is often windy, and mountain storms can develop quite quickly: 80° and calm at the base of the Village may be only 50° and windy on top of Rendezvous. At a minimum a wool hat, lightweight gloves and a wind jacket are recommended gear for this outing.

The new tram system began operating the winter of 2008-09 after 21 months of construction, replacing the double-reversible system that began operation in 1966. It takes 9 minutes for the 100-person capacity tram cars to travel from the valley station at 6,311 feet to the summit dock at 10,450 feet. Like the former tram, the new tram is a double jig-back system: as one

car is ascending the mountain, another is simultaneously going down. Five towers between the valley and summit stations support 12,600 linear feet of track cable.

If you prefer to ride up and walk down, visit www.jacksonhole.com/info/ae.summer.tram.asp for current ticket prices and operating hours Discount coupons are often printed in the *Jackson Hole Daily* or the weekly *Jackson Hole News and Guide*. They are also sometimes offered on the resort's web site.

Or, consider something in-between hiking up or down the entire length of the service road. On evenings when the restaurant at the top of the Gondola is operating, ride the tram up and walk down the service road approximately 3 miles to the eatery. Grab a cold one on The Deck, (Happy Hour starts at 5:30!) and ride the gondola down to the base. The summer of 2009, the gondola restaurant opened July 4th. Call the activity desk at 307-739-2654 to confirm opening/operating hours.

98 Rock Springs/Cody Bowl Loop

Distance: 4.2 miles
Elevation change: Approx. 1,500 ft..
Maximum elevation: 10,450 ft.
Maps: Teton Village, Rendezvous. Book map pg. 265
Use restrictions:
   Mountain bikes prohibited. Hikers are required to stay on the designated trail.
Season: July through early September

The Rock Springs/Cody Bowl interpretive hike at Jackson Hole Mountain Resort is a strenuous 4.2-mile loop through varied, rugged alpine terrain. The loop introduces you to the alpine ecosystem: Engelmann spruce, whitebark pine, subalpine fir and snow buttercups; pink snow; glacial cirques; Teton geology; the fossils and Karst topography of Cody Bowl; and the small animals that den in this high region. This walk's striking beauty is arresting even to long-time valley residents.

The interpretive trail and other hiking routes down the mountain are opened when enough snow has melted off the east face of Rendezvous to allow safe trail travel, usually by early July. Naturally, this varies from year-to-year. For information on trail conditions, tram prices and operating hours, call Jackson Hole Mountain Resort at 733-2292.

Driving Directions

Drive south out of Jackson on U.S. Hwy. 89/191, turning right onto Wyoming Hwy. 22 at the traffic light by Albertsons. Head west five miles to a bridge over the Snake River. Just over the bridge turn right onto Wyoming Hwy. 390 and drive seven miles to Teton Village, the resort complex at the base of the Jackson Hole Mountain Resort. The turn-off is well marked.

Head toward the ticket sales/tram loading dock. The double jig-back tram whisks you to the top of Rendezvous in an average time of 9 minutes, gaining 4,139 vertical feet as the cables pull you skyward. The new aerial tram began operating the winter of 2008-09 after 21 months of construction. It replaced the tram system that had operated since 1966.

Trail Description

Traveling across meadows, talus slopes and occasional snow patches, the

Cody Bowl Lake disappears by late summer.

Top: Rugged Rock Springs Bowl is a scenic highlight of this hike. Bottom: A group carefully negotiates snow in the bowl, which can hold snow well into the summer. Check on conditions before embarking.

Rock Springs Bowl interpretive trail is approximately 40% downhill and 60% uphill—a challenge for those not used to exercising at high altitude. Ski area officials recommend that you allow yourself four hours to complete the loop, which begins by turning left (S) down the ridge trail leading from the tram to Granite Canyon Trailhead.

Stay on the service road/hiking trail as it leaves the ridgetop and drops northeast into Rendezvous Bowl. The steep subalpine slope is buried under 10-12 feet of compacted snow during the winter months. In the summer, small alpine wildflowers and stunted, wind-deformed trees called krummholz cling to the bowl's steep sides and help hold the unstable soil layer on the 35-degree angle slope. At the end of the second switchback, at approximately 1.1 miles, you'll see a clearly marked trail to your right that leaves the road and travels south across Rendezvous Trail, a man-made ski run. Leave the service road and follow the trail into Rock Springs Bowl, a beautiful area that encompasses most of the hike. The steep walls of this glacial cirque were carved during the last ice age 40,000 to 15,000 years ago. Snow clings to the steep slopes well into the summer. Early season you'll probably see "pink snow" created by the red gelatin-like coating that encases algae growing in the snowfields. Do not eat this. Pink snow can cause severe diarrhea and intestinal disorders.

As you begin the uphill walk on the far side of the bowl you may spy bright yellow snow buttercups and animal dens that house ubiquitous ground squirrels, pocket gophers, marmots and pikas. The last is an earless little ball of fur that squeaks out a warning if you get too close.

Near the top of the loop the trail enters Cody Bowl, a small cirque that rests above Rock Springs Bowl. This glacial hollow holds special interest for fossil lovers, as it contains abundant amounts of marine coral and brachiopods deposited in a shallow sea that covered the area 350 million years ago. Uplift of the Teton Range and consequent erosion has brought many of these long-buried fossils to the surface. They are embedded in rocks scattered throughout the bowl.

The bowl is an example Karst topography. Slightly acidic rainwater has dissolved the soft limestone rock in this area, creating a system of underground passages and caverns. Cody Bowl Lake, formed by meltwater, drains completely underground by late summer.

The marked trail climbs out of Cody Bowl and rejoins the ridge trail leading back to the aerial tram dock. Naturalists also lead hikes on top of the peak throughout the summer. Call the activities desk at 307-739-2654 for advance reservations and information.

Persons hiking on top of the mountain are advised that it can be as much as 20-30 degrees cooler than the valley floor, and that the weather can change rapidly. Foul weather can force the tram to stop operating, leaving hikers far from the tram no choice but to wait out the bad weather and hope the tram re-opens, or walk down the 7.2-mile service road to the valley floor. Anyone planning on hiking to Rock Springs and Cody Bowl should come prepared with warm clothing.

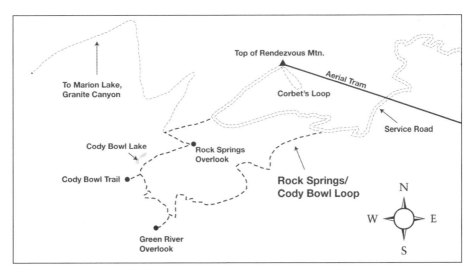

Rock Springs/Cody Bowl Loop Trail

99 Tram to Marion Lake
100 Tram to Moose Lakes

Marion Lake
>   Distance: 6.2 miles
>   Elevation change: Approx. 1,250 ft. gain; approx. 2,410 ft. loss
>   Maximum elevation: 10,450 ft.
>   Maps: Teton Village, Rendezvous Peak. Book map pg. 269
>   Season: July through early September
>   Use restrictions: Mountain bikes prohibited. National Park regulations apply.

Moose Lake
>   Distance: 6.4 miles one-way
>   Elevation change: Approx. 1,350 ft. gain; approx. 2,420 ft. loss
>   Maximum elevation: 10,450 ft.
>   Maps: Teton Village, Rendezvous Peak. Book map pg. 269
>   Season: July through early September
>   Use restrictions: Mountain bikes prohibited. Wilderness regulations apply.
>   Camp 200 ft. from lakeshore and 50 ft. from streams.

Tucked at the base of rocky 10,537-ft. Housetop Mountain, Marion Lake is one of the more popular day and overnight destinations in the southern end of the Teton Range. The up-and-down hike to the lake crosses the South, Middle and North Forks of Granite Creek before climbing a final bench to the small, aquamarine jewel. Moose and deer are often seen browsing in the high meadows and wildflowers abound. Good views of the backside of Rendezvous Peak and Granite Canyon add to this hike's appeal.

In many ways just as pretty as Marion Lake, Moose Lake on the west slope of the Tetons draws far less traffic. The lake is the largest of eight tarns clustered on limestone benches ringed to the west by a wall of 10,300-foot cliffs. This is a superb destination for a day hike or backpacking trip. The outlet to Moose Lake is the headwater of Moose Creek.

Hikers going to either destination share the first 4.1 miles of trail; this pair of hikes is thus presented together.

Driving Directions

Drive south out of Jackson on U.S. Hwy. 89/191, turning right onto Wyoming Hwy. 22 at the traffic light by Albertsons. Head west five miles to a bridge over the Snake River. Just over the bridge turn right onto Wyoming Hwy. 390 and drive seven miles to Teton Village, the resort complex at the base of the Jackson Hole Mountain Resort. The turn-off to the Village to the west is well marked.

Both hikes begin at the top of Rendezvous Peak, accessed by walking 7.2 miles up the service road, or riding the aerial tram to the top. Mileage assumes tram transport.

Top: The alpine scenery around Moose Lake in Jedediah Smith wilderness is second to none. Right: Marion Lake is a popular destination from the tram.

Trail Description

From the tram deck, walk left (S) down a wind-swept ridge toward Cody Peak. The ridge dips at the saddle between Rendezvous Peak and Peak 10,215 to the south. At .5 mile you'll reach a signed trail junction directing you to bear right to reach the Teton Village Parking Area, the Middle Fork Cut-off and Marion Lake. This is the path you want. It drops into Grand Teton National Park as it steeply switchbacks into a rocky cirque on the backside of the ski area.

This shaded enclave often holds patches of snow late into the season. Numerous small streams flowing from the snowfields above are flanked with scores of periwinkle bluebells and snowy white columbine, making this descent particularly scenic.

At the bottom of the cirque the trail climbs north to the top of a ridge on the opposite side of the cirque's horseshoe, offering good views of the valley you just left and the tram station above. It then drops again, angling south as it traverses the base of Peak 10,215 and descends into the upper South Fork of Granite Canyon.

At the head of the canyon the trail turns north, intersecting the Middle Fork Cut-off Trail at 3.5 miles. Bear left at the junction, walking slightly uphill through open slopes. The trail crosses two intermittent streams, usually dry by mid-August, before intersecting the Teton Crest Trail at 4.1 miles.

To continue to Marion Lake

Turn right onto Teton Crest Trail, dropping slightly as you walk toward the headwaters of the Middle Fork at 4.3 miles. Cross the narrow stream and begin the steep 600-foot climb up to a 9,400-foot saddle west of the unnamed 9,814-foot peak to your right. On top of the saddle, 5.2 miles from the trailhead, a little-used trail to your left leads to Game Creek Divide. If you have the time and energy it is worth the .6 mile side trip to the top of the Divide to look down the west side of the range.

From the saddle, the trail steeply drops to a junction with the North Fork Trail at 5.6 miles. This trail descends 8.2 miles down Granite Canyon to the valley floor. Stay on the Crest Trail to reach the lake. The trail crosses the North Fork and steeply climbs the final slope before reaching the lake at 6.2 miles.

Resting at an elevation of 9,240 feet, the popular lake is named after Marion Danford, a frequent guest at the Bar BC Dude Ranch in the early 1900s. Danford later purchased a ranch of her own.

From Marion Lake it is possible to continue north to Fox Creek Pass and walk down either Fox Creek Canyon on the west slope of the Tetons or Death Canyon on the east side. Alternately, you could return to the valley floor by walking back to the North Fork junction and descending Granite Canyon. Those interested in returning via the tram should be sure to allow enough time to catch the last car of the day. For information on tram rates and operating hours, call 733-2292.

To continue to Moose Lakes

Turn left onto Teton Crest Trail and begin the gentle ascent to 9,085-ft. Moose Creek Divide, reached in another .6 mile. The Divide marks the boundary between Grand Teton National Park to the east and Jedediah Smith Wilderness on Caribou-Targhee National Forest to the west. You'll pass a small lake to your left just before you reach the top of the Divide. Horse packers occasionally utilize this area, so if you draw water from the lake be sure to treat it. The Divide provides an excellent view of the upper reaches of Moose Creek and Taylor Mountain to the southwest.

The trail descends via four switchbacks to an intersection with the trail from Phillips Pass. Keep right and walk .1 mile to the intersection with Moose Creek Trail, 5.2 miles from the top of the aerial tram. Turn right onto the unsigned trail and soon cross Moose Creek. You'll recross the willow-lined creek twice as you walk uphill to the lakes.

A short but easy ascent up a 300-foot rock band brings you to the top of the first limestone bench and four of the eight tarns. Moose Lake is the largest. An easy cross-country walk up another 300-foot band at the south end of the lake provides access to the second limestone bench and four more lakes. Cairns mark the trail across the rocky terrain.

Like Death Canyon Shelf and Cody Bowl, much of the water on the limestone benches drains into underground passages.

A hike around Moose Lake reveals a large amount of water funneling down a hole near the lake's shore.

In dry years, all but the largest lake disappears.

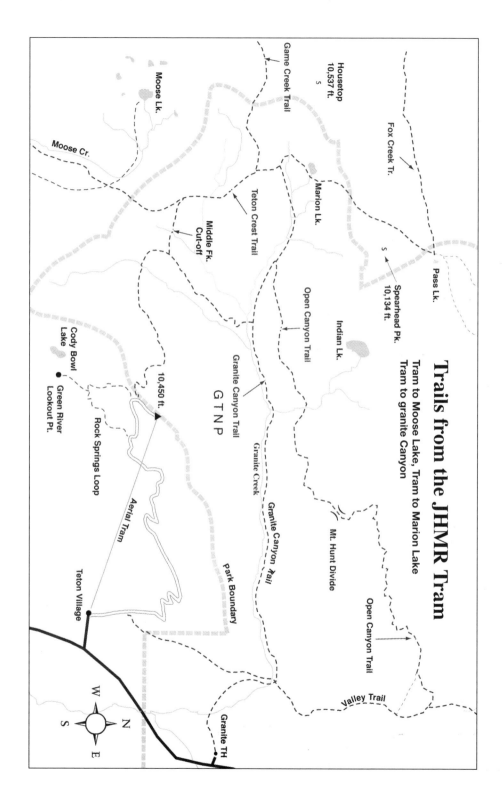

Trails from the JHMR Tram

Tram to Moose Lake, Tram to Marion Lake
Tram to granite Canyon

Housetop
10,537 ft.
S

Game Creek Trail

Moose Lk.

Moose Cr.

Fox Creek Tr.

Teton Crest Trail

Marion Lk.

Middle Fk.
Cut-off

Pass Lk.

Spearhead Pk.
10,134 ft.
S

Open Canyon Trail

Indian Lk.

Granite Canyon Trail

G T N P

Cody Bowl
Lake

Green River
Lookout Pt.

10,450 ft.

Rock Springs Loop

Aerial Tram

Granite Creek

Granite Canyon Trail

Mt. Hunt Divide

Park Boundary

Teton Village

Open Canyon Trail

Valley Trail

Granite TH

W

N

S

E

269

101 Tram to Granite Canyon

Distance:
    To Granite Canyon Trailhead: 11.5 miles
    To Teton Village via Valley Trail: 12.3 miles
Elevation change:
    To Granite Canton Trailhead: Approx. 350 ft. gain, 4,300 ft. loss
    To Teton Village: Approx. 630 ft. gain, 4,710 ft. loss
Maximum elevation: 10,450 ft.
Maps: Teton Village, Rendezvous Peak
Use restrictions: Mountain bikes prohibited. National Park regulations apply.
Season: July through mid-September

This is it: the only trail in the park that starts at the top of a mountain and winds its way down to the valley floor. From the summit of 10,450-ft. Rendezvous Peak, the trail travels predominantly downhill through a scenic canyon characterized by open meadows, scattered forest, rocky cliffs and frequent stretches of dense vegetation. It parallels pretty Granite Creek as it descends. Moose and deer frequent the canyon's lower stretches, an added bonus for wildlife lovers and photographers.

Driving Directions

Drive south out of Jackson on U.S. Hwy. 89/191, turning right onto Wyoming Hwy. 22 at the traffic light by Albertsons. Head west five miles to a bridge over the Snake River. Just over the bridge turn right onto Wyoming Hwy. 390 and drive seven miles to Teton Village, the resort complex at the base of the Jackson Hole Mountain Resort. If you'd like to end at Granite Canyon Trailhead, shuttle a car by driving approximately 2 miles farther on the Moose-Wilson Road. The trailhead is off the left side of the road and is well marked.

This hike begins from the top of Rendezvous Peak, accessed by walking 7.2 miles up the service road, or riding the aerial tram to the top. Mileage assumes tram transport.

A panoramic sweep of mountains and the valley floor thousands of feet below greet you as you unboard—an enticing start for this hike.

Trail Description

From the tram deck, walk left (S) down a windswept ridge toward Cody Peak. The ridge dips at the saddle between Rendezvous Peak and Peak 10,215 to the south. Here, you'll see a sign directing you to turn right to reach the Teton Village parking area, the Middle Fork Cut-off and Marion Lake. This is the trail you want. It rapidly switchbacks down into a rocky cirque that often holds patches of snow late into the season. Numerous small run-off streams are flanked with scores of periwinkle bluebells and snowy white columbine.

From the bottom of the cirque the trail climbs to the top of a ridge on its opposite side, offering good views of the valley you just left and the backside of the tram station. The wildflower displays along the path as you re-ascend is both lush and varied. Penstemon, columbine, larkspur, paintbrush and groundsel, among others,

Top: A hiker ascends Granite Canyon. The trailhead is located on the Moose-Wilson Road approximately 2 miles north of Teton Village, for those who wish to hike up the canyon. Left: Hikers travel through open high country before dropping into Granite Canyon.

can make it appear like someone dropped a paintbox. At the top of the cirque wall, the trails drops again—angling slightly south as it cuts across the forested bottom slope of Peak 10,215.

You'll enter the Middle Fork Camping zone identified on park maps and posted on the ground. The small, flower filled meadows are appealing, but water can become scarce as summer progresses. As the trail continues its descend into the upper South Fork of Granite Canyon, year-round streams eventually appear, often lined by a profusion of water-loving species. Mountain bluebell can grow so think they shimmer like a small pond.

Near the head of the South Fork of Granite Canyon the trail turns north, intersecting the Middle Fork Cut-off Trail at 3.5 miles. Turning left here would bring you to an intersection with Teton crest Trail in another .6 mile. To drop into Granite Canyon, continue straight at the junction The trail descends flowered meadows covering the open ridge between the South and Middle Forks of Granite Canyon.

At the end of the ridge the trail switchbacks down to bridged crossings—first of the Middle Fork of Granite Creek and then the North Fork—to the Upper Granite Canyon Patrol Cabin at 5.2 miles. At this intersection the Granite Canyon Trail ascends left (W) to Open Canyon and Teton Crest Trail beyond, and descends right (E) to an intersection with the Valley Trail and/or the Granite Canyon Trailhead beyond.

Bear right, following rushing Granite Creek as you continue down canyon. The trail is first close to, then above, the stream as it winds in and out of forest, periodically crossing slopes covered with talus and avalanche debris swept down during the winter months. The creek feeds a thriving coniferous forest and luxuriant shrubs and wildflowers. The bright, reddish-orange fruit of mountain ash greets hikers visiting the canyon in autumn.

You'll reach a signed junction with the Valley Trail 9.9 miles beyond the tram station. Turn right onto this. You'll shortly reach a second junction. If you are exiting at Granite Canyon Trailhead, bear left. The path descends through meadow and aspen and fir forest to the parking lot, reached in 1.5 miles.

If you are returning to Teton Village via the Valley Trail, stay right at the intersection. This section of the Valley Trail skirts the western base of Après Vous Peak. There is a lot of horse traffic—and potentially confusing trails—in the area. Most of the horse trails enter the left side of the path. Continue straight at these intersections. If you see a horse party approaching, step off the trail to give the animals the right-of-way and to avoid spooking them.

A half-mile before reaching Teton Village you leave Grand Teton National Park and enter national forest land. Here, the path differs somewhat from the topo map as the base of the ski area has been reconfigured to accommodate recent development. Follow the signage directions to reach Teton Village.

Jackson and
Greater Snow King

Introduction

The Greater Snow King Area lies within Bridger-Teton National Forest and encompasses Cache Creek, Game Creek, Snow King Resort and mountain, and Leeks, Wilson, Adams and Smith Canyons. The mountain complex and watershed are home to numerous wildlife species and contain critical winter range for elk and deer. They have long been important economically and recreationally to valley residents.

Scenic Cache Creek was reportedly named by early settlers for the practice of horse thieves caching their stolen goods at a ranch along the creek. A road was built into the canyon in the early 1900s for settler access to timbering and grazing activity. In the 1920s, Jake Jackson and John Nocker mined coal in the canyon for local heating needs—hard work that netted them $12 a ton. Nocker operated into the 1940s; when oil became heating fuel of choice, he closed the mine.

The town of Jackson drew its culinary water from Cache Creek from 1938 through 1965. During that time frame, the canyon was closed to grazing, timbering and vehicular travel to protect the purity of the watershed. When it re-opened, Cache Creek became both a popular recreation corridor and a semi-permanent camping area for local residents unable to afford local housing options. Escalating concerns led Bridger-Teton to commission an environmental impact study (EIS) that was completed in 1976. The document recommended that Cache Creek transition to a day use area. Bridger-Teton subsequently closed portions of the lower canyon to camping, and established a gate baring onward vehicle traffic. An official trailhead east of today's trailhead/parking area was created. In 1993, the lower portion of the road was closed to summer motorized travel and the present trailhead/ picnic area was developed. Two years later, overnight camping was prohibited in all of lower Cache and Game Creeks.

The recreational importance of Cache Creek Canyon was clearly demonstrated in the 1970s, when a Kansas oil company filed an application to drill test wildcat wells. Three federal oil and gas leases in Cache Creek were issued to the National Cooperative Refinery Association in 1969. The leases totaled 7,680 acres, and were issued without any restrictive stipulations: the 1970 National Environmental Policy Act, landmark legislation that requires assessment of environmental impacts, was not yet adopted.

NCRA filed a drilling application for the Cache Creek test well in 1977. A three-year howl of protest that reached Washington's ears ensued. Faced with a highly controversial application, Bridger-Teton National Forest officials and the USGS recommended that the application undergo an EIS. (At the time, it was only the second EIS prepared for an application to drill an oil well within the continental US.) The EIS, released in August of 1981, reported that Cache Creek Canyon received 16,000 visitor days a year from mostly local hikers, horseback riders, cross-country skiers and snowmobilers. It concluded that full field development of up to eight well pads and six new miles of road construction in the Cache Creek watershed, "could produce long-term significant adverse impacts in valued resources." But, it also concluded that the Secretary of Interior had no legal grounds to deny a drilling permit. Given an apparent mandate, the agencies recommended limited approval for only one test well, that would be accessed through Game Creek. Faced with overwhelming opposition and expensive limitations, NCRA withdrew its application in mid-September of 1981.

Snow King

Snow King Mountain is part of the benchmark Cache Creek Canyon watershed. Like Cache Creek, the mountain has played an important role in Jackson's development and local recreation opportunities. Snow King was known as the Ruth Hannah Simms Ski Hill in 1933, seven years before the first tow lift began operating on its slopes. Mrs. Simms had donated money toward the building of a ski jump, and the mountain was named after her in gratitude. (Ski jumping was then quite popular. At the 1932 Olympics in Lake Placid, jumping and cross-country skiing were the only skiing events.)

In 1935, the Forest Service had CCC crews construct both a horse/hiking/ski trail to the top of the mountain and a small shelter. As the venue's popularity grew in the late 1930s, valley residents Dr. and Mrs. Naegli suggested "Snow King" would be a more appropriate name for the mountain. The name stuck.

The Jackson Hole Ski Club, a forerunner to today's Jackson Hole Chamber of Commerce, was organized in 1938. The following year, the new club called for designs to construct an "uphill facility" at Snow King. Three people submitted plans; Neil Rafferty's was chosen. He was given a permit to run a cable tow and a lease in exchange for building the tow. Rafferty began work in October of 1939. The lift opened for business on January 13, 1940. That day, Rafferty took in $2.95, a profit of $1.65 after he covered his gas expenses. A single ride cost 10 cents for kids and 20 cents for adults. Season passes were $10 for men, $8 for women and $5 for children. The cable was salvaged from an old oil drilling rig from Casper, Wyoming. It ran up the hill over old car tires to keep it from dragging in the snow, and could handle 18 people at a time. Metal clamps with ropes were attached to the cable for skiers to hold as they were towed to the top. Only the lower part of the mountain was skied: the upper sections were too heavily timbered. By 1945, there were two rope tows and a cable lift on the mountain. Lifts were open 3-6 p.m. on Wednesday and Thursday, 11-6 on Saturdays and Sundays, extended hours aided by the fact that the slopes were lit.

The "Town Hill" underwent a major expansion in 1946, when a group of local investors formed the Jackson Hole Winter Sports Association and raised over $40,000 to build a chairlift that went to the top of the mountain. The group located a retired ore tram from a gold mine in Garfield, Colorado. The Taylor Mountain Tramway, nicknamed "Lily," was purchased for a nominal sum and transported to Jackson. A Salt Lake firm was contracted to devise single chairlift seats to replace the ore buckets. The lift opened for business January 7, 1947. It used 4,000 feet of cable and had a vertical rise of 1,670 feet.

The Jackson Hole Winter Sports Association did not operate in the black until 1949, the year the annual report showed that 8,500 people used the chair to travel to the top of Snow King. Its owners agreed to increase profits by operating the lift in the summer. The fledgling summer business grew noticeably after 1959, the year double chairs replaced the lift's single chair arrangement. (Between 1947 and 1959, Rafferty stayed in a shack at the top of Snow King after the lift closed for the day. Since there was no way to turn the lift on from the bottom and he didn't want to walk all the way to the top each morning, he elected to stay overnight. When the double chair was put in, Rafferty installed a remote control device that enabled him to start the lift's diesel engine from the bottom.)

The GSKA Project

From the building of a user trail by the Forest Service in 1935—and addition of summer lift service 15 years later—many hundreds of people presently recreate on some portion of Snow King Mountain every summer day. The heavy usage reflects the growth of the town of Jackson and nearby South Park at its base. Similarly, Bridger-Teton National Forest staff estimate as many as 120 people a day recreate in Cache Creek.

With increased use, reports of conflicts between mountain bikers, dog walkers, hikers and horse riders—as well as wildlife concerns—became commonplace. In the spring of 2000, a coalition that included Bridger-Teton National Forest, Friends of Pathways, Jackson Hole Community Pathways, Wyoming Game and Fish, Jackson Hole Wildlife Foundation, Jackson Hole Conservation Alliance, Snow King Resort, Backcountry Horsemen, the International Mountain Biking Association, Rendezvous Engineering and PAWS sponsored design workshops to address use and concerns in the Greater Snow King Area (GSKA).

The Greater Snow King Area Project, funded by Bridger-Teton National Forest, was formed to implement the management plan developed from a series of workshops and meetings. Through its efforts, hundreds of volunteer hours have been donated to realign and maintain trails in the GSKA, and address future route and ongoing concerns. The GSKA continues to evolve. If signage differs from the descriptions presented here, please follow the posted signage. In addition to forest regulations, GSKA users are asked to adhere to the guidelines listed below

Dog Owners

► Clean up after your dog(s). Carry a mutt-mitt or plastic bag and use it every time. Deposit bag in the can at the trailhead or other trash receptacle.

► Your dog(s) must be under voice control at all times. This means that you only bring the number of dogs that you can reasonably control, your dog is within sight, it comes immediately to your side on command and you are able to physically hold your pet(s) if necessary to let other users, horses or wildlife pass.

► Bring a lease if you have any doubt about your ability to control your dog(s) in the presence of other people, dogs, horses or wildlife. State law prohibits dogs from running after or harassing wildlife and permits game wardens to kill dogs observed to injure or threaten big game.

Walkers/Hikers/Runners

► Stay on designated trails and avoid short cuts. Yield to uphill hikers and equestrian users.

- Give plenty of room for horses to pass. Communicating with a person on a horse will help ensure a safe pass.

- Respect wildlife's needs by providing adequate distance between them and you.

- You are in bear country. Keep yourself and bears safe by packing out what you pack in.

Mountain Bikers

- Ride only on open trails. Avoid short cutting, creating new trails, private property and Gros Ventre Wilderness.

- Always yield the trail. Slow down and/or stop to give other trail users plenty of room to pass. Speak to horse riders so the horse knows you are not a threat.

- Trails are subject to erosion that is hastened by skidding tires. Pedal with an even rhythm consistent with the contour of the trail and brake evenly. If you are climbing and begin to skid, walk your bike to the top of the hill.

- Avoid riding on trails after heavy rain and during spring runoff.

- Always wear a helmet.

Equestrian Users

- Expect to encounter other recreationists. Announce your presence when approaching from behind and offer courteous passing instructions if needed.

- Ride only on designated, open trails. Avoid shortcuts, creating new trails or riding on private property.

- Don't ride on trails after heavy rain and during spring runoff.

- Respect wildlife and its habitat. Keep a safe distance between wildlife and you and your horse.

With the exception of the South Park Management Area, all hikes in this section area administered by the Jackson Ranger District of Bridger Teton National Forest. For questions or further information, contact:

> Bridger-Teton National Forest
> Jackson Ranger District
> Box 1689
> Jackson, Wyoming 83001
> 307-739-5400

102 Hagen/Putt-Putt Loop

103 Hagen/Cache Creek Loop

Hagen/Putt-Putt Loop
Distance: 4 miles
Elevation change: Approx. 740 ft.
Maximum elevation: Approx. 6,940 ft.
Maps: Cache Creek. Book map pg. 281
Season: May through October
Use restrictions: Motorized use prohibited.
　　Dogs must be leashed on Putt-Putt Dec. 1 – April 30.

Hagen/Cache Creek Loop
Distance: 3.7 miles
Elevation change: Approx. 450 ft.
Maximum elevation: Approx. 6,830 ft.
Maps: Cache Creek. Book map pg. 281
Season: May through October
Use restrictions: Motorized use prohibited.

Grant "Tiny" Hagen was an expert skier who served as a ski instructor in the famed 10th Mountain Division in World War II. He worked for many summers as a ranger-naturalist in Grand Teton National Park, supplementing a successful art career begun in the mid-1950s. Hagen was a charter member of the Jackson Hole Winter Sports Association, a group of townspeople who underwrote the cost of installing Snow King's first chairlift in 1946. He successfully led a campaign to prevent Cache Creek from being dammed in the 1960s. It is fitting that the Hagen Trail complex was named in his honor. It traverses above the creek canyon he helped preserve and leads to the ski area he helped grow.

The two loop hikes presented here share a segment of the Hagen Trail on the south side of the Cache Creek drainage. The Putt-Putt Loop returns hikers to the trailhead by traversing the toe of Crystal Butte's southern slope, offering great views of the southern end of the Teton Range, the town of Jackson and the west side of the valley.

The Cache Creek Loop return is via the Cache Creek Trail, whose lower section is a scenic dirt and gravel road that offers an easy descent closer to the creek.

Driving Directions
From the Jackson Town Square, travel east on Broadway for .6 mile to Redmond Street on the right (S) side of the roadway. Turn in and drive .4 mile to Cache Creek Drive on your left. Turn in and drive an additional 1.2 miles to the large trailhead parking area. Park and backtrack a short distance to the signed Cache Creek Trailhead. There are picnic tables, grills and a vault toilet at the trailhead parking area but water is not available. Cache

278

Hikers and mountain bikers enjoy this view from Cache Creek Trail west to the Tetons on both loop hikes.

Creek is a day-use only area.

Trail Description

The path almost immediately crosses a bridge over Cache Creek and splits. Keep right and walk to a three-way split. The trail to the left is the Hagen River Trail. The uppermost trail to the right is a shortcut path. Take the middle branch, which shortly leads to a signed intersection. Turn left onto the Hagen Trail. (Right, the path leads to Snow King Ski Area.)

The well-used trail traverses both open slopes and forested terrain before splitting at about one mile. Bearing left here and crossing a bridge over Cache Creek will bring you back to your car via the Cache Creek Trail—a shorter 2-mile loop option. To complete either of the longer loops, stay right at this junction.

The grade increases to moderate as you approach a short, steep hill with multiple water bars to help control erosion. At the top of the hill, the trail flattens out and cuts across open meadow. Keep right where the trail divides. The path traverses a meadow before entering a pleasant mixed forest of spruce and fir. You'll cross two log bridges over creek tributaries before reaching yet another trail junction. Bear left here and cross the bridge over Cache Creek. You'll soon intersect the old road up Cache Creek drainage at 1.9 miles. Turn left and walk downhill on the road a tenth of a mile farther to a trail on the right side of roadway. This is the Putt-Putt Trail. A sign usually marks it, but occasionally signage is not in place. This junction is also where the two loop options diverge.

To complete the
Hagen/Cache Creek Loop

Remain on the dirt and gravel road. It descends at an easy, steady grade, and is often used by both equestrians and mountain bikers. The upper segment of the road walk is predominantly open, the lower segment shaded by towering trees as you near the trailhead. Moose are occasionally seen near the creek, and both deer and elk inhabit the canyon. You'll pass numerous trails to the right that connect to the Putt-Putt Trail.

As you near the trailhead parking area, a path leaves the left side of the track. This is the handicap accessible boardwalk that closely parallels the creek. It is a nice way to end the hike. Note: If you are hiking after 5:30 p.m., please use the signed Sidewalk Trail, a by-pass route to avoid wagon traffic. Consult the map

To complete the
Hagen/Putt-Putt Loop

Leave the road and bear right onto the trail. It climbs at a moderate grade for a short distance before bending left (W) and opening views of the southern end of the Tetons. It then snakes right (N) and begins

an undulating course in-and-out of folds in the butte. Sunny yellow mule's ears, waterleaf, wild strawberry, lupine, prairie smoke, Oregon grape and wild rose are but a few of the many wildflowers spied in season. After several short drops and climbs you reach the high point of the hike, marked by a rock dressed in orange lichen. The trail then generally descends. You'll enjoy nice views of Glory Bowl and the Tetons in front of you, and—if you are hiking/biking near the end of the summer—amazing waves of blooming fireweed. Continue straight when you reach a sign that indicates a segment of the trail has been relocated to reduce erosion. You'll soon see the parking lot below you. The trail curves toward it and descends at a moderately steep grade to a junction.

Bear left to return to the Cache Creek Trailhead. Continuing right, the trail follows an undulating course, with several short, steep drops and climbs, to its western end off Nelson Drive.

The Hagen Trail from Cache Creek to Snow King Ski Area travels through forest with a rich understory.

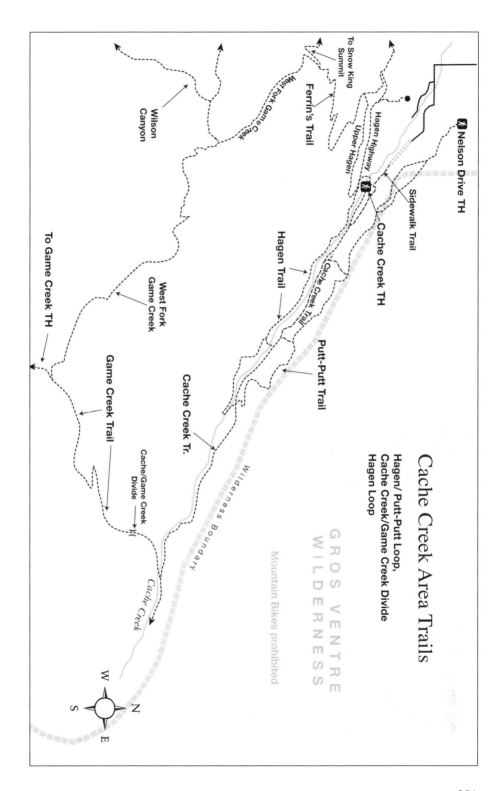

Cache Creek Area Trails

Hagen/ Putt-Putt Loop,
Cache Creek/Game Creek Divide
Hagen Loop

GROS VENTRE
WILDERNESS

Mountain Bikes prohibited

Nelson Drive TH

Sidewalk Trail

Cache Creek TH

Hagen Highway

Upper Hagen

Ferrin's Trail

To Snow King
Summit

Wilson
Canyon

West Fork Game Creek

Hagen Trail

Cache Creek Trail

Putt-Putt Trail

West Fork
Game Creek

Cache Creek Tr.

To Game Creek TH

Game Creek Trail

Cache/Game Creek
Divide

Wilderness Boundary

Cache Creek

N
W   E
S

104 Hagen Loop

105 Ferrin's Slide Loop

Hagen Loop
> Distance: 2.9 miles
> Elevation change: Undulates. Approx. 540 ft. gain and loss
> Maximum elevation: Approx. 6,880 ft.
> Maps: Cache Creek. Book map pg. 285
> Use restrictions: Motorized use prohibited.
> Season: Mid-May through October

Ferrin's Slide Loop
> Distance: 7.3 miles
> Elevation change: Undulates. Approx. 1,620 ft. gain and loss
> Maximum elevation: Approx. 7,870 ft.
> Maps: Cache Creek. Book map pg. 285
> Use restrictions: Motorized use prohibited.
> Season: June through October

The Hagen Loop is a pleasant, forested hike. Its gently undulating course travels west from Cache Creek Trailhead toward Snow King Ski Area. It turns east at an intersection with the Hagen Two-Track Trail to return to the trailhead. Wildflowers, bird song and periodic openings that offer views of the southern Tetons are among the loop's attractions.

The Ferrin's Slide Loop shares the first half of the Hagen Loop hike. Where the routes diverge, Ferrin's climbs at a steady grade to a saddle below the eastern summit of Snow King Mountain. There, hikers access a trail that leads to a dip in Snow King's summit ridge and the intersection with the service road down the front of the ski area. The road is descended to its intersection with a trail that leads to the Hagen Two-Track (aka the Hagen Highway), the closing link for this longer loop hike. Views of meandering Flat Creek and the town of Jackson at the top of this varied hike are superb. Hikers are alerted that the Hagen loop is frequently used by mountain bikers and equestrians, and the popular service road traversing the face of Snow King is very heavily traveled. Be alert for other users and yield appropriately.

Driving Directions
From the Jackson Town Square, travel east on Broadway for .6 mile to Redmond Street on the right (S) side of the roadway. Turn in and drive .4 mile to Cache Creek Drive on your left. Drive up Cache Creek an additional 1.2 miles to the large trailhead parking area. Park and backtrack a short distance to the signed Cache Creek Trailhead. There are picnic tables and a vault toilet at the trailhead parking area. Water is not available.

Trail Description
From the Cache Creek Trailhead, the

Spectacular views west of the Teton Range are enjoyed from the top of the Ferrin's Slide Loop hike.

path crosses a bridge over lively Cache Creek and splits. Continue straight. You'll soon reach a signed three-way split. The trail to the left is the .5-mile Hagen River Trail. The uppermost right branch is a shortcut to the junction just ahead. Take the middle trail. It climbs a short distance then curves to reach the signed junction. The trail traveling uphill to the left is the segment of the Hagen Trail that eventually intersects Ferrin's Trail. The path to the right is the Hagen Two-Track, the path that returns you to the trailhead for both loop hikes. Bear left onto the signed Hagen/Ferrin Trail.

The trail consistently climbs through forest at an easy to moderate grade, its tread a bit rocky and uneven. Rockcress, clematis, columbine, wild strawberry, fra-grant wallflowers and green gentian are among the wildflowers that thrive in the shady forest encountered en route to Snow King. Chattering squirrels, lively bird song and other hikers will likely keep you company .

At a quarter-mile, the trail enters an open meadow where balsamroot, lupine, chicory decorate the grassy slopes. The trail soon gently descends and re-enters the trees, reaching a signed inverted "Y" junction at .4 mile. Left, the Hagen Trail souths south up Cache Creek Canyon. Bear sharp right at the junction to head toward Snow King and the Ferrin Trail.

The path initially climbs steeply for a short distance, then proceeds at a moderate grade through mixed forest dominated by young Douglas fir. The track is lined with twinberry, honeysuckle and luxuriant grasses. Openings to the right provide a glimpse first into Woods Canyon, a box canyon that cuts into the north side of Cache Creek Canyon, then the Grand Teton at .8 mile before splitting. Keep left on the official path, which soon follows a more level course was it traverse a broader bench near the bottom of an obvious slide path. Snapped trees rise above both sides of the trail, evidence of the powerful avalanches that give

283

"Ferrin's Slide" its name. The slide area just east of Snow King Ski Resort is used by out-of-bounds local skiers, and is not without danger. On February 16, 1984, 27-year-old Pierre Muheim was caught in an avalanche that swept him into the trees, resulting in an impact injury that fatally severed his femoral artery.

At 1.1 miles, the trail re-enters the trees and beings ascending at a steeper grade, then levels as it bears right to reach the signed intersection with the Ferrin's Slide Trail at 1.3 miles. Here the two loop hikes part company.

To complete the Hagen Loop

Turn right at the signed junction. The good dirt track descends at a moderately steep grade , crossing under a power line at 1.4 miles. Here, a user trail drops right. Stay on the main trail, which climbs to the high point of the hike before dropping to the signed intersection with the Hagen Two-Track Trail at 1.7 miles. Turn sharp right here.

Throughout its length, the two-track is often wide enough to accommodate two hikers or bikers traveling side-by-side. Its grade is consistently easy to moderate as it traverses through forest.

The trail re-passes under the power lines at 1.9 miles to reach a signed access trail to the left a short distance farther. Continue straight. The trail more steeply climbs then drops as it curves right up a short hill, the grade soon moderating as it travels east. Stay left where a fainter user trail heads right. You'll reach the signed junction with the trail that drops to Cache Creek Trailhead at 2.7 miles. Continue straight and retrace your steps to return to your vehicle.

To complete the Ferrin Loop

Turn left at the signed junction. The path contours at an easy grade through mixed forest of lodgepole pine and Douglas fir that provides favorable habitat for wild roses, sticky geraniums, lupine and rich grasses on the forest floor.

At 2 miles, it ascends a series of switchbacks, then heads generally west for .4 mile before switchbacking up again. En route, the path crosses several open areas cleared by avalanches reflected in the trail's name. At the top of the second set of switchbacks, the trail again contours west at a somewhat steeper grade. It begins the final, winding .3 mile ascent to the low end of a summit, reaching 3.3 miles beyond the trailhead. Here, a signed junction marks the end of the Ferrin's Trail. The trail continuing straight (S) leads to Wilson and West Game Creek Canyons. To complete the loop, bear right at the junction.

This trail heads west/southwest as it climbs open, sage-covered terrain. It bears right then left to reach a small saddle south of Snow King's eastern summit, where it intersects the service road to the radio towers on that apex. This is the high point of the loop hike.

Continue straight, dropping down the service road to its intersection with the path leading to the chairlift at the top of Snow King's western summit. Turn right here and descend the popular service road to Keevert's Corner. Bear right here and follow the trail as it contours the open face of Snow King to an intersection marked by a sign that reads "This section built in 2007 in memory of Adam Denton." Adam Denton was a popular 17-year-old Jackson Hole High School student killed en route to a swim meet on July 21, 2007.

Turning right here leads to the upper Hagen/Ferrin trail. Bear left to return via the Hagen Two-Track Trail, described in detail in the preceding loop hike.

284

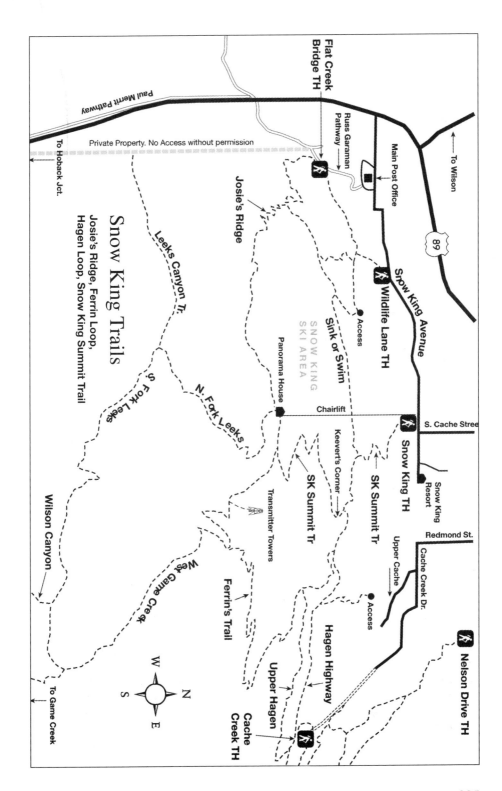

Snow King Trails

Josie's Ridge, Ferrin Loop,
Hagen Loop, Snow King Summit Trail

285

106 Cache Creek/Game Creek Traverse

Distance: 9.7 miles one-way
Elevation change: Approx. 1300 ft. gain, Approx. 1,600 ft. loss
Maps: Cache Creek. Book map pg. 281
  Download trail map at www.friendsofpathways.org
Use restrictions:
  Game Creek is critical wildlife habitat. Pets must be leashed Dec. 1 – April 30.
  Parking at the Game Creek trailhead limited to day use only.
Season: Mid- to late May through October

Located on the eastern outskirts of town, Cache Creek is a popular destination for nearby or after-work forays into the backcountry. The pretty, well-maintained trail winds through wooded Cache Creek Canyon into the Gros Ventre Range.

Shuttling a car or arranging a pick-up at the Game Creek Road south of town can complete a pleasant 9.7-mile excursion. Alternately, those mountain biking can take the pathways trail back to Jackson to complete an 18.6-mile loop

Notable wildflower displays dropping south off the Cache/Game Creek Divide make it a worthwhile out-and-back destination for those who don't wish to bother with a vehicle shuttle.

Driving Directions

From the Jackson Town Square, travel east on Broadway for .6 mile to Redmond Street on the right (S) side of the roadway. Turn in and drive .4 mile to Cache Creek Drive on your left. Drive up Cache Creek an additional 1.2 miles to the large trailhead parking area. There are picnic tables and a vault toilet at the trailhead parking area. Water is not available.

Trail Description

The hike starts on the now closed jeep road left of Cache Creek. At .6 mile you'll pass a Forest Service campsite reserved for special use permitees. The wooded track bears southeast as it gradually climbs to the open, grassy meadows near Gin Pole Draw at 1.4 miles. As you continue upwards the canyon narrows and re-enters the trees. Soon, the early season snow-clad summit of 10,304-ft. Cache Peak pops into view, balanced on both sides by two substantial but unnamed Gros Ventre peaks.

A trail turnoff to your right marked "To Game Creek" is reached at 4 miles. Cross bridged Cache Creek here and begin a sustained, moderately steep to steep climb to the lip of Cache Creek/Game Creek Divide at 4.6 miles. The divide marks the hike's high point of 7,420 feet.

The trail drops into the basin via switchbacks. Early season, impressive wildflower displays are enjoyed on the .5 mile drop to a crossing of a Game Creek tributary at 5.1 miles. The additional drop and mileage is worth considering for wildflower enthusiasts. doing an out-and-back to the divide. Bear in mind that the upper reaches of Game Creek often dry up as the summer progresses, ending the wonderful wildflower display.

The path climbs then drops to cross first a planed board over the southern fork of Game Creek at 5.5 miles, then a

286

Top: Cache Creek Canyon narrows as the trail nears the intersection with the trail traveling over Cache Creek Divide into Game Creek drainage. Bottom: Wolf lichen covers a tree trunk in Cache Creek.

Service two-track road at 7.5 miles and travels southwest on a downward to level course toward the trailhead. In another .3 mile, it leaves the two-track at a bend in the road. The path is slightly shorter than walking the road but has several blind corners. If you choose to take it, proceed cautiously and listen for mountain bikers. The shortcut rejoins the two-track in open, flat terrain.

The canyon narrows as you approach its mouth, and limestone talus from the rock faces above tumbles down toward the creek to your right. You'll soon reach an old fence line and metal cattle guard. Beyond, the old road descends slightly as it travels through a section of willow and aspens.

Game Creek flows into a culvert under the road to re-emerge on the right side just before you reach the parking area.

gap in a section of buck-and-rail fence just ahead. The level trail stays left of the wide, willowed creek drainage. Chiefly open, this section can be a cooker on a hot day.

The trail merges with the closed Forest

107 Snow King Summit

Distance: 1.8 miles one-way
Elevation gain: Approx. 1,570 ft. gain
Maximum elevation: 7,760 ft
Maps: Jackson. Book map pg. 285.
Use restrictions: Pets prohibited on chairlift. Horses prohibited.
Season: Late May through October

The demanding walk up the front face of Snow King Ski Area to its summit yields superb views of Jackson Hole. Starting with a fascinating bird's eye perspective of the town of Jackson, a longer look takes in East and West Gros Ventre Buttes and the National Elk Refuge on the valley floor, the Gros Ventre Range to the northeast, and the Tetons to the northwest. Flat Creek and the Snake River meander through the unbelievably green fields of early summer in this postcard-like scene.

An interpretive nature trail on the ridge near Snow King's western summit describes plants and points of interest. Numerous loops and/or traverses of the Snow King massif also continue or depart from the summit, including the Ferrin's Loop and descents via West Game Creek and Wilson Canyon.

The "town hill," as Snow King is known locally, is one of the oldest ski areas in the country. A rope tow began operating on the mountain in 1940. A lift supported by wooden towers began running to the summit of the peak in 1946. It serviced local skiers until 1981, when the current summit lift replaced it.

Driving Directions

Drive six blocks south of the Jackson Town Square on Cache Street to the intersection of Snow King Avenue. Park in the ballpark parking lot at the corner

of Cache and Snow King and walk to the base of the hill. Those interested in riding up to walk the nature trail must purchase a lift ticket. For fees and operating hours of the chairlift, call 733-5200 or visit /www. snowking.com/Activities_Summer_ Chairlift.aspx

Trail Description

The signed trail angles left above the base of the main chairlift, then traverses east above Aspen Cemetery, switchbacking twice before rejoining the service road. Turn uphill onto the road; keep right a short distance further when the track splits. The road climbs at a moderately steep, sustained grade to Keevert's Corner, an intersection with the Hagen Trail named in honor of Ward Keevert. Keevert was named "King of the King" after climbing Snow King 161 times between Memorial Day and Labor Day, 1998. He was 76.

Continue ascending. You'll soon pass a sign that reminds users horses are prohibited. Stay straight where a spur road to a chairlift midway station angles obliquely left. Bear left at the bend just ahead, straight at the next crossroads. Large trees now shade the track, welcome on a warm summer day. You'll soon reach an old road cut to your left. Bear right here. At the next dogleg, bear left. You are now on the longest switchback segment on the upper mountain. It eventually turns right and leads to a dip in the summit ridge near a snow fence, intersecting the trail that travels east-west between the radio transmission towers and the Panorama House.

Turn right (W) and walk towards the visible ski patrol hut. When you reach it, stay on the path to the left and walk to the Panorama House. Telescopes and engraved metal signs outlining valley features are located on the deck. Inside, vending machines dispense sport drinks, soda, candy bars and bottled water. Picnic tables are available both inside and out and outhouses are maintained behind the building.

Snow King Nature Trail begins on the two-track road behind the Panorama House. The half-mile loop traverses sagebrush meadows before entering a forested area and gently ascending a ridge. A Forest Service pamphlet, available at the trailhead and/or in the Panorama house, describes the plants and features near signed stations along the trail. It also describes a tree-planting project initiated by the Forest Service and Jackson Hole Winter Sports Association. Between 1960 and 1965, Jackson Hole grade school students planted lodgepole pine trees to act as a barrier against drifting snow and prevent cornice formation at the ridgetop.

There are numerous return hiking options from the top of the mountain outlined in this section. The simplest is to retrace your route or ride the chairlift down for a modest fee. A PDF trail map of Greater Snow King Area trails may be downloaded from www.friendsofpathways.org.

Every summer, from Memorial Day to Labor Day, residents participate in "Climb the King," a fundraiser for the local metal health counseling center that garners pledges for each ascent. For information, visit www.climbtheking.org

Top: Wonderful views of the Tetons, National Elk Refuge and Town of Jackson are enjoyed from the summit of Snow King Mountain and, as pictured in the bottom photograph, riding down the chairlift.

108 Snow King to Game Creek

Distance: 8.2 miles one-way
Elevation change: Approx. 570 ft. gain, approx 2,220 ft. loss
Maximum elevation: 7,900 ft
Maps: Jackson, Cache Creek.
Use restrictions: Pets prohibited on chairlift.
    Daylight recreational parking only at the Game Creek trailhead
Season: Late May through chairlift closure
    (Note: Call Snow King Resort at 307-733-5200 to confirm current operating hours, fees and seasonal opening/closing dates.)

Close to town, this predominantly open hike down the south side of Snow King Mountain and the West Game Creek and Game Creek drainages is a good early season choice. The first wildflowers of the season, sweeping views of the southern aspect of the Snow King massif and its drainage canyons and the chance to see moose, elk and great blue heron await late May and June visitors. As summer temperatures rise, the open terrain in West Game and Game Creek drainages can be uncomfortably hot and the trail quite dusty. This outing is best done late spring/ early summer or on cool days throughout the season.

Driving Directions

Begin by shuttling a car to the Game Creek trailhead, reached by driving south through Jackson on Hwy. 89 to the traffic light at the intersection of the highway with Maple Way near Kmart. Continue straight (S) on Hwy. 89/ Broadway 5.9 miles beyond the light to signed Game Creek Road on your left (E). Turn in and drive one mile on paved road to a small parking area bordered by large rocks at the bend of the road. The trail begins on the closed dirt-and-gravel two-track left of the parking area. Park a vehicle here and drive to the Jackson Town Square. Turn right (S) on Cache Street and continue six blocks to the base of Snow King Ski Area near the corner of Cache Street and Snow King Avenue. Park your vehicle and ride the chairlift to the top of Snow King's 7,760-foot west summit.

Trail Description

From the top of the chairlift, walk left (E) past the ski patrol building on the wide gravel path/two-track. The track hugs the ridge, dipping to a low point and intersection with the service road up the north slope of Snow King. (If you walked up the mountain, turn left onto the two-track at this intersection.) Continue straight toward the radio transmission towers ahead. The two-track dirt road bends right and climbs to a ridge at .6 mile. This is the high point of the hike. Leave the road at the ridge, turning sharply left onto a trail that descends toward a trail junction below. Larkspur, waterleaf, yellowbells, spirea, violets, balsamroot and sugarbowl are but a few of the blooming wildflowers lining the path early season. The trail reaches

View of Cache Creek Canyon, seen dropping off Snow King's summit ridge en route to West Game Creek.

a junction in three switchbacks. At the junction, Ferrin's Trail descends left (N). Bear right and continue descending open, sagebrush-covered terrain at a moderate to moderately steep grade. The path levels as it reaches a flat grassy expanse at the toe of a slope. Narrow but clear, it travels left of predominantly lodgepole forest and crosses the length of the expanse, soon paralleling the meager beginning of an seasonal stream that flows down Wilson Canyon.

At 1.2 miles, an old road cut left of the trail, aged stumps to the right and occasional weathered slash piles mark former timbering activity in the drainage. The path stays in the old, grassed-in roadbed, soon passing stretches of willow. Be alert for moose in this favored habitat.

At 1.9 miles, the path bends right and splits near a copse of willow. It rejoins on the far side of the stand; early season, the left fork is typically drier. The path soon splits a second time in a "Y" configuration.

Right, the trail leads to Wilson and the South Fork of Leek's Canyon. Stay left to eventually reach the Game Creek trailhead.

The level path soon turns east and climbs at a moderately steep grade up open slopes to the crest of a ridge, marked by a pair of towering Douglas fir silhouetted on the skyline. On the ridge, it bears right and travels the crest, opening up nice views of 11,180-ft. Gros Ventre Peak ahead at the 2 o'clock position.

Two short, steep drops interspersed with almost level sections carry you to a sustained, steep descent through forested terrain. The steep descent ends at the bottom of the ridge, start of the upper reaches of West Game Creek drainage. The trail hugs the toe of predominantly open slopes and soon begins paralleling tiny, frequently dry West Game Creek. Shortly after traversing a willowed area, it bends right and crosses open terrain colored with a garden of blooming wildflowers mid-

June to early July. The grade steepens a bit as the creek drainage narrows. Generally, this is the first point you can reliably expect to encounter moving water in the creekbed.

The path hops the small creek and weaves in-and-out of forest, contouring on a level to slightly downhill grade to an open section of the drainage and a plank bridge crossing. It then bears right and parallels the willow-lined creek to reach a second plank crossing. Here, the trail again turns right and gently descends as it traverses open terrain, staying left of a long stretch of willows.

You'll pass a series of small, beaver-created ponds before reaching an open park and crossing the creek via a third plank bridge. Beyond, the path turns right and skirts the willows, shortly bearing left to a bridged crossing of Game Creek and an intersection with the Game Creek Trail at 5.1 miles. Turning left here would take you to the Cache Creek/Game Creek Divide and down Cache Creek, another trip option. To continue to the Game Creek trailhead, bear right.

The wider, well-used path gently descends through open forest and soon crosses a planed board over the southern fork of Game Creek, then a gap in a section of buck-and-rail fence just ahead. The level trail stays left of the wide, willowed creek drainage. Chiefly open, this section can be a cooker on a hot day

At 6.1 miles, the path merges with a now closed Forest Service two-track road. The track travels southwest on a downward to level course toward the trailhead. At 6.4 miles a trail leaves the two-track at a bend in the road. The path is slightly shorter than walking the road, but it has several blind corners. If you choose to take it, proceed cautiously and listen for mountain bikers. The shortcut rejoins the two-track in open, flat terrain at 6.8 miles. You'll cross a metal cattle guard and pass through the narrower, scenic portal of lower Game Creek drainage to reach the trailhead parking area at 8.2 miles.

A hiker drops into West Game Creek. West Game Creek intersects the Game Creek Canyon Trail.

109 Josie's Ridge

Distance: 2.4 miles to Snow King Summit
Elevation gain: Approx. 1,640
Maximum elevation: 7,760 ft
Maps: Jackson (Not plotted) Book map pg. 285
Use restrictions: Closed to all human activity Dec. 1 – April 30.
 Because of its very steep grade, this trail is recommended for hiking only.
Season: Late May through October

Josie's Ridge Trail offers an alternative route to the more heavily trafficked service road that leads to Snow King's summit. Its predominantly west-facing aspect means it is typically snow-free earlier in the season.

The trail switchbacks many times before accessing the summit ridge. Numerous trails bisect its route. The Forest Service is working hard to eliminate redundant trails on the mountain. If you come across branches and other obstacles placed across a path, it is an indication the Forest Service is trying to eliminate that particular trail. Please stay on the trail not barricaded.

Josie's Ridge Trail can be accessed off Hidden Ranch Lane in south Jackson, or from the Russ Garaman pathway behind the main post office at Maple Way. Because parking is limited at Hidden Ranch, the trail branching off the Russ Garaman pathway is the preferred access. Trailhead directions and the trail description are written for that option.

Driving Directions

Turn south off Broadway onto Scott Lane and drive to the stop sign at the intersection of Scott Lane and Maple Way. Turn right here and drive the short distance to the main Jackson Post Office.

Park in the back of the post office lot, or park on Elk Run Road behind the post office. The signed Russ Garaman Pathway begins on the south side of Elk Run Road.

Trail Description

The paved Russ Garaman Pathway closely follows bubbly Flat Creek to a bridged crossing. Here, the paved trail curves right. A second dirt trail turns 90 degrees left and parallels Flat Creek. The path you want is the middle trail that angles obliquely left and uphill off the paved pathway. It climbs at a moderate grade through a grove of young aspen and divides. Take the right fork and ascend at an easier grade to a Forest Service sign that reminds users the trail is closed December 1 to April 30.

The path contours at a level grade across open sagebrush and divides again. Go left here. The path soon turns south and steeply climbs the open slope. The grade moderates somewhat as the path arcs southwest and enters a grove of aspen. It soon bears left (E) and continues its ascent. Early season, this segment of the path is lined with blooming pasque flowers, sugarbowl and shooting stars.

The trail passes under a powerline and enters a pleasant stand of subalpine and Douglas fir forest as it continues ascending at an easy grade. When you reach an inverted Y intersection, bear right. Please walk to a second junction a short distance ahead; the Forest Service is trying to reclaim a triangle of redundant user trails.

The path switchbacks five times in quick succession before reaching a "T" intersection. Bear right here and at the next split, generally heading southwest and re-entering the trees. The trail now contours at an easy grade for a longer distance before turning left and ascending east at a steeper incline. Pass the next two intersections to your left. The trail soon leaves the trees and opens up expansive views of the southern Jackson Hole.

Three short zigzags carry you to a

Top: The view from Josie's Ridge Overlook. Bottom: Delicate pasque flowers thrive on the lower portion of Josie's Ridge early season.

dip on the low end of the summit ridge at 1.5 miles. Here, you'll enjoy views of both South Park and the Snake River Range beyond. The trail divides on the ridge. The path to the right travels a short distance to the overlook. To continue to the top of Snow King take the left fork. It travels through open terrain, and dips slightly before ascending via five short switchbacks and bearing more directly south. It continues contouring up the slope, traveling just below a rocky spur on the ridge crest. You'll bear northeast near the head of Leek's Canyon. Westerly winds spiraling up this defile attract soaring red-tailed hawks.

As the trail bears more directly left, it flattens and opens views of the Gros Ventres and the radio transmission towers on top of Snow King. Shortly after this viewscape opens, you'll reach a maze of trails. Take the lower path that angles left to reach the Panorama House at the end of this hike, hidden just around the bend.

Retrace your steps, or walk down the front side of Snow King Mountain to the 3-mile Sink or Swim Trail to loop back to your vehicle. Consult the map.

Josie's Ridge honors Josie Horn, who moved to the valley with her husband, Maurice, and their two sons in 1946. The Horns bought the Frew's Four Lazy F Ranch in South Park and renamed it the Powderhorn Ranch. When Maurice died in 1959, Josie sold the ranch back to the Frew family. She eventually bought Hidden Hills Ranch south of town and renamed it the Powderhorn Ranch. Josie donated a portion of the ranch to the town in 1977 to form Powderhorn Park.

Josie had a keen sense of the future of the valley, and purchased several key pieces of real estate at opportune times— including the Million Dollar Cowboy Bar and the former Spirits of the West liquor store. She died April 9, 1997.

110 High School Hill

Distance: 1.6 miles RT
Elevation change: 624 ft. gain and loss.
Maximum elevation: 6,794 ft
Maps: Jackson (Not plotted)
Use restrictions: Stay on trail to prevent erosion of steep slope.
Season: Early May through November

This prominent hill in south Jackson derives its name from its proximity to Jackson Hole High School. Its south facing slopes are snow-free earlier than Snow King, making it a popular early season after work or school exercise option. Paragliders, Red-tailed and Swainson's Hawks take advantage of the strong updraft created when south/southwestern winds sweep over the steep hillside. The summit offers good views of the Teton Range, the town of Jackson and South Park. Hardy souls hike to this lofty vantage point to listen to Grand Teton Music Festival's Fourth of July outdoor concert in the athletic fields below.

Driving Directions

From the intersection of Hwy. 89/191 with Hwy. 22, drive south .4 mile to South Park Loop Road. Turn right and drive .6 miles to the stop sign. Turn left, then left again into the school parking lot, or park off-road during school hours. Carefully cross busy South Park Loop Road to the start of the trail.

Trail Description

The obvious path immediately begins climbing at a steep grade. Although it is somewhat more direct, do not hike the trail that climbs straight up. Its very steep grade is creating erosion problems on the hill. Stay on the switchbacks, which are steep enough! The path zigzags 10 times on its way to the summit.

Early season, ground-hugging phlox and rocks covered with pincushion orange lichen add color to the bare slopes. Scattered, hardy Rocky Mountain and common juniper also find the dry, open slope to their liking. The female seed cones resemble bluish-purple berries. They are produced in May and June and eaten by mammals and birds. Passage through the mammals' and birds' digestive tracts removes the bluish, fleshy covering, releasing the seeds for germination. Although they look like berries, the small cones of these hardy coniferous trees and shrubs should never be ingested, particularly by people with kidney disease or by pregnant women. The authors of the *Lone Pine Field Guide to Plants of the Rocky Mountains* note that juniper was nicknamed "bastard killer" in Europe, where it was historically used to induce abortions—occasionally killing the mother as well.

As you gain elevation, expansive views of South Park, the Tetons from Teton Pass to the Grand, Snow King Mountain and the high peaks of the Gros Ventre pop into view. Hidden by the slope itself, the town of Jackson is not visible until you reach the crest. After a breather, hikers

Top: View of the Snake River Range and the Tetons, looking west from the summit of High School Hill. Left: the Town of Jackson from High School Hill.

have two options: return the way you came, or descend the hill's north-facing slope and traverse the base to complete a loop. Although a well-established user trail indicates this option is often done, this author does not recommend it as the traverse requires walking a stretch of busy highway.

If you choose to do the loop, stay on the obvious path at the crest. It gradually then more steeply drops down the northeast ridge of the hill, wetter terrain studded with Douglas fir, scattered aspen and limber pine. The trail itself skirts the edge of the treeline at a moderately steep to very steep grade. It eventually parallels a wire and post fence a short distance before bearing right (S) and dropping to the highway, reaching it opposite Albertson's parking lot. From here, it is a 1-mile walk back to your vehicle. Turn right on the path and walk to the intersection of Maple Way. Cross at the light and walk south on the sidewalk to the traffic light at the intersection of South Park Loop Road. Carefully recross the highway at the traffic light and walk via sidewalk down South Park Loop Road to return to your vehicle.

296

111 Wilson Canyon

Distance: 3.4 miles to West Game Creek intersection
Elevation gain: Approx. 1,300 ft.
Maximum elevation: 7,360 ft
Maps: Jackson, Cache.
Use restrictions: Closed to motorized vehicles.
    Closed to recreation use Dec. 1 – April 30.
Season: Mid-May through October

This wooded canyon close to Jackson has much to offer for both birders and wildflower enthusiasts. It's narrow, steep mid-section make this trail best suited for walkers, but the path draws other recreational users as well. Be aware that horses and bikes may be encountered on the trail.

Driving Directions

From the intersection of Maple Way and Broadway in Jackson, drive south on U.S. Hwy. 89/191 for 3.4 miles to the turn-off for the Lower Valley Power and Light building on the left. Turn in and park at the back of the lot. The trailhead is left of the fenced, high-voltage power station.

Trail Description

The trail begins as a two-track that soon narrows to trail width. It gently ascends open sage grasslands sprinkled with penstemon, sticky geranium, cinquefoil, sulfur buckwheat, bull thistle and blue flax. The path curls right, then left has it contours up a hillside left of the canyon's approach to skirt private property. You'll contour around the hill at a flat to easy grade before bearing right in about 10 minutes and descending at a moderate grade into the mouth of the canyon. Look for sun-loving sego lilies on the sunny slope as you descend.

The trail again broadens into a two-track as it enters the canyon, proceeding at a flat to easy grade through an open section of grasses, scattered junipers, Douglas fir, serviceberry, wild rose bushes and a garden of wildflowers too numerous to list. The grade gradually increases to moderate as you head up-canyon and the vegetation changes to reflect the moister, shaded areas of the draw. Junipers are replaced with spruce, and clematis, wintergreen and mint replace the sun-loving plants. Avian friends find the habitat to their liking: bird song will accompany you as you continue your ascent.

At roughly .8 mile, you'll pass through the remnants of an old buck-and-rail fence. Here, rock faces soar to the right above the trail and talus fields tumble down the slopes to your left. The path tunnels through a section of towering chokecherries before climbing through open forest. The host of wildflowers has created a natural butterfly garden. Swallowtails, cabbage, blue copper, coral hairstreak, northern checkerspots and callippe fritillary were but a few of the species observed on a walk through the lower canyon one June.

At 1.2 miles, the path divides, with

a fainter use trail to the right. Keep left here. The tread becomes rocky and bushes overhang portions of the trail as it continues climbing at a moderately steep grade. Sizeable squirrel middens cover the forest floor at the base of Engelmann spruce on both sides of the trail. Squirrels perch in the branches above and pull apart the scales of the cones to get to the seeds. Over time, the scales form large piles, called middens, under the host tree.

As you continue ascending, the trail passes several large trees charred by lightning, and the steep tread becomes quite rocky. As you near the head of the canyon, the grade moderates and the terrain opens. Green gentian and orange agoseris dot the terrain near a seep left of the trail. Just ahead, to the right of the trail,

Top: Old log crib dam in Wilson Canyon. Bottom: Limestone faces and wooded terrain characterize the mid-section of the canyon. Early settlers logged the canyon to built homes in South Park.

is a section of old, abandoned log cribbing that long-time Jackson hole resident Ernie Wampler says dates to some of the valley's earliest settlers. The cribbing was used to dam up the small spring-fed creek to provide a general water supply source and possibly water for grazing. Wampler characterized the dam has a "bad idea that someone put a lot of work into," since most of the water from the nearby springs and the creek disappears into the underground channels and vaults often found in limestone canyons.

Beyond the old cribbing, the grade flattens and gently ascends open, sage grassland. Moose pellets are evidence that this ungulate frequents the small, willow-lined creek right of the trail. The trail itself gently climbs and contours the open hillside left of the creek, eventually reaching a faint "T" intersection with the trail from Leek's Canyon. A short distance ahead, you'll reach a more pronounced intersection and the end of the Wilson Canyon Trail. Retrace your steps, or bear left to access the top of Snow King Mountain, right to descend Game Creek.

Wilson Canyon is named after Sylvester Wilson, who homesteaded in South Park in 1889. Wilson presided over the first Latter Day Saints church service in the valley on Easter of 1890; he organized the first formal branch of the Mormon Church in the valley three years later. The first official school in Jackson Hole was held in his home, and sadly, the first cemetery begun when two of his 12 children, Joseph and Ellen, died of diphtheria in 1891.

Wilson Canyon provided much of the wood for homestead cabins built in South Park. Residents cut timber during the winter and skidded the logs down the snow to the mouth of the canyon, where a man named Grundy operated a sawmill.

112 Lower Game Creek

Distance: 6 miles RT
Elevation change: Approx 580 ft. gain and loss
Maximum elevation: 6,670 ft
Maps: Cache Creek. Book map pg.
Use restrictions:
 The slopes north of the trail are closed from Dec. 1 – April 30 to protect critical wildlife habitat. Dog owners who bring their animals must be able to keep them under control. Game Creek trailhead parking is day-use only.
Season: Mid-May through early November

As its name suggests, moose, deer and elk find this pleasant riparian corridor to their liking. Aspen groves and plentiful willow provide both food and protective cover for all three ungulate species.

The comparatively low elevation and open aspect of Lower Game Creek means it is typically snow-free by early spring. This, plus Lower Game Creek's lack of substantial elevation change, proximity to town and nearby paved pathways trail make it a well-used destination for hikers, mountain bikers and equestrians. Conflicts between different users in Game Creek have resulted in litigation—an unfortunate situation that can be avoided if users respect the land and each other. Hikers and mountain bikers are reminded to yield right-of-way to horseback riders; all users should approach blind corners carefully to avoid mishap, and dog owners must be able to control their pets. If separate routes for mountain bikers and horse riders are established, please adhere to new routes/designations posted on the ground.

Driving Directions

Travel south through Jackson on Hwy. 89 to the traffic light at the intersection of the highway with Maple Way near Kmart. Continue straight (S) on Hwy. 89/Broadway 5.9 miles beyond the light to signed Game Creek Road on your left (E). Turn in and drive one mile on paved road to a small parking area bordered by large rocks at the bend of the road. The trail begins on the closed dirt-and-gravel two-track left of the parking area.

Trail Description

The first portion of this hike is on the closed U.S. Forest Service road. Placid Game Creek is first to the right, then left of the road after flowing under it through a large culvert. As the dirt two-track climbs at a barely perceptible grade, it soon cuts through a narrow section of the drainage. Willows and aspens line the road and exposed limestone faces rise to your left. You'll soon reach a cattle guard and old fence line. Here, talus slopes from the rock faces above tumble down to the creek.

The grade steepens a bit beyond the cattle guard but is still quite easy. It flattens out as the road crosses an open section of sage grassland. Keep left where the road splits. At just over two miles, you'll see a trail leave the right side of the road; this is your return path. Continue straight to reach the remains of an old fence a short distance ahead. When you reach it, bear

Lower Game Creek Canyon is a hot, open choice by mid-summer, but offers a nice early season outing.

right and walk approximately 20 feet, skirting two willows to reach a plank bridge crossing of the placid creek.

The track continues at a level grade on the two-track, Game Creek now out-of-sight at the toe of the slope across the large willowed drainage. You may glimpse hikers or bikers across the expanse. A short distance after passing ponds to your right, the old roadbed splits where the creek crosses the track. Walk a short distance left to cross a plank over the creek, and bear slightly right as you cross a grassy area where the trail is indistinct. You'll quickly reach a log crossing of the creek.

Beyond, the trail travels a short distance before intersecting the main trail for hikers doing the Cache/Game Creek traverse and the walk from Snow King to Game Creek. Bear right onto the trail. The wider, well-used path stays left of the wide, willowed creek drainage. Chiefly open, this section can be quite hot.

The trail merges with the closed Forest Service two-track road and travels southwest on a downward to level course toward the trailhead. In another .3 mile, a trail leaves the two-track at a bend in the road. The path is slightly shorter than walking the bend in the road but has several blind corners. If you choose to take it, proceed cautiously and listen for mountain bikers.

The shortcut rejoins the two-track in open, flat terrain in .4 mile. You'll reach the metal cattle guard you crossed on your initial leg. The trailhead and return to your vehicle is a short distance farther.

113 South Park Management Area

Distance: 1 to 2.5 miles RT
Elevation change: Negligible
Maximum elevation: 6,670 ft
Maps: Cache Creek.
Use restrictions:
　　Closed Jan. 1–April 30. No unauthorized vehicles beyond Flat Creek Bridge May 1–June 30. Vehicles must stay on established roads. Overnight camping prohibited. Pets must be under verbal or physical control. Wyoming fishing license required.
Season: May through November

Situated just south of Jackson between Flat Creek and the Snake River is one of the prettiest wetland areas in Jackson Hole: the South Park Management Area. Administered as an elk feedground closed to human activity in the winter, Wyoming Game and Fish opens the triangle of land to recreational use the rest of the year. Fishermen try their luck in the river, families use scattered picnic tables and equestrians, hikers and mountain bikes enjoy the access road and trails located under the towering cottonwoods.

Birders are drawn to the avian paradise as well. On a recent May bird count, volunteers recorded sightings for the International Migratory Bird Day. Forty-two species were recognized in a two-hour period. Trumpeter swans, great blue herons, sandhill cranes, Swainson's and red-tailed hawks, killdeer, yellow-headed blackbirds, osprey and bald eagles are among the many common species spotted in the management area.

Driving Directions

From the intersection of U.S. Hwy. 89/191 and Wyoming Hwy. 22, drive south 5.7 miles to the turn-off on the right (W) side of the highway, a short distance beyond a deer crossing sign. After you turn in, you'll see the Wyoming Game and Fish sign. Carefully cross the community bike path and cattle guard, and drive downhill past horse corrals to a parking area located behind the hay storage sheds, a distance of .9 mile from the highway. Walk across the bridge over Flat Creek. The trail begins near the information sign.

Trail Description

Users have several options. The first is a 1-mile interpretive wildlife walk, a cooperative project begun in the fall of 1994 between Wyoming Game and Fish and Mrs. Foster's seventh grade class at Jackson Hole Middle School. The students helped design the scenic loop and wrote an educational pamphlet available at the information kiosk. Regrettably, the pamphlet is often out-of-stock. Its content is reproduced in abbreviated form below.

After you cross the bridge, begin the walk on the trail to the right. Cross the planks over a wet section of ground to reach the first wood marker.

No. 1: Wetlands

Wetlands are a type of riparian area, defined by abundance of water and a special plant community. They are important because they hold water like a sponge and help prevent floods. They also help clean the water. These wetlands are man-made. They were created to replace natural wetland habitat lost when Jackson Lake Dam was built. The wetlands were made by excavating soil, diverting water from a stream and impounding the water with a dike. The water level is controlled by checkboards inside the culvert. The floating islands are for waterfowl to use for safer nesting and resting areas. Very soon after this pond was built, ducks, geese, swans and herons appeared to feed on the riparian plants, insects and fish.

Top: An old elk trap on the feedgrounds used to capture cows and calves fort tagging and testing. Bottom: An osprey feeds her chicks. Osprey are one of many bird species found in the management area.

No. 2: Osprey

Look west to see an osprey nest high on a pole. Osprey, sometimes called fish hawks, almost always nest near water. Their main diet is fish, but they also eat rodents, birds and other prey found in or near water. These large birds are often mistaken for bald eagles, but unlike that eagle, osprey have a dark brown eye stripe and white underside. Bald eagles and ospreys have been known to live within 200 yards of each other. An eagle will occasionally bombard an osprey carrying a fish. When the osprey drops the fish, the eagle dives down to catch it.

No. 3: Elk Trap

This old trap was used to catch cow elk and calves on the feedground (antlers of bull elk prevent it from passing through the narrow gate). Hay would be scattered in the corral to lure the elk in. The trap door would close when the elk stepped on a trip wire in the corral. Biologists would then let the elk out through a narrow chute, separating each elk by a partition so it could be ear-tagged and/or blood tested. Hunters return ear tags with a report on where the animals were found, allowing biologists to learn about and track migration patterns.

After signpost 3, the trail crosses a metal bridge over a marshy area and enters the pleasant shade of a stand of cottonwoods.

No. 4: Birds at South Park

Up to 100 species of birds can be seen at South Park on a good day, drawn by the meadows, bushes, forests, oxbow ponds and the river. Chickadees, nuthatches, woodpeckers and jays stay all year; others nest in the area and fly south for the winter. For the largest diversity, visit in the spring or fall when neotropical migrants pass through the area. These birds spend winter in the tropics and fly north in the summer.

No. 5: Biodiversity and riparian areas

Riparian areas have the most wild-life diversity of any kind of habitat in Wyoming. More than 75% of the wild-life species in the West use riparian areas. South Park is a good example of a diverse riparian area because it has cottonwoods, shrubs, meadows, tall grass, flowers, shady places, ponds and willows, offering homes for a wide spectrum of plants, animals and birds. If riparian areas are lost, so are many plants and animals.

No. 6: The Snake River

The Snake River flows from Yellow-stone to Portland, Oregon, where the Columbia River meets the Pacific Ocean. This section of the Snake has a steep gradient and flows very fast. During spring run-off, its strong flow allows the river to carry big rocks. As the run-off abates, the big rocks are left in place. Changes in the seasonal amount of water make the river change course, resulting in braided channels.

No. 7: Munger Mountain

Munger Mountain, straight ahead, has an elevation of about 8,400 feet and covers an area of roughly 15 square miles. It is part of the Snake River Range. Munger is named after William Munger, a miner who prospected for gold at the base of the mountain. On August 23, 1934, a large forest fire burned part of the mountain. For many years, a fire lookout station was located on top of the peak. It has since been removed.

No. 8: Snake River Levees

Levees are man-made berms of rock and dirt that prevent the river from flooding, protecting nearby homes. But,

what may be good for man has serious environmental side effects. These include preventing fish from accessing creeks and side channels and damaging plants and trees, such as cottonwoods, that have to be flooded in order to grow.

No. 9: Cottonwoods

Cottonwoods live here because there is abundant water. When these trees die, however, they may not be replaced. The flood control levees have affected the natural flooding that creates fertile seedbeds for young cottonwoods to spread. Cottonwoods that manage to sprout can't get started because elk on the feedground eat the suckers in the winter. Hopefully, a strategy will be developed that will give the cottonwoods a chance.

No. 10: Cabin

Amos Davis, who homesteaded the area, built this sod-roofed cabin in 1902. When he died, his adopted son John inherited the structure. John eventually married his stepmother and the Davis family moved into town.

No. 11: Hayfields and Feedgrounds

South Park is one of numerous elk feedgrounds in northwest Wyoming. The property was purchased in 1939 for the purpose of providing elk winter range. Subsequent land was added in 1941. Approximately 1,000 elk winter at South Park. They eat available grasses and alfalfa hay delivered by horse-drawn sleighs. Wyoming Game and Fish is re-assessing management and continuation of feedgrounds, as it has become clear that concentrating elk fosters the spread of disease, particularly brucellosis.

No. 12: Fish Habitat Improvement

In 1991, fish biologists brought in rocks to constrict this portion of Flat Creek.

The constriction created a wider, slow stretch of creek above the rocks, creating a favorable environment for aquatic plants and insects that fish and ducks fed upon. The faster current below the constriction created deeper water, where eagles and osprey cannot see the fish as easily.

No. 13: Weeds

Noxious weeds take over large areas and outcompete native plants that wildlife would normally eat. Their seeds are brought in by vehicles, animals, hay and the river. They grow on roadsides, corrals, areas trampled by elk and other disturbed sites. Some weeds, such as hounds tongue and common tansy, contain a toxic alkaloid that if cattle ingest in sufficient quantities stops their liver cells from reproducing.

After completing the interpretive loop, visitors may extend their outing by walking or riding along the old jeep tracks to the end of the game management area. Double-back to No. 8 to pick up a track by the levee. Turn right. The track parallels a fast-moving channel of the Snake River. It splits near a pond; the left branch dead-ends at a main channel of the Snake. Continue straight for 120 yards to another split. If you turn right here, you will return to your vehicle via the outer dirt and gravel road. Continue straight on the dirt road. It eventually bends left to intersect the main levy. Continue straight (W) on the grassy roadbed through a quieter, less visited riparian area graced by a grove of cottonwoods.

You'll reach an open pasture at the end of the feedgrounds, marked by a fence. Retrace your route to the intersection with the outer track. Turn left and return to your vehicle.

Photos, top to bottom: Cottonwoods; the Davis Cabin, built in 1902; yellow-headed blackbirds are one of many species in South Park; a quiet side channel of the Snake River.

114 South Park Levee

Distance:
    1.5 miles to gate
    2.5 miles to fence
Elevation change: Negligible
Maximum elevation: Approx. 6,000 ft.
Maps: None needed
Use restrictions: Winter wildlife area.
    No unauthorized vehicles November 15-April 30; closed to human presence
    January 1 – April 30. Wyoming fishing licensee required to fish.
Season: May through November

Like its counterpart in Wilson, the South Park Levee—known locally as the South Park Dike—is a popular recreation corridor for walkers, anglers, picnickers and dog walkers. It parallels a channel of the Snake River and winds in and out of South Park's signature cottonwood groves. Visitors to this scenic levee enjoy the pastoral setting, historic structures, luxuriant grasses and wildflowers and the chance to sight an array of riparian corridor inhabitants, including eagles, pelicans, moose and otters. This author watching a family of five river otters cross the dike to a nearby pond one June day.

Unlike the Wilson levees, the South Park levee is not open year round. It marks the boundary of a Wyoming Game and Fish Elk Management Area, and is closed to winter use as noted in the information capsule above.

Driving Directions

From the traffic light at the intersection of U.S. Hwy 89/191 and High School Road by Smiths, drive south on US Hwy 89/191 5.5 miles to the unsigned gravel turn-off on the right side of the highway. The abrupt turn-off is just after crossing a low bridge over a Snake River side stream. Park so access to the locked metal gate just ahead remains clear.

Trail Description

Beyond the gate, visitors almost immediately enter a stretch of impressive wildflowers. Early season wild rose, lupine and hollyhock are dominant; later, goldenrod and sulphur buckwheat provide bursts of color. They thrive among luxuriant grasses that grown under the 60-plus foot cottonwoods towering above you.

A short distance in, you'll reach a quiet side channel of the Snake as Munger Mountain and a gravel operation on the south bank of the Snake come into view. The track is cobbled with river rock in this open stretch, where a sign reminds users at the .6-mile mark that the levee is closed to human presence November 15-April 30.

At .9 mile, the levee re-enters an extensive cottonwood grove, where it remains until reaching a metal gate at 1.5 miles. In season, this section is home to impressive sweeps of lupine. In the distance to the right, an old wood elk trap and the historic 1902 Davis Cabin are viewed, both described in hike no. 113. Just before the gate, at 1.4 miles, you'll

Top: Impressive, mature cottonwoods are a highlight of the South Park Levee hike. Left: A calm channel of the Snake draws local fishermen to the levee.

pass a "Wildlife Walk" sign on the right. The path is little used and grassed over.

The gate is a fine turn-around point for a 3-mile outing. To continue, walk around the gate and proceed through the cottonwood grove. At 1.9 miles, you'll pass small algae covered ponds on both sides of the levee. Yellow-headed blackbirds are frequently seen among the cattails that fringe the ponds. A short distance farther, you'll see an arm of the levee that extends left into a Snake side channel, and a road intersection to the right. This leads into the South Park Management Area, offering an alternate return to the highway for mountain bikers. Continue straight. You'll pass another cross dike to the left used by anglers. Near the end of the levee, the dirt and gravel track becomes a trail through grasses. Three planks over side rivulets are crossed before reaching a pond. Here, the trail turns 90 degrees left and parallels fenced private property before reaching a dead end at 2.5 miles.

Appendix

BEAR COUNTRY GUIDELINES

The future of bears and the safety of others depend on you. If a bear gets food or garbage from you, it's likely to be nuisance or even aggressive to the next person it meets. Aggressive behavior often results in human injury and/or the bear being destroyed. Wildlife managers state it succinctly: a fed bear is a dead bear. Take the time to learn about bears and how to avoid confrontations.

The guidelines below have been co-operatively developed by the Forest Service, National Park Service, U.S. Fish and Wildlife Service, BLM, and state game and fish agencies in the Greater Yellowstone area.

Plan your trip

- Before you head out into bear country, check if special regulations apply.
- Contact the local Forest Service or Game and Fish Department office to get the most recent report on bear activity.
- Avoid packing smelly, greasy foods like bacon and fish.
- Plan your trip so you don't leave food and containers (ice chests, bags, cans) in cars at the trailhead. If available, use trailhead food storage boxes. Bears can break into vehicles if they see or smell signs of food.

Visiting Bear Country

- Properly Store all food and attractants
  The most important part of visiting bear country is keeping all food and attractants (pop, beer, canned goods, toothpaste, chapstick, game meat, garbage, dog food, livestock feed, etc.) unavailable to bears. COOLERS, BACKPACKS, WOODEN BOXES, AND TENTS ARE NOT BEAR RESISTANT!
- Do not leave food or other bear attractants in open vehicles at trailheads, campgrounds or along forest roads.
- View and photograph all wildlife from a distance and don't approach a bear even if it looks calm.
- Learn to recognize bear tracks, diggings and scat. Avoid camping in these areas.
- Hike in groups rather than alone.

- Bears are most active at night. Hiking after dark or at dawn or dusk may increase your chances of meeting a bear.
- Bears don't like surprises! Use extra caution in places where visibility or hearing is limited such as bushy areas near streams. Talking, singing or wearing bells reduce your chances of surprising a bear.

Camping in Bear Country: Established Front Country Campgrounds

Store your food and any other item with odors in one of the following places:
- Place the items in the metal storage boxes located throughout the campground. Keep in mind that you must share these food boxes with other campers.
- Put everything inside your locked car, preferably in the trunk (be warned, some bears will break into your car if they smell or see items).
- Hang your items from a provided bear pole.

Camping in Bear Country: Backcountry Camps

- Choose a campsite free of fresh bear signs.
- Cook and store your food, garbage and other bear attractants well away (100 yards) from sleeping area. Attractants must be hung 10 feet off the ground and 4 feet out from any vertical support. Bring 100 feet of rope and storage bags for hanging. Small pulleys and carabiners are helpful. Alternately, store food and attractants in a bear resistant container. They can be purchased at many outdoor shops or in some cases can be rented from outdoor shops.

  Hanging food is not permitted in GTNP below 10,000 ft. in elevation. When backpacking below 10,000 ft. all food, garbage, toiletries and any odorous item that may attract a bear, must be stored in an Interagency Grizzly Bear Committee (IGBC) approved bear-resistant food canister when not in immediate use, day and night. Bear canisters are available for use in the park for free at back-country permitting locations.

A bear-clawed tree.

- Keep a clean camp. Food and odors attract bears.
- Don't burn or bury garbage. Bears will dig it up.
- Bears are active both day and night. At night and any time you are away from camp, remove all food from your pack and store it properly. Leave your pack on the ground with flaps and pockets open.
- When you leave an area, take all your garbage with you.
- If a bear does get your food, please take the responsibility for cleaning up and packing out all debris.
- Report any encounter to the nearest Forest Service or Park Service Office

Note: These regulations and precautions help decrease the chance of personal injury or property damage. However, bear damage and confrontations are still possible, even when all guidelines are followed.

Encounters

The decisions you make and the actions you take when you encounter a bear can greatly effect the outcome of the situation. Keeping a cool head and knowing what your options are very important. If you encounter a bear...

► First try to slowly back out of the situation. Keep calm, avoid direct eye contact, back up slowly and speak in a soft monotone voice. Never turn your back to the bear and never kneel down. Most encounters end with the bear leaving the area. Stay close together if in a group.
► NEVER RUN, and do not try to climb a tree unless you are sure you can climb at least 10 feet before the bear reaches you. Remember, you cannot out run a bear! Climbing a tree may not work for black bears as they are agile climbers.
► If a bear charges, stand your ground. Bears often "bluff charge" or run past you. The bear may charge several times before leaving the area. Shooting a charging bear should be your last resort. Shot placement is difficult and the bear almost always lives long enough to maul the shooter. A wounded bear can be very dangerous.
► As a last resort, play dead. Curl into a ball or lie flat, covering your neck and head with your hands and arms. If you have a backpack, leave it on as it will help protect your back. If the bear swats at you, roll with it. Stay face down and do not look at the bear until you are sure it is gone. Many people have survived bear attacks using this method.

If you kill a grizzly bear in self-defense, there will be a thorough investigation. Remember, grizzlies are federally protected species and unwarranted killings can result in criminal charges. Unnecessary killing of grizzly bears contributes to their decline. Report all bear encounters to the Game & Fish Department or the U.S. Forest Service, no matter how insignificant. Your report may help wildlife managers prevent further conflicts.

Pepper Spray

An increasing number of backcountry hikers carry pepper spray as a possible deterrent against aggressive bears. This aerosol red pepper derivative affects an animal's upper respiratory system and mucous membranes, triggering temporary incapacitating discomfort. It is intended to be a non-toxic and non-lethal means of deterring bears. Throughout North America, pepper spray has apparently repelled aggressive or attacking bears. However, there are accounts where pepper spray has not worked as well as expected. Many factors influence the effectiveness of pepper spray. Spray distance, wind, wet or rainy weather, extremes of heat or cold, and product shelf life all may affect its usefulness. The decision to carry pepper spray as a bear deterrent comes down to a personal choice. If you decide to carry spray, it is your responsibility to use it wisely and only in situations where aggressive bear behavior justifies its use. Keep in kind the considerations below:

► You can purchase pepper spray from most sporting goods stores in Montana, Wyoming, and Idaho. The spray cans are generally good for 2-3 seasons. After that, they should be replaced. Call your local recycling center for proper disposal of unused pepper spray.

► If using the spray for bear repellent, get the biggest can possible, generally the 9 -15 oz. size. The cost of these range from $30 - $50. The can should have an EPA Registration number.

► Most large cans come with a holster, make sure yours has one. Have your spray can on your belt and available. Don't put it in your pack when you hike. It must be available in a split-second.

► Make sure you know how to use your spray - read the manufacturer's instructions and give it a test spray.

► Do not leave pepper spray in a vehicle. On a warm summer day, temperatures inside your vehicle can get high enough that the canister will explode. You will not be able to enter your vehicle if this happens. It will have to be towed to an automotive center capable of stripping the inside of your vehicle and washing it down to remove the oil-based residue.

Using Bear Canisters
► Prepare food, eat, and store your bear-resistant food canister at least 100 yards downwind from your tent.

► Store your canister on the ground hidden in brush or behind rocks.

► Take care not to place canister near a cliff or any water source, as a bear may knock the canister around or roll it down a hill.

► Keep your eyes out for approaching bears. Be prepared to put your food away in a hurry.

► Keep your bear canister closed and locked, even while you're around your campsite. The bear canister only works if it's closed and locked!

► Do not hang or attach anything to the canister (ropes attached to the canister may enable a bear to carry it away).

USEFUL WEB SITES

Bear & Wolf Sighting forms
> http://www.fs.fed.us/r4/caribou-targhee/wildlife/bear_sighting_form.shtml
> http://www.fs.fed.us/r4/caribou-targhee/ wildlife/wolf_reporting_form.shtml

Bear Resistant Containers (park approved):
> http://www.backpackerscache.com/ (Model 812-C)
> http://www.bearvault.com (Models BV350, BV400)
> http://www.counterassault.com/
> http://www.bareboxer.com/

Campground Information & Reservations
> http://www.forestcamping.com/
> http://www.recreation.gov/
> http://www.nps.gov/grte/planyourvisit/campgrounds.htm

Fire information:
> http://www.tetonfires.com/

Grand Teton National Park
> http://www.nps.gov/grte/

GPS plotted trails:
> http://www.redtrails.com/base.asp

Maps: USGS topos, paper or digital to upload: http://www.usgs.gov/pubprod/
> Forest Service Travel Maps:http://www.grandtetonpark.org/default.asp

National Forests: Bridger-Teton National Forest: http://www.fs.fed.us/r4/btnf/
> Caribou-Targhee National Forest: http://www.fs.fed.us/r4/caribou-targhee/

Road and Travel Conditions, State of Wyoming: http://www.wyoroad.info/

State Game and Fish Departments/Professional Outfitting Associations
> Wyoming Game and Fish: http://gf.state.wy.us/
> Wyoming Outfitters & Guides Association: http://www.wyoga.org/

State Travel and Tourism site: http://www.wyomingtourism.org/

Stop Poaching reporting
> http://gf.state.wy.us/wildlife/enforcement/stoppoaching/submitTip.aspx

Weather
> http://forecast.weather.gov/ • http://www.weather.com/

Wildflowers
> http://www.fs.fed.us/wildflowers/ • http://plants.usda.gov/

Wildlife
> http://www.fs.fed.us/r4/caribou-targhee/wildlife/

PHONE NUMBERS

Emergencies.. 911
Accidents
    Wyoming Highway Patrol..800-442-9090
Law enforcement assistance
    Sublette County Sheriff Office 307-367-4378
    Teton County Sheriff Office...307-733-2331
Medical
    Alpine Clinic...307-654-7138
    Eastern Idaho Regional Medical Center, Idaho Falls.......................208-529-6111
    St. John's Hospital, Jackson...307-733-3636
Poison Control
    WY Poison Control..800-955-9119
    ID Poison Control 800-860-0620

General Numbers
Campground Reservations, Forest Service 1-877-444-6777
Campground Information, GTNP
    Colter Bay, Gros Ventre, Jenny Lake...800-628-9988
    Flagg Ranch Campground 800-443-2311
    Lizard Creek , Signal Mtn. Campgounds...800-672-6012
Bridger-Teton Ranger Districts
    Jackson...307-739-5400
    Supervisors Office..307-739-5500
Caribou-Targhee Ranger Districts
    Palisades..208-523-1412
    Supervisors Office..208-524-7500
Grand Teton National Park 307-739-3300
    Craig Thomas Discovery and Visitor Center 307-739-3399
    Laurance S. Rockefeller Preserve 307-739-3654
Road & Travel Information
    Idaho 1-888-432-7623
    Wyoming... 1-888-996-7623
State Game and Dish Departments/Outfitting Associations
    Idaho Dept. of Fish & Game 208-334-3700
    Idaho Outfitters & Guides Association 1-800-635-7820
    Wyoming Game and Fish..307-777-4600
    Wyoming State Board of Outfitters... 1-800-264-0981
Stop Poaching tip line 1-877-943-3847
Travel & Tourism Organizations
    Eastern Idaho Visitors Center 208-523-3278
    Idaho Travel Council.. 1-800-VISIT-ID
    Wyoming Travel and Tourism..800-225-5996

Index

Order Form

To order additional copies of *Jackson Hole Hikes*, please check with your favorite bookseller/outdoor retailer, or send a copy of this form with your personal check or money order to:

White Willow Publishing • Box 6464, Jackson, Wyoming 83002

Please enter the address you wish to send this order to:

Name _____

Mailing Address _____

City/State/Zip _____

Enclose $18.95 per copy, plus $3 shipping per book. Shipping discounts available for multiple books. Email whitewillow@bresnan.net to inquire. Wyoming residents add 6% sales tax ($1.13) per copy.

Order Form

To order additional copies of *Jackson Hole Hikes*, please check with your favorite bookseller/outdoor retailer, or send a copy of this form with your personal check or money order to:

White Willow Publishing • Box 6464, Jackson, Wyoming 83002

Please enter the address you wish to send this order to:

Name _____

Mailing Address _____

City/State/Zip _____

Enclose $18.95 per copy, plus $3 shipping per book. Shipping discounts available for multiple books. Email whitewillow@bresnan.net to inquire. Wyoming residents add 6% sales tax ($1.13) per copy.

For updated trail information,
wildflower and wildlife reports
and/or to view photographs of trails in
this publication in color, visit
http://jacksonholehikes.blogspot.com/